THE NOTEBOOK

THE NOTEBOOK

JOSÉ SARAMAGO

Translated by Amanda Hopkinson and Daniel Hahn

VERSO
London • New York

English edition published by Verso 2010
© Verso 2010

First published as *O Caderno* © José Saramago &
Editorial Caminho, SA, Lisbon 2008–2010
by arrangement with Literarishe Agentur Mertin Inh.
Nicole Witt e. K., Frankfurt am Main, Germany

English translation © Amanda Hopkinson and Daniel Hahn 2010

1 3 5 7 9 10 8 6 4 2

Verso
UK: 6 Meard Street, London W1F 0EG
US: 20 Jay Street, Suite 1010, Brooklyn, NY 11201
www.versobooks.com

Verso is the imprint of New Left Books

ISBN-13: 978-1-84467-614-9

British Library Cataloguing in Publication Data
A catalogue record for this book is available from the British Library

Library of Congress Cataloging-in-Publication Data
A catalog record for this book is available from the Library of Congress

Typeset by Hewer Text UK Ltd, Edinburgh
Printed in Sweden by ScandBook AB, Smedjebacken 2010

This book is dedicated to my collaborators at the José Saramago Foundation, and in particular to Sérgio Letria and Javier Muñoz. They are the ones who wait night after night, in Lisbon and Lanzarote, sometimes till late, for me to send them my short pieces of writing. They are the ones who, one leaf at a time, have collected a volume I never imagined would be this extensive. They are the craftsmen of my blog.

There is no need for this book to be dedicated to Pilar, because it has belonged to her ever since the day she said to me, "Here's a job for you. Write a blog."

Contents

Preface

When Pilar and I settled in Lanzarote in February 1993, while still keeping our Lisbon house, my sister- and brother-in-law, María and Javier, who had already lived there for some years, along with Luis and Juanjo, who had recently arrived, offered me a notebook, which I was to use to record our days in the Canary Isles. They imposed just one condition: that I should give them a mention every once in a while.

I never wrote anything in that notebook, but it was thanks to this gift, and for no other reason, that the *Lanzarote Notebooks*[1] were born and lived for five years. Today I find myself in an unexpectedly similar situation. This time, however, the motivating forces are Pilar, Sérgio and Javier, who take care of the blog. They told me they had reserved me a blog space and that I ought to write for it—commentary, reflections, simple opinions about this and that, in short whatever happened to occur to me. Being much more disciplined than I often seem, I replied yes, indeed, I would do it, on the condition that this notebook would not demand the same diligence that I had obliged myself to show with the others. For what that is worth, you can count on me.

---

1 Published in the 1990s, the *Lanzarote Notebooks* are an account of Saramago's life as a writer on the island. They have not yet been translated into English.

September 2008

September 15: *Words for a City*

While shuffling around a few bits of paper that have lost that fresh quality of newness, I came across an article about Lisbon I wrote a few years ago, and I'm not ashamed to admit that it moved me. Perhaps because it isn't really an article, but a love letter—expressing my love for Lisbon. So I decided to share it with my friends and readers, making it public once again, this time on the infinite page of the Internet, and with it inaugurate my personal space on this blog.

WORDS FOR A CITY

There was a time when Lisbon didn't go by the name Lisboa. They called it Olisipo when the Romans arrived there, Olissibona when it was taken by the Moors, who immediately began saying Aschbouna, perhaps because they couldn't pronounce that barbaric (Latin) word. But in 1147, when the Moors were defeated after a three-month siege, the name of the city wasn't changed right away; if the man who would become our first king had written to his family to announce the news, he would most likely have headed his letter Aschbouna, October 24, or Olissibona, but never Lisboa. When did Lisboa start being Lisboa in law and in effect? At least a few years would have to pass before the birth of the new name, as they would for the Galician conquerors to begin to become Portuguese . . .

One might think these historical minutiae uninteresting, but they interest me a great deal: not just knowing but actually seeing—in the precise meaning of the word—how Lisbon has been changing since those days. If cinema had existed at the time, if the old chroniclers had been cameramen, if the thousand and one changes through which Lisbon has passed over the centuries had been recorded, we would have been able to see Lisbon growing and moving like a living thing across eight centuries, like those flowers that we see on television opening up in just a few seconds, from a still, closed bud to a final splendor of shapes and colors. I think I'd love that Lisbon above all else.

In physical terms we inhabit space, but in emotional terms we are inhabited, by memory. A memory composed of a space and a time, a memory inside which we live, like an island between two oceans—one the past, the other the future. We can navigate the ocean of the recent past thanks to personal memory, which retains the recollection of the routes it has traveled, but to navigate the distant past we have to use memories that time has accumulated, memories of a space that is continually changing, as fleeting as time itself. This film of Lisbon, compressing time and expanding space, would be the perfect memory of the city.

What we know of places is how we coincide with them over a certain period of time in the spaces they occupy. The place was there, the person appeared, then the person left, the place continued, the place having made the person, the person having transformed the place. When I had to recreate the space and time of the Lisbon where Ricardo Reis lived his final year, I knew in advance that our two concepts of time and place would not coincide—that of the shy adolescent I used to be, enclosed within his own social class, and that of the lucid and brilliant poet who frequented the highest planes of the spirit. My Lisbon was always that of the poor neighborhoods, and when, many years later, circumstances brought me to live in other environments, the memory I always preferred to retain was that of the Lisbon of my early years, the

Lisbon of people who possess little and feel much, still rural in their customs and in their understanding of the world.

Perhaps it isn't possible to speak of a city without citing a few notable dates in its history. Here, speaking of Lisbon, I have mentioned only one, that of its Portuguese beginnings, the day it was first called Lisboa: the sin of glorifying its name is not such a dreadful one. What would be a grave matter would be to succumb to that kind of patriotic exaltation that, in the absence of any real enemies over whom to assert one's assumed power, resorts to the facile stimuli of rhetorical evocation. Exalted rhetoric, which is not necessarily a bad thing, does however bring with it a sense of self-satisfaction that leads to confusing words with deeds.

On that October day, Portugal—still barely begun—took a great step forward, a step so decisive that Lisbon was not lost again. But we will not allow ourselves the Napoleonic vanity of exclaiming: "Eight hundred years look down on us from the height of that castle," and pat ourselves on the back for having survived so long . . . Rather we recall that blood was shed, first on one side and then the other, and that all sides make up the blood that flows in our own veins. We, the inheritors of this city, are the descendents of Christians and Moors, of blacks and Jews, of Indians and Orientals, in short, of all races and creeds considered good, along with those that have been called bad. We shall leave to the ironic peace of their tombs those disturbed minds that not so long ago invented a Day of the Race for the Portuguese, and instead reclaim the magnificent mixing, not only of bloods but above all of cultures, that gave Portugal its foundation and has made it last to this day.

In recent years Lisbon has been transformed, has managed to reawaken in the conscience of its citizens that strength that hauled it out of the mire into which it had fallen. In the name of modernization, concrete walls have been erected over ancient stones, the outlines of hills disrupted, panoramas altered, sightlines modified. But the spirit of Lisbon survives, and it is the spirit that makes a city eternal. Entranced by that crazy love and divine enthusiasm that inhabit poets, Camões once wrote that Lisbon was "... a princess among other cities." We will forgive his exaggeration. It is enough that Lisbon is simply what it should be—cultured, modern, clean, organized—without losing any of its soul. And if all these virtues end up making her a queen, well, so be it. In our republic, queens like this will always be welcome.

September 17: *An Apology to Charles Darwin?*

A piece of good news, naïve readers would say, assuming that after so many disappointments there could still be any good news out there. The Anglican Church, the British version of Catholicism established in the time of Henry VIII and the official religion of the kingdom, has announced an important decision: they are apologizing to Charles Darwin, on the bicentenary of his birth, for how badly they treated him following the publication of *The Origin of Species*, and how much worse after *The Descent of Man*. I have nothing against all these apologies that seem to be cropping up almost every day for one reason or other, other than to question how useful they are. Even if Darwin were still alive and inclined to be magnanimous, saying, "Yes, I forgive you," those generous words could not erase a single insult, a single calumny, a single one of the many contemptuous remarks that were thrown at him. The only institution to benefit from this apology will be the Anglican Church, which will see its store of goodwill increased at no expense. Nonetheless, I'm grateful for a repentance, however belated, that might perhaps prompt Benedict XVI—currently engaged in a diplomatic maneuver in relation to secularism—to ask forgiveness of Galileo Galilei and Giordano Bruno, especially the latter, who was tortured in the Christian manner, most charitably, right up until the moment when he was burned on the bonfire.

This apology by the Anglicans won't please North American creationists one bit. They will feign indifference, but quite clearly this goes against their plans. And against those of the Republicans, who, like their vice-presidential candidate, have raised the flag of that pseudoscientific aberration that goes by the name of creationism.

September 13: *George W. Bush, or the Age of Lies*

I wonder why it is that the United States, a country so great in all things, has so often had such small presidents. George W. Bush is perhaps the smallest of them all. This man, with his mediocre intelligence, abysmal ignorance, confused communication skills, and constant succumbing to the irresistible temptation of pure nonsense, has presented himself to humanity in the grotesque pose of a cowboy who has inherited the world and mistaken it for a herd of cattle. We don't know what he really thinks, we don't even know if he does think (in the noble sense of the word), we don't know whether he might not be just a badly programmed robot that constantly confuses and switches around the messages it carries around inside it. But to give the man some credit for once in his life, there is one program in the robot George Bush, president of the United States, that works to perfection: lying. He knows he's lying, he knows we know he's lying, but being a compulsive liar, he will keep on lying even when he has the most naked truth right there before his eyes—he will keep on lying even after the truth has exploded in his face. He lied to justify waging war in Iraq just as he lied about his stormy and questionable past, and with just the same shamelessness. With Bush, the lies come from very deep down; they are in his blood. A liar emeritus, he is the high priest of all the other liars who have surrounded him, applauded him, and served him over the past few years.

George Bush expelled truth from the world, establishing the age of lies that now flourishes in its place. Human society today is contaminated by lies, the worst sort of moral contamination, and he is among those chiefly responsible. The lie circulates everywhere with impunity, and has already turned into a kind of *other truth*. When a few years ago a Portuguese prime minister—whose name for charity's sake I will not mention here—stated that "politics is the art of not telling the truth," he could never have imagined that some time later George W. Bush would transform this shocking statement into a naïve trick of fringe politics, with no real awareness of the value or the significance of words. For Bush, politics is simply one of the levers of business, and perhaps the best one of all—the lie as a weapon, the lie as the advance guard of tanks and cannons, the lie told over the ruins, over the corpses, over humanity's wretched and perpetually frustrated hopes. We cannot be sure that today's world is more secure, but we can have no doubt that it would be much cleaner without the imperial and colonial politics of the president of the United States, George Walker Bush, and of the many—quite aware of the fraud they were perpetrating— who allowed him into the White House. History will hold them to account.

September 19: *Berlusconi and Co.*

According to the North American magazine *Forbes*, the *Gotha* of global wealth, Berlusconi's fortune comes to nearly ten thousand million dollars. Earned honorably, of course, albeit not without the assistance of many other people, including, for instance, my own. Being published in Italy by the Einaudi publishing house, owned by the aforementioned Berlusconi, I must have earned him some money. An infinite drop of water in the ocean, to be sure, but at least enough to be keeping him in cigars, assuming that corruption is not his only vice. Apart from what is public knowledge, I don't know very much myself about the life and miracles of Silvio Berlusconi, il Cavaliere. The Italian people, who have sat him once, twice, three times in the prime minister's chair, must know far more than I do. Well, as we often hear it said, the people are sovereign, and they are not only sovereign, they are also wise and prudent, especially since the continual exercise of their democratic rights allows citizens to learn certain useful things about how politics works and about the different means of attaining power. This means that the people are very well aware of what it is they want when they are called to vote. In the particular case of the Italian people, since that is who we're talking about and no one else (the time for others will come), it is obvious that the sentimental feelings they have for Berlusconi, which they have demonstrated three times, are quite impervious to any consideration of moral order. Really, in the land of the Mafia and the Camorra, what importance could the proven fact that the prime minister is a criminal possibly have? In a land where justice has never had much of a reputation, who cares if the prime minister gets approval for laws aimed at defending his own interests and protecting himself against any attempt to punish his excesses and abuses of authority?

Eça de Queiroz used to say that if we were to send a laugh around an institution, that institution would fall to pieces. That was then. What can be said about the recent prohibition—ordered by Berlusconi—against Oliver Stone's film *W.* being shown there? Have il Cavaliere's powers already stretched so far? How has it been possible for such senseless acts to have been committed, especially since we know that however many times we might send a laugh around the Quirinale it will not fall? Our outrage may be just, but we should make an effort here to understand the complexity of the human heart. *W.* is a film that attacks Bush, and Berlusconi, a man of heart just as any Mafia boss might be, is a friend, colleague, buddy of the man who is still president of the United States. They are good for one another. What would be no good at all would be for the Italian people to place Berlusconi in the seat of power for a fourth time. No amount of laughter will be able to save us then.

September 20: *The Pulianas Cemetery*

Once, perhaps seven or eight years ago, we were sought out, Pilar and I, by a man from León by the name of Emilio Silva, who was asking for support for an undertaking he was planning to embark upon: to find the remains of his grandfather, assassinated by the Francoists at the start of the civil war. He asked us for moral support, no more than that. His grandmother had expressed a wish that his grandfather's bones should be recovered and given a dignified burial. Rather than just taking these words as the will of a bitter old woman, Emilio Silva took them as an order that it was his duty to fulfill, whatever might happen. This was the first step in a mass movement that quickly spread across all Spain: retrieving from ditches and ravines the tens of thousands of victims of fascist hatred that had been buried there, identifying them, and handing them over to their families. It was a massive task that did not enjoy universal support—and mention should be made of the continuous efforts of the Spanish political and social right to block it when it was already a thrilling reality, when the relics of those who had paid with their lives for fidelity to their ideas and to the legitimacy of the Republic were being raised from the dug-up and turned-over earth. Let me introduce here—in a symbolic bow to so many who have dedicated themselves to this work—the name of Ángel del Río, a brother-in-law of mine, who has given the best part of his time to it, including writing two books of research on the disappeared and those killed in reprisal.

It was inevitable that the rescuing of the remains of Federico García Lorca, buried like thousands of others in the Viznar ravine in the province of Granada, would quickly become a genuine national imperative. One of Spain's greatest poets, the most universally known, there he is in that desert, that place we know almost as a certain fact is the ditch where the author of *Romancero Gitano* lies, along with three other men who had been shot—a primary school teacher called Dióscoro Galindo and two anarchists who had worked in the bull ring as banderilleros, Joaquín Arcollas Cabezas and Francisco Galadí Melgar. Strangely, however, García Lorca's family has always opposed his exhumation. To a greater or lesser extent their arguments concern what we might call questions of social decorum, such as the unhealthy prurience of the media and the spectacle that would be made of the excavation of the skeletons, and these are undoubtedly respectable reasons, but, if I might be allowed to say this, today they are outweighed by the simplicity with which Dióscoro Galindo's granddaughter replied when asked in a radio interview where she would take her grandfather's remains if they were to be found: "To the Pulianas cemetery." I should clarify that Pulianas, in the province of Granada, is the village where Dióscoro Galinda worked and where his family still lives. Pages in books are for turning over, pages in life are not.

September 22: *Aznar, the Oracle*

We can sleep easy: global warming doesn't exist. It is a malicious invention by ecologists, a strategic part of their "ideology of totalitarian inclinations," as defined by that implacable observer of planetary politics and universal phenomena who is José María Aznar. There is no way we could live without this man. No matter that one day flowers will begin to grow in the Arctic, no matter that the Patagonian glaciers are diminishing each time someone sighs and makes the environmental temperature go up by a tiny fraction of a degree, no matter that Greenland has lost a significant part of its territory, no matter that droughts and devastating floods take so many lives, no matter that there is less and less difference between the seasons of the year—none of this matters if the distinguished sage José María denies the existence of global warming, based on the meandering pages of a book by Czech president Vaclav Klaus that Aznar himself, in a lovely piece of scientific and institutional solidarity, will soon be presenting. We're already listening. And yet we are tortured by a very serious doubt, which it is now time to offer up for the reader's consideration. What could be the origin, the spring, the source of this systematic attitude of denial? Might it have resulted from a dialectic egg deposited by Aznar in the uterus of the Partido Popular when he was its lord and master? When Rajoy, with his characteristically calm seriousness, told us that some professor cousin of his—a professor of physics, apparently—told him that this business with global warming was nonsense, this ever so daring statement was merely the fruit of an overheated Celtic imagination that had been unable to understand what was being explained to it. That dialectic egg is now a doctrine, a rule, a principle recorded in small print in the Partido Popular's primer; and in that case, if Rajoy had just unfortunately repeated the words of the professor cousin, then his former boss turned oracle clearly didn't want to miss an opportunity to teach the ignorant people one more lesson.

I have little space remaining, but perhaps there is room for a brief appeal to common sense. Since we know that our planet has already been through six or seven ice ages, could we not be on the threshold of another? Could it not be that the coincidence between this possibility and the ongoing activities carried out by human beings against their environment is very like those common examples of one illness hiding another illness? Please think about this. In the next ice age, or in this one that is just beginning, the ice will cover Paris. We can relax; it will not happen tomorrow. But we do at least have a duty for today: Let's not help the forthcoming ice age along. And don't forget, Aznar is merely a brief episode. Don't be afraid.

September 23: *Biographies*

I believe that all of the words we speak, all of the movements and gestures we make, whether completed or merely sketched, can each and every one of them be understood as stray pieces of an unintended autobiography, which, however involuntary, or perhaps precisely because it is involuntary, is no less sincere or truthful than the most detailed account of a life put into writing and onto paper. This conviction that over time everything we say and do, however devoid of significance and importance, is—cannot but be—a biographical expression once led me to suggest, with more seriousness than might have appeared at first sight, that every human being should leave a written account of his or her life, and that these thousands of millions of volumes, when there is no longer room for them on earth, should be taken to the moon. This would mean that the big, enormous, gigantic, vast, immense library of human existence would have to be split first into two parts, and then, as time went on, into three, then four, or even into nine, assuming that the eight other planets of the solar system had atmospheres benign enough to respect the fragility of paper. I would imagine that accounts of the many lives that, being simple and modest, would fit on a mere half-dozen pages, or even fewer, would be dispatched to Pluto, the most distant of the sun's children, where researchers would doubtless want to travel only rarely.

I am sure that a number of problems and doubts would arise when the time came to establish and define the criteria for making up these so-called libraries. It would be beyond dispute, for example, that books like the diaries of Amiel, Kafka, and Virginia Woolf, Boswell's life of Samuel Johnson, Cellini's autobiography, Casanova's memoirs, Rousseau's confessions and many other works of comparable human and literary significance ought to remain on the planet on which they were written, in order to bear witness to the passage through this world of men and women who for good or bad reasons have not only lived but also left a mark, a presence, an influence, which, having survived to this day, will continue to affect generations to come. The problems will arise when the choice of what will stay and what will be sent into space begins to reflect the inevitably subjective value judgments, prejudices, fears, hatreds both ancient and new, impossible excuses, belated justifications, everything in life that constitutes terror, despair and agony—in other words, human nature. I think that after all it might be better to leave things as they are. Like most of the best ideas, mine is impracticable. So be it.

September 24: *Divorces and Libraries*

On two occasions in recent years—or it might have been three—I have been approached at the Lisbon Book Fair by readers, in twos and threes, weighed down by dozens of new volumes, freshly purchased, usually still in their plastic wrappers. I asked the first of these who approached me what seemed the most logical question: whether he had come across my work recently and, it would appear, been overwhelmed by it. He replied no, that he had been reading my work for a long time but that he had got divorced, and his ex-wife—another enthusiastic reader—had taken the dismantled family's library with her into her new life. It then occurred to me, and I wrote a few lines about this in the old *Lanzarote Notebooks*, that it would be interesting to study the subject from the point of view of what I described at the time as the significance of divorces in the multiplication of libraries. I acknowledge that this was a somewhat provocative idea, which was why I let it go, to save myself from accusations of putting my own material interests before others' marital harmony. I don't know, I can't imagine, how many conjugal splits have led to the formation of new libraries without any harm befalling the old ones. Two or three cases—which are as many as I'm aware of—were not enough to make a summer, or, to spell it out, they were not enough to improve either the publisher's profits nor the royalties I was able to extract.

What I frankly never expected was that the economic crisis that has kept us in a state of permanent alarm should have made divorces even more difficult, and therefore incidentally slowed down the intended arithmetical progression of libraries—and I'm sure we'd all agree that this represents a real crime against culture. What is to be said, for example, about the complex, often insoluble problem of finding a homebuyer nowadays? If so many divorce proceedings are stalled, if court cases do not go ahead, then this alone is the real reason. Worse still, how should one proceed against certain examples of scandalous behavior already in the public domain, such as the (regrettably common and utterly immoral) case of a couple still living in the same house, perhaps not sleeping in the same bed but using the same library? There is no longer any respect, no longer any sense of decorum—this is the wretched situation we have come to. No one ever says that Wall Street is to blame: in the television comedies they finance there is never a book to be seen.

September 25: *Nothing but Appearances*

I suppose that right at the very beginning, before we invented speech, which is, as we know, the supreme creator of uncertainties, we were not troubled by any serious doubts about who we were or about our personal and collective relationship with the place where we found ourselves. Of course, the world could only be what our eyes saw from one moment to the next and—which was equally significant information—what the remaining senses—hearing, touch, smell, taste—were able to perceive of it, too. In its earliest phase, the world was nothing but appearances and nothing but surface. Matter was rough or smooth, bitter or sweet, acidic or bland, noisy or silent, scented or odorless. All things were just what they seemed, simply because there was no reason for them to seem one thing and to be altogether another. In those most ancient of days it never occurred to us that matter was porous. Today, however, even though we know that from the smallest of viruses to the universe as a whole we are all no more than compositions of atoms, and that inside them, beyond the mass that is inherent to them and defines them, there is still enough space for emptiness (absolute density doesn't exist; everything is permeable), we still—just like our ancestors in their caves—continue to learn about, identify, and recognize the world according to the way it repeatedly shows itself to us. I would imagine that the spirits of philosophy and of science must have appeared one day when someone suspected that although this appearance was an external image that could be captured by consciousness and used as a map of knowledge, it could also be a delusion of the senses. We all know the popular expression derived from this realization, though it is more often used to refer to the moral world than the physical one: "Appearances can mislead." Or deceive, which comes to the same thing. There would be no shortage of examples had we but space for them.

This scribbler has always worried about what is hidden behind mere appearances, and I'm not talking now about atoms or subparticles. What I am talking about are current, common, everyday questions about, for example, the political system that we call democracy, the system that Churchill described as "the worst form of government, except for all the others that have been tried." He didn't say it was good, only the least bad. One might say that we consider the government we can see to be more than sufficient, and I think this is an error of perception for which—without our noticing—we are paying the price every day. This is a subject to which I will return.

September 26: *The Whiteness Test*

According to the Universal Declaration of Human Rights, Article 12, "No one shall be subjected to arbitrary interference with his privacy, family, home or correspondence, or to attacks upon his honor and reputation." And further, "Everyone has the right to the protection of the law against such interference or attacks." That's what it says. The piece of paper shows, among others, the signature of the representative of the United States, which thereby acknowledged the commitment of the United States to the effective fulfillment of the articles contained in this Declaration; however, to their shame and our own, these articles are worthless, especially when the very law that is supposed to protect us not only does not do so but is used to justify the most senseless acts, including those that this same Article 12 condemns. To the United States, any person, whether an immigrant or a simple tourist, and regardless of his profession, is a potential delinquent who is obliged, like Kafka's hero, to prove his innocence without knowing the charge of which he stands accused. Honor, dignity, reputation—these are words that provoke nothing but laughter from the Cerberuses who guard the entrances to the country. We already know this, we have already experienced it in deliberately humiliating interrogations, we've already been looked at by the official in charge as if we were the most repulsive of worms. In short, we have already become used to being mistreated.

But something new is happening now, a further turn of the oppressor's screw. The White House, which houses the most powerful man on the planet, as journalists are prone to say when suffering from a crisis of inspiration—the White House, I say again, has authorized officers of the border police to inspect and scrutinize the documents of any foreign citizen or North American, even if they have no reason to suspect this person of any intention of participating in a crime. Such documents will be retained "for a reasonable period of time" in a vast library where all manner of personal data are kept, from simple address books to supposedly confidential e-mails. There, too, will be kept an incalculable quantity of copies of hard disks from our computers each time we present ourselves at any of the borders of the United States. With all their contents: scientific, technological, or creative research work, academic theses, simple love poems. "No one shall be subjected to arbitrary interference with his privacy," says poor old Article 12. To which we say, see how little the signature of a president of the most powerful democracy in the world is worth.

So there it is. We are trying out an infallible whiteness test on the United States, and this is what we have ascertained: it is not merely dirty, it is absolutely filthy.

29 September: *Clear as Water*

As has always been the case, and as will always be the case, the
central question concerning any kind of human social organization, and the one from and into which all others flow, is the question of power, and the theoretical and practical problem we are
presented with is identifying who holds it, discovering how they
attained it, checking what use they make of it, by what means and
for what ends. If democracy really were what we continue (with
real or feigned ingenuousness) to say it is, government of the
people by the people for the people, any debate on the question
of power would lose a lot of its meaning, since if power resides
in the people it is the people who control it, and people controlling the power clearly would only do so for their own good and
to secure their own happiness, compelled by what I call, with no
pretension to conceptual rigor, the law of the preservation of life.
Well, only a perverse spirit, Panglossian even to the point of cynicism, could dare to proclaim the happiness of a world that, on the
contrary, nobody should expect us to accept as it is, just by virtue
of its being, supposedly, the best of all possible worlds. This is the
right and actual situation of the so-called democratic world, where
if it is true that the people are governed, it is also true that they are
not governed by or for themselves. It's not a democracy that we
live in, but a plutocracy, which has ceased to be local and close but
has become instead at once universal and inaccessible.

Democratic power must by definition always be provisional
and circumstantial; it depends on the stability of the vote, on the
fluctuation of class interests or ideologies, and therefore can be
understood as an organic barometer that registers variations in
a society's political will. But in the past, just as today—albeit to
an increasingly great degree today—there have been numerous
cases of apparently radical political changes that have resulted
in radical changes in government but that were not followed by
the radical economic, cultural, or social changes that the results

of the vote had promised. Today, calling a government socialist, social democratic, conservative, or liberal is to ascribe power to it, that is, purport to identify something in it that is not really there but in some other place far out of reach—a place where you can see the filigree outlines of economic and financial power, a power that invariably eludes us when we try to get closer, that inevitably counterattacks if we whimsically wish to reduce or regulate its domain, subordinating it to the common good. In other, clearer words, then, what I'm saying is that people do not choose a government that will bring the market within their control; instead, the market in every way conditions governments to bring the people within its control. And if I talk about the market in this way it is only because today, and more with each day that passes, it is this that is the instrument par excellence of authentic, unitary, simple power, global economic and financial power, which is not democratic because the people never elected it, which is not democratic because the people do not govern it, and finally which is not democratic because it does not have the people's happiness as its aim.

Our forefathers in their caves would say, "It is water." We, being a little wiser, warn, "Yes, but it is contaminated."

September 30: *Hopes and Utopias*

A lot has been written and much more chattered about the virtues of hope. Utopias have always been and always will be Paradise as dreamed of by skeptics. Yet not only skeptics but also fervent believers, the Mass and Communion kind of believers who look forward to Heaven, still ask the compassionate hand of God to shade their heads, protect them from rain and heat, and deliver in this life at least a small portion of the rewards that he has promised in the next. Which is why anyone who isn't satisfied with what has fallen to his lot in the unequal distribution of the planet's assets, especially the material assets, clings to the hope that it won't always be the devil who is at the door and that one day—sooner rather than later—it will be wealth that comes in through the window. Someone who has lost everything, but has been lucky enough to retain at least his sad life, considers that he is owed the most human right of hoping that tomorrow will not be as wretched as today. Presuming, of course, that there is justice in the world. Well, if in this place and in these times there did exist something worthy of the name *justice*, not the mirage of a tradition able to deceive our eyes and our mind but a reality that we could touch with our hands, it is obvious that we wouldn't have to carry hope around with us every day, cradling it to us, or be carried around cradled by it. Simple justice (not that of courtrooms, but the justice of that fundamental respect that should preside over relations between human beings) would take charge of putting things in their proper places. In the past, the poor man asking alms would be denied with the hypocritical words "Have patience." I don't think advising someone to have hope is all that different from advising him to have patience. It is common to hear recently elected politicians say that impatience is antirevolutionary. Perhaps so, but I incline toward the view that, on the contrary, many revolutions have been lost through an excess of patience. I have nothing against hope, obviously, but I prefer impatience. It's time for impatience to make itself felt in the world, to teach a thing or two to those who would prefer us to feed on hopes. Or on dreams of utopia.

October 2008

October 1: *Where Is the Left?*

Three or four years ago, in an interview with a South American newspaper, from Argentina, I think, I came out with a statement I subsequently thought would provoke discomfort, discussion, even a scandal (such was my naïveté), beginning with local left-wing groups and continuing, who knows, like a wave growing in concentric circles, out into the international media—at least such political, trade union or cultural organs of the media that are the tributaries of the said left. The paper reproduced my argument word for word, in all its harshness, not shying away from actual obscenities, as in the following: "The left has no fucking idea of the world it's living in."

The left responded to my deliberate challenge with the iciest of silences. No communist party, for instance, beginning with the one of which I'm a member, emerged from its stockade to refute what I had said or simply to argue about the propriety or the lack of propriety of my language. Even more to the point, nor did any of the socialist parties then in government in their respective countries—I'm thinking especially of those in Portugal and Spain—consider it necessary to demand a clarification from the impudent writer who had dared to throw a stone into a fetid swamp of indifference. Nothing of anything at all, absolute silence, as if there were nothing but dust and spiders in the ideological tombs where

they had taken refuge, or nothing more than an ancient bone that
was no longer solid enough for a relic. For several days I felt as
excluded from human society as if I were carrying the plague, or
were the victim of a kind of cirrhosis of the mind, no longer able to
speak coherently. I even ended up thinking that the compassionate line going the rounds among those people who were keeping
so quiet was something like, "Poor thing, what can you expect at
his age?" It was clear that they didn't think my opinions worthy of
their consideration.

Time went on, and on, the state of the world grew increasingly
complicated, and the left continued fearlessly to play out the roles,
whether in power or in opposition, that had been handed to them.
I, who had in the meantime made another discovery, that Marx
was never so right as he is today, imagined, when the cancerous
mortgage scam broke in the United States a year ago, that the left,
wherever it was, if it was still alive, would finally open its mouth
to say what it thought of the matter. I already have an explanation:
the left doesn't think. It doesn't act, it doesn't risk taking a step.
What happened then has gone on happening, right up to today,
and the left has continued in its cowardly fashion not thinking, not
acting, not risking taking a step. Which is why the insolent question in my title should not cause surprise: "Where is the Left?" I
am not suggesting any answers; I have already paid too dearly for
my illusions.

October 2: *Enemies at Home*

That there is a crisis in the family is something nobody would dare
to deny, however much the Catholic Church might seek to disguise
the disaster with a mellifluous rhetoric that doesn't even deceive
itself. Nor can we deny that many so-called traditional values of
family and social cohabitation have gone down the drain, dragging with them even those values that ought to be defended from
the constant attacks coming from the highly conflictive society in

which we live; nor that today's schools—the successors to those old schools that for many generations were tacitly charged (in the absence of anything better) with making up for the educational failings of the family unit—are paralyzed, riddled with contradictions and mistakes, disoriented by successive pedagogical methods that are not in fact pedagogical methods, that too often are no more than passing fashions or amateur experiments doomed to fail. They are doomed by the very lack of intellectual maturity of those who formulated them, without being able to formulate or answer a question that to my mind is essential: "What kind of citizens are we trying to produce?"

The social landscape is not a pretty sight. Strangely, our more or less worthy rulers do not seem as concerned with these matters as they should be, perhaps because they think that since these are universal problems the solution—whenever it is found—will be automatic, for everyone.

I disagree. We live in a society that seems to have made violence a way of social interaction. The aggression that is inherent in this species of ours, and which at times we think that we have managed to control through education, burst brutally up from the depths in the past twenty years, manifesting itself right across the social sphere, prompted by modes of idleness that have stopped using simple hedonism to condition the consumer's mentality and instead use violence: led by television, where ever more perfect fake blood gushes out every hour of the day and night, and video games that are like instruction manuals for teaching total intolerance and perfect cruelty, and, because all of this is connected, the avalanche of ads for erotic services, welcomed by all newspapers, including the more right-thinking ones, while they cram their editorial pages (if any still remain?) with hypocritical instructions to society on how it should behave. Do I exaggerate? Then explain to me how it is we have reached the point where many parents are afraid of their children—those sweet adolescents, our hope for tomorrow, from whom the word "no" from a father or mother grown tired of irrational demands instantly unleashes a fury of insults, of outrageous behavior, of aggression. Physical aggression, in case you had any doubt about my meaning. Many parents harbor their worst enemies in their own home: their children. Ruben Darío innocently wrote of "that divine treasure, youth." He would not write so today.

October 6: *On Fernando Pessoa*

He was a man who knew languages and wrote poetry. He earned his bread and wine replacing words with words. He wrote poetry as one must write poetry, as if for the first time. To begin with he called himself Fernando, a person like anyone else. One day he remembered to announce the imminent appearance of a super-Camões, a Camões much greater than the old one, but since he was a man who was known to be discreet, who used to walk through Douradores in a light-colored gabardine, a bow tie, and featherless hat, he did not say that the super-Camões was in fact himself. After all, this super-Camões could not become a still greater Camões; he was merely waiting to become Fernando Pessoa, a phenomenon the like of which Portugal had never known. Naturally, his life was made up of days, and we know that days may be alike but each never happens more than once, which is why it is not surprising that on one of those days when Fernando passed in front of a mirror he spied in it, at a glance, another person.[1] He thought this was just another optical illusion, those ones that happen when you're not paying attention, or that the last glass of *eau de vie* had not agreed with his liver and his head, but he cautiously took a step back just to make sure that—as is usually assumed—when mirrors show something they do not make mistakes. This one, however, had indeed made a mistake: there was a man looking out at him from inside the mirror, and that man was not Fernando Pessoa.

---

1 Translators' note: The Portuguese word for "person" is "pessoa."

He was a little shorter, and his face was somewhat dark-skinned and completely clean-shaven. Unconsciously Fernando brought his hand to his upper lip, then breathed deeply in childlike relief: his moustache was still there. One can expect many things from an image that appears in a mirror, but not that it will speak. And because these two, Fernando and the image that wasn't an image of him, were not going to stay watching one another forever, Fernando Pessoa said, "My name is Ricardo Reis." The other man smiled, nodded, and disappeared. For a moment the mirror was empty, bare, then right away another image appeared, of a thin, pale man who looked as if he were not long for this world. It seemed to Fernando that this must have been the first one; however, he made no comment, merely saying, "My name is Alberto Caeiro." The other did not smile; he merely nodded slightly, agreeing, and left. Fernando Pessoa waited, having always been told that whenever there are two a third will always follow. The third figure took a few seconds to arrive, and he was one of those men who look as if they have more health than they know what to do with, and he had the unmistakable air of an engineer trained in England. Fernando said, "My name is Álvaro de Campos," but this time he did not wait for the image to disappear from the mirror, but moved away from it himself, probably tired from having been so many people in such a short space of time. That night, in the small hours of the morning, Fernando Pessoa awoke wondering whether Álvaro de Campos had stayed in the mirror. He got up, and what he found there was his own face. So he said, "My name is Bernardo Soares," and went back to bed. It was after assuming these names and a few others that Fernando thought it was time for him, too, to be ridiculous, and he wrote the most ridiculous love letters in the world. He made great progress in his work of translation and poetry, and then he died. His friends had told him he had a great future ahead of him, but he can't have believed them—believed them so little, in fact, that he unfairly decided to die in the prime of life, aged forty-seven, if you can believe such a thing. A moment before the end he asked to be handed his glasses: "Give me my glasses," were his last, formal words. To this day nobody has sought to learn what he wanted them for, such is the way the final wishes of the dying are ignored or despised, but it seems quite likely that what he wanted was to look in a mirror to see who was there in the end. But he was not allowed enough time. Actually, there wasn't even a mirror in the room. Fernando Pessoa never did find out for sure who he was, but thanks to his doubts we can manage to learn a little more about who it is we are.

October 7: *The Other Side*

What might things be like when we are not looking at them? This question, which seems less absurd to me every day, is one that I asked often as a child, but only asked myself, not my parents or my teachers, because I guessed that they would smile at my naïveté (or at my stupidity, according to a more radical opinion) and would give me the only answer that would never convince me: "When we are not looking at them, things look just the same as when we are looking at them." I always thought that things, whenever they were alone, were other things. Later, when I had reached that phase of adolescence characterized by the disdainful conceit with which it judges the childhood from which it has emerged, I thought I had found the definitive solution to the metaphysical concern that had tormented my tender years: I thought that if you were to set up a camera in such a way that it would shoot a picture automatically in a room where there were no human presences, you would be able to catch things unawares, and in this way learn their true appearance. I forgot that things are smarter than they seem and don't allow themselves to be tricked quite so easily: they know perfectly well that inside each camera there is a human eye hidden. . . Besides, even if the equipment had cunningly been able to capture the image of the thing face-on, its other side would have remained beyond the reach of the optical, mechanical, chemical, or digital system of that photographic record. And it would have been toward that hidden side that at the last moment, ironically, the photographed thing would have turned its secret aspect, that twin sister of darkness. When we enter a room that is immersed in absolute darkness and turn on a light, the darkness disappears. So it is not strange that we should ask ourselves, "Where has it gone?" And there can only be one reply: "It didn't go anywhere; darkness is simply the other side of light, its secret aspect." It is a pity that nobody told me earlier, when I was a child. Today I would know all about darkness and light, about light and darkness.

October 8: *Getting Back to the Subject*

The lessons of life have taught us how little use a political democracy will be, however well-balanced it may appear in its internal structures and institutional functioning, if it is not constituted as the basis for an effective and real economic democracy and for a no less real and effective cultural democracy. It may seem a worn-out old commonplace to say such a thing today about certain ideological concerns of the past, but it would be shutting our eyes to the simple historical truth if we were not to recognize that the democratic trinity—politics, economics, culture, each part complementing and enabling the others—at the height of its prosperity as an idea for the future represented one of the most passion-inspiring civic flags that in recent history has ever managed to awake consciences, mobilize wills, move hearts. Today, scorned and thrown into the rubbish heap of formulas that have been worn down by use and stripped of their true nature, the idea of economic democracy has given way to a market that is obscenely triumphant, even at the moment of an extremely serious crisis on its financial axis, whilst the idea of a cultural democracy has ended up being replaced by an alienating industrialized mass marketing of culture. We are not progressing, we are regressing. And it becomes ever more absurd to speak of democracy if we insist on mistakenly identifying it exclusively with the quantitative and mechanical expressions of it that we call political parties, parliaments, and governments, without paying any attention to their actual content and the distorted, abusive use they tend to make of the vote that justified them and placed them where they are.

You should not conclude from what I have just written that I am against the existence of parties: I am a member of one of them myself. You should not think that I abhor parliaments or their members: I would wish both to be better, more active and responsible in all things. Nor should you believe that I am the Providential creator of a magic recipe that will allow people henceforth to live without having to put up with bad government and waste time on elections that rarely solve the problems: I just refuse to accept that it is only possible to govern and wish to be governed according to the supposedly democratic models currently in use, which to my mind are distorted and incoherent, and which certain politicians (not always in good faith) want to make universal, along with the false promises of social development that barely manage to disguise the egotistical and relentless ambitions that really motivate them. We nurture these ills in our own home, then behave as though we were the inventors of a universal panacea capable of curing all the ills of the body and the spirit of the planet's six thousand million inhabitants. Ten drops of our democracy three times a day and you will be happy forever. The truth is, the only really deadly sin is hypocrisy.

October 9: *God and Ratzinger*

What might God think of Ratzinger? What might God think of the Roman Catholic and Apostolic Church of which this Ratzinger is sovereign pope? As far as I know (and it is fair to say that I know rather little), no one has ever yet dared to formulate these heretical questions, perhaps knowing in advance that there are not nor will there ever be answers to them. As I once wrote during a

spell of vain metaphysical inquiry, a good fifteen years ago, God
is the silence of the universe and man is the cry that gives meaning to that silence. It is in the *Lanzarote Notebooks* and it has been
quoted frequently by theologians of the neighboring country who
have been so kind as to read my work. Of course, for God to think
something of Ratzinger or of the church that the pope has been
trying to rescue from a totally predictable death—whether from
starvation or from failing to find ears to hear it or faith to reinforce its foundations—it would be necessary to demonstrate the
existence of said God, the most impossible of tasks, in spite of the
supposed proofs offered by Saint Anselm; even Saint Augustine
confessed that trying to explain the Trinity was like emptying the
ocean with a bucket into a hole in the sand. The reason that God, if
he exists, ought to be grateful to Ratzinger is the concern the pope
has shown in recent times for the delicate condition of the Catholic
faith. People do not go to mass, they have stopped believing in
the dogmas and acting on the prejudices that generally made up
the basis of spiritual life for their forefathers, and of their material life too, as happened, for example, with many of those bankers
established in the very first years of capitalism, who were strict
Calvinists and, as far as one can gather, of a personal and professional honesty that was proof against any devilish temptation of a
subprime variety. The reader might perhaps be thinking that this
sudden switch in the transcendent subject I began by broaching—
that is, the Episcopal synod gathered in Rome—was a more or less
dialectic ploy to introduce a critique of the irregular behavior (to
say the least) of contemporary bankers. That was not my intention, nor is this my area of expertise, if I have such a thing.

So then, let us return to Ratzinger. Something occurred to this
man, who is undoubtedly intelligent, with an extremely active life
within and around the Vatican (suffice it to say that he was head of
the Congregation for the Doctrine of Faith, the successor, though
using other methods, of the ominous Holy Office, formerly better
known as the Inquisition), something that one might not expect

from someone with his degree of responsibility, whose faith we
should respect while not respecting the expression of his medie-
val thinking. Scandalized by secularism, frustrated at the church's
abandonment by the faithful, he opened his mouth at the mass with
which the synod began to let loose such outrageous remarks as
"If we look at history, we are forced to admit that this distancing
alienation and rebellion of inconsistent Christians is not unique.
As a consequence, God, though never breaking his promise of
salvation, had to resort frequently to punishment." In my village
they used to say that God punishes with neither stick nor stones,
and that's why we have to be afraid of another one of those floods
coming to drown all the atheists, the agnostics, the secularists in
general, along with other promoters of spiritual disorder en masse.
But God's designs are boundless and unknown, so perhaps the
current president of the United States has already been a part of
the punishment reserved for us. Anything is possible if God wills
it. On the crucial condition that he exists, of course. If he doesn't
exist (or at least he has never spoken to Ratzinger), then these are
all just stories that no longer frighten anyone. God, they say, is
eternal, and he has time for everything. Eternal he may be; we can
allow that much so as not to contradict the pope, but his eternity is
only that of eternal not-being.

October 13: *Eduardo Lourenço*

I have stubbornly remained in debt to Eduardo Lourenço since
1991—for exactly seventeen years. It is a rather unique debt,
because although it would be natural for him, as the creditor, never
to have forgotten it, it is rather less common that I, the debtor,
contrary to the nature of my kind, have never denied it. However,
if it is indeed true that I have never pretended to be oblivious to
my debt, it should also be said that he has never allowed me to
be deceived by his tactical silences on the subject, which he intermittently breaks, saying, "So what about those photographs?" My

response is always the same: "Oh hell, I've been very busy with work, but the worst thing is I've still not been able to send them off to get the copies made." And he, every bit as consistent as I am, "There are six of them: you keep three and give me back the rest." "No, never, that would be absurd, you should have them all," I always reply, hypocritically magnanimous. Now, the time has really come for me to explain what these photos are. We were— he and I—in Brussels, at Europalia, and were wandering about like any other curious people from hall to hall, commenting on the beauties and opulence displayed, and Augusto Cabrita was with us, camera at the ready, in search of the immortal moment. What he was expecting to find at the moment when Eduardo Lourenço and I stood with our backs to a baroque tapestry of some historical or mythical scene, I don't really know. "Right there," commanded Cabrita, with that fierce air that photographers have in what I imagine they consider critical situations. To this day I have no idea what little demon made me not take the solemnity of the moment seriously. I began by straightening Eduardo's tie, then invented something about his glasses not being on straight and devoted myself to putting them in their proper place, where in fact they had been all along. We started laughing like two little boys, he and I, while Augusto Cabrita with one shot after another took advantage of the occasion that had been offered him on a platter. That is the story of the photographs. A few days later, Augusto Cabrita, who died two years ago, sent me the pictures, thinking no doubt that they would be in good hands. They were indeed good hands, or not altogether bad hands, but, as I have explained, not very effective ones.

Some time after that I came to write the novel *All the Names*, which, as I thought at the time and continue to believe today, could have had no one better than Eduardo to present it. I made this known to him, and he, good chap that he is, agreed at once. The day came, the biggest room in the Altis Hotel was bursting at the seams, and no sign or word of Eduardo Lourenço. You could breathe the concern in the heavy air—something must have happened. On top of this, the great essayist has a reputation for haplessness, and he might have got the wrong hotel. So hapless, so hapless indeed, that when he finally did arrive he announced, in the calmest voice in the world, that he had lost his speech. There was a general "Ah" of consternation, in which I did not join. For a terrible suspicion had assailed my soul: that Eduardo Lourenço had decided to take advantage of the occasion to avenge himself for the episode of the photographs. I was wrong. With or without his notes, the man was as brilliant as ever. He started off on some ideas, weighed them up with the misleading air of someone who was thinking about something else, left a few of them to one side for a second examination, arranged others on an invisible tray, allowing them to develop the necessary connections between themselves and other minor ideas that in fact turned out to be more valuable than had first appeared. The final result, if I might be permitted the metaphor, was a nugget of solid gold.

My debt had increased, had expanded wider than the hole in the ozone layer. The years went by. Until—and there is always an "until" to set us straight at last, as though time, after a lot of waiting, has lost patience. In this case it was my recent reading of an essay by Eduardo Lourenço, 'Do immemorial ou a dança do tempo' ["On the Immemorial or the Dance of Time"] , in the journal *Portuguese Literary and Cultural Studies 7* from the University of Massachusetts at Dartmouth. It would be insulting to summarize this extraordinary piece. I will limit myself to assuring you that the famous copies are now finally in my possession and that Eduardo will receive them in a few days. With the greatest friendship and deepest admiration.

October 14: *Jorge Amado*

For many years Jorge Amado wanted to be, and knew how to be, the voice, meaning, and joy of Brazil. It is not often that a writer manages to become as much the mirror and portrait of an entire people as he was. A significant part of the reading world outside the country started learning about Brazil when they started reading Jorge Amado. And many people were surprised to discover in Jorge Amado's books, on the clearest of evidence, the complex heterogeneity of Brazilian society, not only in racial but in cultural terms too. The generalized, stereotyped view that Brazil could be reduced to the mechanical sum of white, black, mulatto, and Indian populations—a view that in any case has been progressively corrected, albeit unequally, owing to the dynamics of development in the country's multiple sectors of social interaction—received in Jorge Amado's work the most serious and at the same time pleasing rebuttal. We were not unaware of early Portuguese immigration, nor (on a different scale and at different times) German and Italian immigration, but it was Jorge Amado who placed what little we knew about the subject right there before our eyes. The fresh breeze that fanned Brazilian culture came from an ethnic richness and diversity you would never believe if you looked through the eyes of Europeans, whose view was obscured by the insular habits of colonialism. In fact, from the nineteenth century through the twentieth and up to the present day, hordes of Turks, Syrians, Lebanese and *tutti quanti* left their countries of origin to transport themselves body and soul to the seductions, but also the perils, of the Brazilian El Dorado. And Jorge Amado opened wide the doors of his books to them.

I will give as an example of what I'm saying a small and delightful book whose title—*The Discovery of America by the Turks*—is capable of mobilizing the immediate attention of the most apathetic readers. It begins by telling the story of two Turks, who are not Turks, Jorge Amado says, but Arabs called Raduan Murad and Jamil Bichara, who have decided to emigrate to America in pursuit of money and women. It does not take long, however, for the story (which seemed to start out by promising unity) to divide up into other stories, in which dozens of other characters

appear—violent men, whorers and drunkards, women as thirsty
for sex as for domestic harmony, all peopling the district of Itabuna
(Bahia), precisely where Jorge Amado had been born. (Is this a
coincidence?) The picaresque land of Brazil is no less violent than
the Iberian Peninsula. We are in the land of hired guns, cocoa
plantations that once were gold mines, arguments resolved with
machete cuts, lawless colonels who exert a power nobody can
understand how they came to hold, brothels where prostitutes are
fought over like the most chaste of wives. Here the people think
only of fornicating and accumulating money, lovers and opportunities for drunkenness. They are flesh for the Final Judgment, for
eternal damnation. And yet. . . and yet, throughout this stormy
story of persons of ill repute there breathes (to the reader's bewil-
derment) a kind of innocence, as natural as the wind that blows
or the water that flows, as spontaneous as the weeds that spring
up after the rains. A wonder of narrative skill, *The Discovery of
America by the Turks*, notwithstanding its almost schematic brevity
and apparent simplicity, deserves to occupy a place alongside the
great Romanesque panoramas, such as *Jubiabá*, *A Tenda dos mila-
gres* [*The Tent of Miracles*] or *Terras do Sem-fim* [*The Violent Land*].
They say that you can recognize a giant from his finger. Well then,
here is the finger of the giant, the finger of Jorge Amado.

October 15: *Carlos Fuentes*

*Carlos Fuentes, who created the expression "La Mancha territory," a
happy formula that came to express the diversity and complexity of the
existential cultural experiences that connect the Iberian Peninsula with
South America, has just received the Don Quixote Prize in Toledo.
What follows is my tribute to the writer, to the man, and to the friend.*

The first Carlos Fuentes book I read was *Aura*. Although I have
not returned to it, I have retained to this day (and more than forty
years have gone by) the impression of having penetrated a world

unlike anything I had known before, with an atmosphere composed of realist objectivity and mysterious magic, and that these opposites—which after all are not as opposed as they seem—merged to captivate the reader's spirit in a wholly unique way. Few of my encounters with books have left me with such an intense and lasting recollection.

That was not a time when American literatures (I am referring to South America) enjoyed the special favor of the learned public. Having been fascinated for generations by the French *lumières*, which today have faded, we watched with a certain carelessness (the feigned carelessness of ignorance that suffers from having to recognize itself as such) what was going on below the Rio Grande, a movement that, just to aggravate the situation, might have been traveling with relative freedom to Spain but barely paused in Portugal. There were lacunae, books that simply never appeared in the bookshops, and the distressing lack of competent criticism that could help us to find among the little that was being placed within our reach the excellent things at which those literatures, often fighting against similar odds, kept persistently working away. Deep down, there might have been another explanation: the books traveled little, but we traveled even less ourselves.

My first trip to Mexico was to Morelia, where I participated in a congress on the chronicle as a literary form. I didn't then have time to visit bookshops, but I had already begun to peruse assiduously the work of Carlos Fuentes, reading key works such as *La region más transparente* [published in English as *Where the Air Is Clear*] and *The Death of Artemio Cruz*. It became clear to me that this was a writer of the highest artistic standard and of a rare conceptual richness. Later there was another extraordinary novel, *Terra Nostra*, which opened new perspectives for me, and I need not mention any further titles here (with the exception of *The Buried Mirror*, a key work indispensable to any sensitive and aware understanding of South America, as I have always preferred to call it) to affirm that from then on I saw myself definitively as an admiring devotee of the author of *The Old Gringo*. I knew the writer; I had yet to meet the man.

Now for a confession. Personally I am not easily intimidated, quite the contrary, but my first encounters with Carlos Fuentes, which of course were always polite, as one would have expected of two well-brought-up people, were not easy, not through any fault of his but because of a kind of resistance on my part to accepting naturally something which in Carlos Fuentes is extremely natural—that is, his style of dress. We all know that Fuentes dresses well, with elegance and good taste, his shirt never wrinkled, but for some mysterious reason I thought that a writer, especially one from that part of the world, should not dress in that way. My mistake. Carlos Fuentes managed to make the greatest critical demands and the greatest ethical rigor—both of which he has—compatible with a well-chosen tie. Believe me, that's no small thing.

October 16: *Federico Mayor Zaragoza*

The Frankfurt Book Fair begins: gathered there all together, the great entrepreneurs of the book world announce hard times for the object from which we have long derived a living and to which we still owe so much. Apparently all the big publishing houses are there, but there are countless small publishers who cannot travel, who cannot afford the stands that others can, and who are nevertheless fighting against the fulfillment of that fatal prediction: the span of ten years that will see paper books come to an end and digital ones take over. What will the future be like? I don't know. Although we have not yet reached that day, a day that will go hard for the inhabitants of the Gutenberg galaxy, I offer here a brief tribute to small publishers, for example Spain's Ânfora, which is about to publish a book by my friend Federico Mayor Zaragoza, the man who wanted Unesco to be something more than just an acronym or an elite place—in other words, a real forum for solving problems, using culture and education as the basic, if not the only, ingredients. I wrote the prologue to Mayor Zaragoza's book *En pie de paz* [*At the Feet of Peace*], which was more a vow than a title, and I have brought it to this blog today as a modest offering, hoping that it might add to the number of those who struggle to improve the lives of others—the lives of the anonymous people who are the substance of the planet.

EN PIE DE PAZ

Federico Mayor Zaragoza translates the pains of his conscience into poems. Of course, he is not the only poet to do this, but the difference—to my mind a fundamental one—lies in the fact that they, these poems, almost without exception, are an appeal to the conscience of the world, delivered this time without the illusions of his earlier almost systemic optimism. Speaking to the conscience of the world could easily be taken as yet another vague gesture to add to those that have lately been infecting the ideological discourse and so-called thinking of certain sectors of the left. That is not so. Federico Mayor Zaragoza knows humanity and the world better than most; he is not a fickle tourist of ideas, one of those who devote their attention to discovering which way the wind is blowing and then consistently setting their course wherever they consider most convenient. When I say that in his poems Federico Mayor Zaragoza appeals to the conscience of the world, I mean that he is addressing himself to people, to each and every one of them, people who wander about, confused, disoriented, stunned, amid intentionally contradictory messages, trying not to inhale the atmosphere of organized lies that has come to compete with simple oxygen and simple nitrogen.

Some would say that Federico Mayor Zaragoza's poetry has been feeding from the inexhaustible store of good intentions. Personally, I disagree. Federico Mayor feeds—poetically and vitally—from another store, the one that holds the treasure of his inexhaustible and extraordinary kindness. His poems, more sophisticated than their formal simplicity admits, are the expressions

of an exemplary personality, a man who has not cut himself off
from the living masses, who belongs to them through feeling and
reason, two human attributes that have reached a higher level in
Federico. We owe this man, this poet, this citizen much more than
we can imagine.

October 17: *God as a Problem*

On the list of all the most unlikely things in the world, the possibility
of Cardinal Rouco Varela reading this blog would be close to the top.
Be that as it may, since the Catholic Church continues to maintain that
miracles do happen, I'll put my trust in that assertion and hope that
one day the eyes of the illustrious, erudite, and pleasant empurpled one
might light upon the lines that follow. There are many more pressing
problems than secularism, which his eminence considers responsible for
Nazism and communism, and it is precisely about one of these problems
that I speak here. So read, Senhor Cardinal, read. Get some spiritual
exercise.

GOD AS A PROBLEM

I have no doubt that this discourse, beginning with its very title,
will achieve the prodigious wonder of bringing into agreement,
at least for this once, the two irreconcilable enemy brothers
called Islam and Christianity, particularly as regards the universal (that is, catholic) pinnacle to which the first aspires and which
the second still mistakenly believes itself to occupy. In the most
benign of possible reactions, the well-meaning will cry that it is
an inexcusable provocation, an unforgivable offence to the religious feelings of believers on both sides, and in the worst (assuming there is anything worse than this) I will be accused of irreverence, sacrilege, blasphemy, profanation, disrespect, and whatever
other offences of the like order they might be able to discover,
and thus, who knows, deserving of a punishment that would be

a badge of dishonor for the rest of my life. If I belonged to the Christian club myself, Vatican Catholicism would have to interrupt the Cecil B. de Mille–style spectacles it currently indulges in to take the trouble to excommunicate me; however, once they had fulfilled this disciplinary obligation they would find themselves losing their nerve. They already lack the strength for bolder deeds, now that the tears wept by their victims have dampened—forever, we hope—the firewood that made up the technological arsenal of the first Inquisition. As for Islam, in its modern fundamentalist and violent variety (as violent and fundamentalist as Catholicism was in its imperial version), the watchword par excellence, insanely proclaimed every day, is Death to the infidels. Or, in a free translation, If you don't believe in Allah you are a filthy cockroach, which, even though it, too, is a creature born from the divine fiat, any Muslim who cultivates expeditious methods has the sacred right and duty to crush under the slipper with which he will enter Muhammad's paradise to be received into the voluptuous bosoms of the houris. Allow me therefore to say now that God, who has always been *a* problem, is now *the* problem.

Like any other person who is not indifferent to the pitiful situation of the world in which he lives, I have read some of what has been written by others about the political, economic, social, psychological, strategic and even moral motives in which aggressive Islamic movements have taken root, movements that have cast the so-called Western world (and not only here) into a state of disorientation, fear, even the most extreme terror. Relatively low-powered bombs (we should remember that they have almost always been carried to the site of attacks in rucksacks), just a few here and there, have been enough to shake and begin to crack the foundations of our so very luminous civilization, bringing nearer the grand collapse of the ultimately precarious structures of collective security that have been set up and maintained at such labor and cost. Our feet, which we thought were shod in the strongest steel, have turned out to be feet of clay.

You might say it is the clash of civilizations. Perhaps, but that is not how it seems to me. The more than six thousand million inhabitants of this planet, all of them, live in what we might accurately call a global oil civilization: even those who are deprived of the precious "black gold" are not outside its domination. This oil civilization creates and satisfies (unequally, as we know) multiple needs that bring to the same well the Greeks and Trojans of classical renown, along with Arabs and non-Arabs, Christians and Muslims, not to mention those who, being neither one thing nor another, still, wherever they may be, have a car to drive, a digger to set to work, a cigarette lighter to light. Clearly this does not mean that beneath this civilization that is common to all we should not be able to discern the traces (or more than mere traces in some instances) of ancient cultures and civilizations now engaged in the technological processes of westernization as though on a forced march—a westernization that has managed to penetrate the substantial core of these cultures' personal and collective mentalities only with great difficulty. And for some reason they say that the habit doesn't make the monk . . .

An alliance of civilizations, were it to be realized, could represent an important step toward the reduction of global tensions, a step from which we seem to be ever further away, but it would be inadequate, if not totally impracticable, if it did not include an interdenominational dialogue, for without one there would not be even a remote possibility of an alliance . . . As there is no reason to fear that the Chinese, Japanese, or Indians, for example, might be finalizing their own plans to take over the world, spreading their various beliefs (Confucianism, Buddhism, Taoism, Hinduism) by peaceful or violent means, it should be more than obvious that when I speak of an alliance of civilizations I am thinking particularly of Christians and Muslims, the enemy brothers who across history have alternated—now one, now the other—in their tragic and apparently eternal roles of executioner and victim.

Hence, whether you like it or not, we have God as a problem, God as a rock in the middle of the road, God as a pretext for hatred, God as an agent of disunity. But no one dares mention this most prima facie evidence in any of the many analyses of the question, be they political, economic, sociological, psychological, or strategically utilitarian in nature. It is as if a kind of reverential fear, or a resignation to what is established as politically correct, has prevented the analyst from seeing what is present in the threads of the net, the labyrinthine weave from which there has been no escape—that is to say, God. If I were to tell a Christian or a Muslim that the universe is made up of more than four hundred thousand million galaxies, and that each one of them contains more than four hundred thousand million stars, and that God, whether Allah or some other, *could not have made this,* and even better *would have had no reason to make this,* they would reply indignantly that for God, whether Allah or some other, nothing is impossible. Except apparently—I would argue—making peace between Islam and Christianity, by way of reconciling the most wretched of the animal species said to have been born from his will, the one made in his image, that is, the human species.

In the physical universe there is neither love nor justice. Nor is there cruelty. No power presides over the four hundred thousand million galaxies and the four hundred thousand million stars that exist in each one. No one makes the sun rise each day and the moon every night, even when it is not visible in the sky. Since we were put here without knowing why or what for, we have had to invent everything. We have invented God too, but he didn't go beyond our thoughts; rather, he stayed inside our heads, at times as a fact of life, almost always as an instrument of death. We're able to say, "Here is the plough we have invented," but we cannot say, "Here is the God that invented man who invented the plough." We cannot eliminate this God from our minds—even an atheist such as myself cannot. But let us at least discuss it. It is no use saying that killing in God's name makes God a killer. To those who kill in God's name God is not only the judge who will absolve them, he is also the powerful Father who in their minds used to provide the firewood for the *autos-da-fé* and now prepares and orders the planting of bombs. Let's discuss this invention, let's solve this problem, let's recognize at least that the problem does exist. Before we all go crazy. And from there on, who knows? Maybe that will be how we'll manage not to go on killing one another.

October 20: *A (Financial) Crime against Humanity*

I was thinking of writing in the blog about the economic crisis that is upon us, but had to devote myself instead to fulfilling an obligation to another medium of communication. I offer you here my thoughts, which have already been published in Spain in the newspaper Público, *and in Portugal in the weekly* Expresso.

A (FINANCIAL) CRIME AGAINST HUMANITY

The story is well known, and in the old days when schools considered themselves the ideal instruments of education, it was taught to children as an example of the modesty and discretion that should remain in us when the devil tempts us to hold an opinion on a matter about which we know nothing or little. Apelles would allow a cobbler to point out a mistake in the shoes of the figure he had painted, because shoes are the cobbler's business, but the same cobbler ought never dare to give an opinion on, for example, the anatomy of the knee. In short, a place for everyone and everyone in his place. At first glance, Apelles was right: he was the master, he was the painter, he was the authority, and as for the cobbler, he would be called for at the appropriate time when it was a matter of putting half-soles on a pair of boots. And really, where would we be if any person, including the most universally ignorant, could allow himself to offer an opinion on things he didn't know? If someone hasn't completed the necessary studies, he should keep

silent and leave the responsibility of making the most suitable decisions (suitable for whom?) to those who know.

Yes, at first glance Apelles was right, but only at first glance.
The painter of Philip and Alexander of Macedon, considered a
genius in his day, forgot one important aspect of the matter: the
cobbler has knees, so by definition he is competent in these joints,
even if it is only to complain about the pains he feels in them (if he
does). By now an attentive reader will have understood that these
lines are not really about Apelles nor about the cobbler. What they
are about is the extremely serious economic and financial crisis that
is convulsing the world, to the extent that we cannot escape the
distressed feeling that we have come to the end of an era without
being able to glimpse what the next will be, or bring, nor how after
an intermediate period, a span of time impossible to predict, we are
going to restore the ruins and open up new paths.

How so? How can an ancient legend explain today's disasters?
Well, why not? The cobbler is us, those of us who sit impotently
by as the great economic and financial powers approach, crushing,
mad to conquer more and more money, more and more power,
by any legal or illegal means within their grasp, however clean or
dirty, commonplace or criminal. And Apelles? Apelles is precisely
those bankers, those politicians, those insurers, those big specula-
tors, who with the complicity of the media have for the past thirty
years responded to our timid protests with the arrogance of those
who consider themselves the possessors of ultimate wisdom. That
is, even if our knee hurts we are not allowed to speak of it, denounce
it, hold its injury up to public condemnation. Those three decades
were the era of the absolute empire of the Market, that supposedly
self-balancing and self-correcting entity charged by immutable
destiny to arrange and defend for all time our personal and collective happiness, even if in reality it was constantly denying it to us.

So what now? Will fiscal paradises and numbered accounts
come to an end at last? Will there be tireless investigations of the
origins of enormous bank deposits, blatantly criminal financial

machinations, opaque investments that frequently have been no
more than mass laundering of dirty money, of drug-trafficking
money? And since we're talking about crimes... will ordinary
citizens have the satisfaction of seeing those responsible for the
earthquake that is shaking our homes, the lives of our families, and
our jobs brought to judgment and condemned? Who will solve the
problem of the unemployed (I have not counted them, but I don't
doubt there are already millions) who are victims of the crash and
who will continue to be unemployed for months or years, strug-
gling to live on wretched state subsidies while the big executives
and administrators who deliberately brought their companies to
the wall enjoy millions and millions of dollars, protected by cast-
iron contracts that the fiscal authorities, paid from taxpayers'
money, pretend to know nothing about? And the active complicity
of the governments, who will investigate that? Bush, that malignant product of Nature at one of her worst moments, will say that
his plan has saved (will save?) the North American economy, but
there are questions he will have to answer: Did you not know what
was happening in those plush meeting rooms, which even cinema
has allowed us into, and not just allowed us in but shown us the
criminal decisions being taken, sanctioned by every penal code in
the world? What good are the CIA and the FBI to you, or the
dozens of other institutions of national security that have prolifer-
ated in the misnamed North American democracy, where a traveler coming into the country has to hand his computer over to an
officer of the border police officer and allow him to copy his hard
disk? Did Mr. Bush not realize that he had an enemy at home, or
rather, did he realize but not care?

In every respect what is happening is a crime against humanity, and it is in this light that it should be examined in every public
forum and in every conscience. I am not exaggerating. Crimes
against humanity are not limited to genocide, ethnocide, death
camps, torture, targeted assassinations, deliberately provoked
famines, massive pollution, the repressing of victims' identities

through humiliation. A crime against humanity is what the financial and economic powers of the United States, with the actual or tacit complicity of their government, have been perpetrating in cold blood against millions of people all over the world, who are threatened with losing whatever money they have left, after many of them—I don't doubt that there are millions—have already lost their only, often inadequate, source of income: work.

The criminals are known, they have names and surnames, yet they take limousines to the golf course, so sure of themselves that they do not even think of hiding. They would be easy to catch. Who dares bring these gangsters to court? Even if an action against them didn't succeed, we would all be so grateful. It would be a sign that for honest people all is not yet lost.

October 21: *Constitutions and Realities*

The Portuguese Constitution came into effect on April 25, 1976, two years after the revolution and the end of a troubled period of partisan struggles and social unrest. Since then it has been through seven revisions, the most recent in 2005. In many of its constituent articles, a political constitution is a declaration of intent. Constitutionalists should not rend their garments when I say this: I am not trying to minimize the importance of these documents, which I am considering here along with the Universal Declaration of Human Rights, which has been in force (or rather, we should say, in latency) since 1948. As we all know, changes to a constitution are a form of operational correction, adjustments to social reality, when they are not simply the result of the political will of a parliamentary majority that is able to promote or impose its own preferences. On the other hand, maybe through superstition or inertia, it is not unusual for constitutions, or at least some of them, to retain fossilized remains of articles that have entirely or partly lost their original meaning. There is no other way to explain how the preamble to the Portuguese Constitution has retained, as if untouchable, even if as a purely rhetorical concession, the phrase "to open a path to socialism." In a world dominated by the cruelest economic and financial liberalism ever imagined, this reference, the last echo of a thousand popular aspirations, risks raising a smile. A tearful smile, that is. Constitutions exist, and it is by their light that I believe we should judge the administration of our governments. The law of the jungle that has ruled these past thirty years would not have produced the consequences we see today if governments, all of them, had each made the constitution of its country into a vade mecum to be used day and night, the primer for all good citizens. It may be that the terrible shock the world is experiencing will lead us to treat our constitutions as something more than the simple declarations of intent they remain in so many respects. Let us hope so.

October 22: *Chico Buarque de Holanda*

Do parallel universes exist? Faced with the various "proofs" presented to the court of public opinion by those writers who dedicate themselves to science fiction, it is not hard to believe that they do, or at least to concede to this audacious hypothesis that which we would deny no one—that is, the benefit of the doubt. Now, supposing such parallel universes do exist, it would be logical and I think inevitable that we should acknowledge the existence of parallel literatures, parallel writers, parallel books. A sarcastic soul would not fail to remind us that you needn't go that far to find parallel writers, better known as plagiarists, who nonetheless never actually become real plagiarists at all because they feel obliged to put something of their own labor into the work they sign in their own name. Absolute plagiarism was what Pierre Menard did, who according to Borges copied *Quixote* word for word, and even in this case Borges himself warned us that the word *justice* in the twentieth century does not mean the same thing (or the same justice) as when it was written at the beginning of the seventeenth. . . Another kind of parallel writer (nowadays called a "ghost") is the writer who writes for others, so that they can enjoy the supposed or actual glory of seeing their names on a book jacket. It is this type of author that Chico Buarque de Holanda's novel *Budapest* is apparently about, and if I say apparently it is only because the ghost whose grotesque adventures we follow (entertained, and at the same time filled with pity) is merely the unconscious cause of a series of repetitions, which, if not actually repeated universes or literatures, are certainly, disconcertingly, repetitions of authors and books. What is most unsettling, however, is the feeling of vertigo that continually overtakes the reader, who from moment to moment knew where he was but from moment to moment does not know where he is. Without seeming to be trying to do so, each page of the novel expresses a "philosophical" question and an "ontological" provocation: What is reality, after all? What and who am I, after all, in this scheme they have taught me to call reality? A book exists, stops existing, will exist again. One person wrote it, another person signed it; if the book disappears, will they both disappear, too? And if they disappear, will they disappear altogether or only in part? If one survives, will he survive in this universe or another? Who would I be, if by surviving I were no longer who I was? Chico Buarque shows great audacity in this book; he writes crossing a chasm on a high wire and makes it to the other side. To the side where we find his work masterfully accomplished, demonstrating a mastery of language, of narrative construction, of just *doing*. I don't think I am wrong when I say that something new happened in Brazil with the appearance of this book.

October 23: *Do Torturers Have Souls?*

Over the past few days Judge Garzón has been made the object of target practice. Even those who defend him would argue that his personality is controversial, as if we were each obliged to be identical to our next-door neighbor. . . The thing is that Garzón, with his highly individual edicts, is the judge who has given the most joy to those who—in spite of everything—expect a lot from justice, or, to be more accurate, from those tasked with administering it. Following some complaints that were brought to his attention, Garzón waded into an issue that is bigger than he and all judicial institutions are put together: the Spanish Civil War, the illegality of Francoism, the dignity of those who defended the Republic and an entire way of life. He knows that he might have to abandon the battlefield, but he will have left the doors open for certain truths to be recognized, and for the dead to be identified and, ultimately, decently buried. The Spanish transition, a period that was lived through in the hope of what might be possible, is not a safe conduct: the left yielded because military and civilian Francoism were beginning to appear. But they did not give up, they didn't say, "This is the last word," they simply waited for the day to come when they could count their dead and call things by their proper names. Garzón has used his position of authority to help, and no one felt greater joy at this than the war victims who have managed to survive to this day.

Judge Garzón is no partisan. He understands that nothing human can be alien to him, and he delves into matters he considers to be criminal because he has the authority to do so. He also wonders whether torturers have souls, which is more than enough of an indication that he approaches an analysis from both sides. A few months ago he asked me to write a prologue for a piece of work he had carried out with the journalist Vicente Romero. This, I repeat, was an investigation into the behavior of torturers. I enthusiastically recommend reading this book—El Alma de los Verdugos [*The Torturers' Soul*], *published by RBA*—*and until you have a copy in your hands I shall leave you with these lines that I wrote in the manner of a prologue for Baltasar Garzón and Vicente Romero.*

DO TORTURERS HAVE SOULS?

The idea of a soul that can be considered responsible for any and every act we commit must necessarily lead us to recognize the complete innocence of the body, reduced to being the passive instrument of a will, of a yearning, of a desire impossible to locate in any specific part of itself. A hand in repose, with its bones, nerves, and tendons, is ready to fulfill an order within the instant it is given, an order for which the hand is not responsible, whether it is to offer someone a flower or to stub out a cigarette on someone's skin. On the other hand, attributing a priori the responsibility for all our actions to an immaterial entity, the soul, that, mediated by our conscience, is also the judge of those actions, leads us into a vicious circle, in which in the end no culprit is answerable for his deed. Yes, we do accept that his soul is responsible, but where is this soul for us to put into cuffs and send off to trial? Yes, we can show that the hammer that destroyed the victim's skull was wielded by this hand, but if the hand that killed might have just as readily—or unconsciously—held out a flower, how can we incriminate it? Does the flower absolve the hammer?

I mentioned above that will, need, desire (synonyms that, strictly speaking, cannot be kept apart) cannot be specifically located in the body. That much is certain. No one can state, for example, that the will is to be found between the middle and index finger of the hand that is currently employed in strangling someone with the help of its partner to the left. However, we all imagine that if the will has a home, and it must, then it can only be inside the brain, that highly complex universe (the cerebral cortex is about five millimeters thick and contains seventy thousand million nerve cells arranged in six interconnected layers) whose function still largely remains to be studied. We are the brain we have at any given moment, and that is the only essential truth we can state about ourselves. What, then, is the will? Is it something material? I cannot imagine, do not think anyone could imagine, what sort of argument you could

use to defend the alleged materiality of the will without presenting
some material demonstration of that same materiality. . .

Voluntarism, as is widely known, is the theory that maintains that
the will is the basis of being, the root of action, and, in addition, the
essential function of animal life. Voluntarist tendencies are already
to be found in classical antiquity in Aristotelianism and Stoicism.
In contemporary philosophy, voluntarists include Schopenhauer
(will as the essence of the world, but beyond cognitive representation) and Nietzsche (the will to power as a principle for achieving
success in life). This is a serious matter, and all the evidence requires
someone here (not the person writing these lines) who is capable of
relating these and other philosophical reflections on the will to the
contents of this book, whose title, let us not forget, is *The Torturers'
Soul.* I should perhaps have stopped here, to the benefit of my sense
of honor, had my eyes not lighted—my hand leafing distracted
through a humble dictionary—on the following definition: "Will.
The capacity for determining to do or not to do something. Liberty
is rooted in it." Nothing could be clearer, as you see: through my will
I can determine to do or not to do something, and liberty renders me
free to determine myself one way or another. Since language has
accustomed us to consider the will and liberty as inherently positive concepts, we are suddenly aware of an instinctive fear that the
sparkling medals that we call liberty and will can show the complete
and utter opposite on their reverse sides. It was through the use of
his freedom (shocking though the use of this word might seem to
us in such a context) that General Videla became, through his own
will—I insist on that, through his own will—one of the most loathsome participants in the bloody and seemingly unending world
history of torture and murder. It was likewise by using their will and
their freedom that the Argentine torturers carried out their dreadful
work. They wanted to do it, and they did it. So no forgiveness is
possible. No national or personal reconciliation is possible.

Knowing whether or not they have souls does not matter much.
In fact, the person who should know most about this subject is

the Argentine Catholic priest Christian von Vernich, who a few
months ago was sentenced to life imprisonment for genocide. His
service record shows six murders, the torture of thirty-four people,
and forty-two cases of kidnapping. And if I might be allowed a
tragic irony, it is even possible that at some point he gave one of
his victims the last rites. . .

October 24: *José Luis Sampedro*

This afternoon I heard mention of José Luis Sampedro, an economist, a writer, and above all a wise man, with the sagacity that
doesn't come with age (though age can help a little) but from
reflection as a way of life. He was asked on television about the
crisis of '29, which he experienced as a child and which he subsequently studied as an academic. He gave intelligent answers,
which anyone interested in understanding what is going on will
find in his books (he has written so much, José Luis Sampedro),
or by seeking out his journalism on the Web, but there was one
question that he himself—rather than the interviewer—asked,
and which remained engraved in my memory. The master asked
us, and himself, how to explain why the money used to rescue
the banks appeared so quickly and was given unconditionally,
and whether this money would have appeared with the same
speed had it been solicited to help with an emergency in Africa,
or to fight AIDS. . . It did not take us long to guess the answer.
The economy we can save, but not the human being, who should
take absolute priority, whoever and wherever he or she may be.
José Luis Sampedro is a great humanist as well as an exemplar
of lucidity. Contrary to what is sometimes said, the world is not
completely lacking in deserving people like him, so we should
pay him careful attention. And do what he tells us: intervene,
intervene, intervene.

October 27: *When I Grow Up I Want to Be like Rita*

The Rita I want to be like when I grow up is Rita Levi-Montalcini, winner of the Nobel Prize for Medicine in 1984 for her research into the development of neural cells. Given that I already have a Nobel Prize, it is not with any ambition for that greater or lesser glory (opinions of those in the know are divided) that I am ready to stop being who I am in order to become Rita. Increasingly so, since I am of an age when any sort of change, however promising, always seems to be a sacrifice of the routines that we more or less all end up adopting.

So why do I want to be like Rita? It's simple. At her investiture as a Doctor (*Honoris Causa*), delivering the inaugural lecture of the Complutense University in Madrid, this woman, who will be a hundred years old in April, made a few statements (a shame we weren't able to get hold of a complete transcript of her improvised speech) that left me alternately amazed and grateful, however hard it is to imagine these two extreme feelings together and united. She said: "I have never thought about myself. Living or dying, they're the same thing. Because naturally, life is not in this little body. What matters is the way in which we live and the message we leave behind. That is what survives us. That is immortality." And she said too, "The obsession with aging is ridiculous. My brain is better now than it was when I was young. It's true that I don't see well and my hearing is even worse, but my head has always worked well. The crucial thing is always to keep the brain active, to try to help others and retain your curiosity about the world." And these words, which made me feel as if I had found a kindred spirit: "I am against reform or any other kind of subsidy. I have survived without it. In 2001 I didn't earn a thing and I had money problems until President Ciampi named me Senator for Life."

Not everyone agrees with such radicalism. But I would bet that many of you reading this will also want to be like Rita when you grow up. So be it. If you do we can be sure that the world will soon change for the better. Is that not what we have been saying we want? Rita is the way to do it.

October 28: *Fernando Meirelles & Co.*

The story of the adaptation of *Ensaio sobre a cegueira*[2] for the cinema has been filled with highs and lows since Fernando Meirelles, in 1997 or thereabouts, asked Luiz Schwarcz, my Brazilian editor, if I might be interested in giving up the rights to it. He received a peremptory negative as a reply: No. However, in the offices of my literary agent in Bad Homburg, Frankfurt, a heavy shower began and lasted for years, a shower of letters, e-mails, telephone calls, messages from every kind of producer from other countries, in particular from the United States, asking the same question. I had them all given the same answer: No. Was this arrogance? No, it wasn't a question of arrogance; it was just that I wasn't sure, or even hopeful, that the book would be treated with respect. So the years went by. Then one day two Canadians turned up in Lanzarote, accompanied by my agent; they had come straight from Toronto, and they were hoping to make the film: Niv Fichman, the producer, and Don McKellar, the scriptwriter. They belonged to a new generation, neither of them reminded me of Cecil B. de Mille, and after a frank conversation, without any hidden trapdoors and without any mental reservations, I gave them the job. We still didn't know who the director would be. More years would have to pass before the day they asked me what I thought of Fernando Meirelles. Having completely forgotten what had happened back in that already distant year of 1997, I replied that I thought well of him. I had seen and liked *Cidade de Deus* [*City of God*] and *The Constant Gardener*, but I still wasn't associating the name of this director with a real person. . .

---

2   Published in the UK in a translation by Margaret Jull Costa, under the title *Blindness*.

And now the upshot of all this is finally with us. It goes by the title *Blindness*, which it is hoped will make it easier for people on the international circuit to connect it with the book. I saw no reason to dispute this decision. Today in Lisbon this *Blindness* of mine was presented in images and sounds. The audience was made up of a good number of journalists who I hope will be able to give a good account of it. The preview will be tomorrow. When we were talking about these episodes of recent history, at one point Pilar—the most practical and objective of all the individuals I know—came out with an idea: "As I understand it, the book anticipated the effects of the crisis we are suffering today. Those people desperately running down Wall Street, from bank to bank, before the money runs out are no different from the ones who move, blind, directionless, through the novel and now the film. The difference is that they don't have a doctor's wife guiding and protecting them." Come to think of it, this Andalusian woman may be right.

October 29: *A New Capitalism?*

A few days ago, a number of us from different countries and different political positions signed the text that I am reproducing below. It is a wakeup call, a protest, and an expression of the alarm we feel faced with the crisis and the possible solutions being put forward. We cannot be complicit.

A NEW CAPITALISM?

The time has come for change on a collective and individual scale. The time has come for justice.

The financial crisis is again destroying our economies, hitting our lives hard. This past decade its disruptions have been increasingly frequent and dramatic. East Asia, Argentina, Turkey, Brazil, Russia, the massacre of the New Economics, prove that these are not just random accidents happening on the surface of economic life but are inscribed in the very heart of the system.

These ruptures that have ended up producing a disastrous contraction of contemporary economic life, and are used to justify unemployment and the spread of inequality, and mark the shattering of financial capitalism and the definitive ankylosis of the global economic order in which we live. So it is necessary to transform it radically.

In his discussion with President Bush, Durão Barroso, president of the European Union, stated that the current crisis should lead to "a new global economic order," a solution that is acceptable as long as this new order is guided by the democratic principles—which should never be abandoned—of justice, liberty, equality and solidarity.

The laws of the market led to a state of chaos that brought a rescue of thousands of millions of dollars—to the culprits, not the victims. In other words, "rescue" meant "privatize the profits, nationalize the losses." This is a unique opportunity to redefine the global economic system in favor of social justice. There was no money to fund the fight against AIDS, nor to support feeding the world. . . and finally, in a real financial whirlwind, it turns out that there were enough funds to save from ruin those very same people who, by overly favoring dotcom and property bubbles, have destroyed the world economic edifice of "globalization."

This is why it is completely wrong for President Sarkozy to speak of the realization of so many efforts under the aegis of the interested parties aiming at "a new capitalism"! And for President Bush, as one might have expected, to have agreed that "the freedom of the market" should be safeguarded (without getting rid of farm subsidies!). . .

No: now it is we, the citizens, who should be rescued, and we should with speed and courage favor the transition from an economy of war to an economy of global development, in which the collective embarrassment of three thousand million dollars a day being invested in arms while more than sixty thousand people are dying of starvation would be overcome. An economy of development that would eliminate the abusive exploitation of the natural resources currently taking place (oil, gas, minerals, coal) and apply norms under the supervision of a reconstituted United Nations—including the International Monetary Fund, the World Bank "for reconstruction and development," and the World Trade Organization, which should not be a private club for nations but a U.N.O. institution— using whatever personal, human and technical means were necessary to exercise its judicial and ethical authority effectively.

Investment in renewable energy, food production (agriculture and aquiculture), the obtaining and distribution of water, and in health, education, housing. . . so that the "new economic order" might at last be democratic and beneficial to individuals. The errors of globalization and of the market economy must stop! Civil society will no longer remain a resigned spectator, and if necessary will apply all the power of the citizenry together with every modern means of communication it now has at its fingertips.

A new capitalism? No!

The time has come for change on a collective and individual scale. The time has come for justice.

Federico Mayor Zaragoza
Francisco Altemir
José Saramago
Roberto Savio
Mário Soares
José Vidal Beneyto

October 30: *The Question*

"And I would ask the political economists, the moralists, if they have already calculated the number of individuals who must be condemned to wretchedness, to overwork, to demoralization, to infantilization, to despicable ignorance, to insurmountable misfortune, to utter penury, in order to produce one rich person?"

Almeid

November 2008

November 3: *Falsehood, Truth*

On the eve of the presidential elections in the United States, this little observation is not, I think, out of place. Some time back a Portuguese politician, then in government, said to anyone prepared to listen that politics is primarily the art of not telling the truth. The worst thing was that after he said it there wasn't, as far as I know, a single politician, left or right, who corrected him, saying absolutely not, truth should be the first and last aim of politics, for the simple reason that this is the only way that both can be saved—truth saved by politics, and politics saved by truth.

November 4: *The War that Wasn't*

And what about this? In March 1975, and increasingly the following month, rumors reached us in Portugal of the displeasure of the Spanish government—at the time led by Carlos Arias Navarro—at the path, dangerous in Navarro's view, that was being taken by the Portuguese revolution. The defeat of the right-wing military coup of March 11, whose inspiration and leader had been General Spínola, had as its immediate consequence the reinvigorating of the political forces of the left, including trade unions. Arias Navarro, it would appear, went into a panic, to the point where in a meeting with the North American Deputy Secretary of State, Robert

Ingersoll, he raised the idea that Portugal was a serious threat to Spain, not only because of the way in which the situation there was developing but also because of the external support the country would be able to obtain from quarters hostile to Spain. The next development—according to Arias Navarro—might be war. In his report to Secretary of State Henry Kissinger, made immediately after this meeting, Ingersoll said that "Spain would be prepared to launch itself into combat against communism on its own if needs be. It is a strong and prosperous country. Arias Navarro doesn't want to ask for help, but trusts that they would have the cooperation and understanding of their friends, not only in Spain's interests but in the interests of all those who think in the same way." In another conversation, on April 9, with Wells Stabler, United States ambassador to Spain, Arias Navarro said that "the Spanish army is aware of the dangers of communism through its experience of the Civil War, and it is absolutely united."

And what about this? Here we were, concerned about establishing a more worthy future for Portugal against the thousand internal winds and tides, and other forces prepared against us from outside, and our neighbors, our brothers, were plotting with the United States to fight a war that would probably ruin us and no doubt would leave Spain herself badly injured too. Ever since the conversations that Franco had with Hitler with a view to sharing out—one for me, one for you—the Portuguese colonies, the explicit threat of an invasion had hovered over our heads, an invasion that might have needed no more than a yes from the United States.

Do I have to tell you that this was not the reason I wrote *A Jangada de Pedra* [*The Stone Raft*]?

November 5: *Guantánamo*

As I write, the Electoral College still has a few more hours of work ahead. It will not be till the early hours of the morning that the first projections of who will be the next president of the United States will start emerging. In the deeply unappealing event that it is Senator McCain who wins, what I'm writing will seem like the work of someone whose ideas about the world in which he lives suffer from a complete lack of realism, a complete ignorance of the threads with which political facts are woven and of the planet's various strategic objectives. Senator McCain, especially because (as the propaganda never tires of saying, and a wretched civilian such as myself would never dare to dispute) he is a war hero, a veteran of Vietnam, would never knock down the concentration and torture camp installed in the Guantánamo military base and dismantle the base itself, down to the very last screw, returning the space it occupied to its legitimate owners, the Cuban people. Because, like it or not, though the habit certainly doesn't always make the monk the uniform really does always make the general. Knock down? Dismantle? What kind of naïve person had that idea?

And yet this is precisely the issue. A few minutes ago a Portuguese radio station wanted to know what would be the first act of government I would propose to Barack Obama in the event of his being—as so many of us have been dreaming for a year and a half—the new president of the United States. I was able to answer quickly: dismantle the military base at Guantánamo, send back the marines, destroy the shame that the concentration camp (and torture camp, let's not forget) represents, turn the page and ask Cuba's forgiveness. And while he's at it, end the blockade, the garrote with which the US tried—uselessly—to strangle the will of the Cuban people. It might happen—and here's hoping that it will—that the final results of this election will invest the North American population with a new dignity and a new respect, but I would like to remind those who pretend not to be paying attention what genuinely dignified lessons, from which Washington could have learned, the people of Cuba have been giving on a daily basis during almost fifty years of patriotic resistance.

But surely it's not possible to do everything, just like that, in a single sitting? True, perhaps it isn't possible, but please, Mr. President, at least do something. Contrary to what you might have been told in the corridors of the Senate, that island is more than just a dot on the map. I hope, Mr. President, that one day you will want to visit Cuba to meet those who live there. At last. I assure you that no one there will hurt you.

November 6: *106 Years*

The 106-year-old woman, Ann Nixon Cooper, whom Obama referred to while delivering his first speech as president-elect of the United States, might come to occupy a place in the gallery of characters beloved by North American readers, beside the woman who refused to stand up and give up her place on a bus to a white man. Not a lot has been written about the heroism of women. What Obama told us about Ann Nixon Cooper included no acts of public heroism, only everyday ones, but the lessons of silence can be every bit as powerful as those of words. One hundred and six years of watching the world go by, watching its convulsions, its successes and its failures, its lack of piety, its joy at being alive in spite of everything. Last night this woman saw the picture of one of her race on a thousand posters and understood—she couldn't not have understood—that something new was happening. Or she simply kept the repeated image in her heart, in the hope that her joy would be justified and confirmed. Old people are like that sometimes: they suddenly abandon commonplaces and go against the tide, asking impertinent questions and maintaining stubborn silences that spoil the party. Ann Nixon Cooper suffered slavery of various kinds—being black, being a woman, being poor. She lived a life of submission; laws may have changed in the outside world but they didn't change the things she feared, as she looked around her and saw women mistreated, used, humiliated, and murdered, always by men. She saw that women were paid less than men for the same work; that they had to take on domestic responsibilities that kept them invisible, necessary though those duties were; she saw how their determined steps were obstructed, and how still they continued to walk forward, or refused to stand up on the bus—we should mention her again, that other black woman, Rose Banks, who made history, too.

A hundred and six years watching the world go by. Perhaps she sees it as beautiful, as did my grandmother, not long before she died, old and lovely and poor. Perhaps the woman Obama told us about yesterday felt the serenity of perfect joy, a loveliness that perhaps we, too, will know one day. However, we congratulate the president-elect for having offered her a tribute that she probably didn't need, but we did. As Obama was talking about Ann Nixon Cooper, we understood that with each word her example made us better, more human, closer to the verge of absolute brotherhood. Whether we know how to make this feeling last is up to us.

November 7: *Words*

Fortunately there are words for everything. Fortunately there are words that will always say that he who gives should give with both hands, so that his hands retain nothing that rightfully belongs to someone else. Just as kindness should not be ashamed of being kindness, so justice should never forget that above all it is restitution, the restitution of rights. All of them, beginning with the basic right to live in dignity. If I were asked to put charity, kindness, and justice in order of precedence, I would give first place to kindness, second to justice, and third to charity. Because kindness already dispenses justice and charity of its own accord, and because a fair system of justice already contains sufficient charity within it. Charity is what is left when there is neither kindness nor justice.

November 9: *Rosa Parks*

Rosa Parks, not Rose Banks. A regrettable lapse of memory, which wasn't the first and certainly won't be the last, made me perpetrate one of the worst slips that it is possible to make in the always complex system of interpersonal relations: giving someone a name that is not hers. Apart from the patient reader of these modest lines, I have no one to ask for forgiveness, but I am punished enough for the error by the sense of intense embarrassment that seized me when I immediately realized the seriousness of my mistake. I even contemplated letting it go, but I pushed the temptation away and here I am to confess the mistake and promise that henceforth I'll be careful to check everything, even things of which I think I am certain.

Good things can come of bad, according to popular wisdom, and perhaps it's true. So I have the opportunity to return to Rosa Parks, that forty-two-year-old seamstress who, traveling on a bus in Montgomery, in the state of Alabama, on December 1, 1955, refused to give her place up to a white person as the driver had told her to. This crime got her sent to prison on a charge of having disturbed public order. It should be made clear that Rosa Parks was sitting in the part of the bus reserved for black people, but since the whites' section was fully occupied, the white person wanted her seat.

In response to the imprisonment of Rosa Parks, a relatively unknown Baptist pastor, Martin Luther King, Jr., led the protests against the Montgomery bus company, which forced the public transport authority to end the practice of racial segregation in those vehicles. It was the signal that triggered other protests against segregation. In 1956 the Parks case finally reached the US Supreme Court, which declared segregation on the buses to be unconstitutional. Rosa Parks, who had been a member of the National Association for the Advancement of Colored People since 1950, found herself transformed into an icon of the civil rights movement, for which she continued to work throughout her life. She died in 2005. Without her, Barack Obama might not be president of the United States today.

November 10: *Recipe for Killing a Man*

The reference to Martin Luther King in the last post reminded me of a column published in 1968 or 1969 under the title "Recipe for Killing a Man." I include it here again as a tribute to a true revolutionary who opened the way for the imminent and definitive end to racial segregation in the United States.

RECIPE FOR KILLING A MAN

Take a few dozen kilos of flesh, bones, and blood, according to the relevant patterns. Arrange them harmoniously into head, torso, and limbs, fill them with innards and a network of veins and nerves, being careful to avoid the manufacturer's flaws that can result in the appearance of teratological phenomena. The color of the skin has no significance whatsoever.

Give the product of this tricky piece of work the name Man. Serve hot or cold, depending on the latitude, the season of the year, age, and temperament. When you mean to launch your prototypes on the market, instill in them a few qualities that will make them stand out from the common stock: courage, intelligence, sensitivity, character, a love of justice, active kindness, a respect for one's neighbor and for those further away. Second-rate products will have one or another of these positive attributes, to a greater or lesser degree, alongside those opposite qualities that tend to predominate. Modesty demands that we do not consider products that are wholly positive or wholly negative as viable. In any case, be aware that in these matters the color of the skin still has no significance whatsoever.

But a man is classified by a personal label, so as to distinguish him from his associates who have come off the production line just like him, and assigned to live in a building called Society. He will occupy one or another of the floors of this building, but only rarely will he be allowed to go up the stairs. Going down is permitted, and at times even facilitated. The floors of the building contain many homes, assigned sometimes by social standing, at other times by profession. Movement comes about through channels called habit, custom, and prejudice. It is dangerous to swim against this current, though some men do so their whole lives. These men, into whose fleshly mass are born the qualities that almost touch perfection, or who have chosen these qualities deliberately, cannot be distinguished by the color of their skin. There are some who are white and some who are black, some who are yellow and some who are brown. There are fewer copper-colored ones, these being a near-extinct species.

Man's ultimate destiny, as we have known since the beginning of the world, is death. At its precise moment, death is the same for everyone. What immediately precedes it is not. One can die simply, like someone falling asleep; one can die in the clutches of one of those illnesses said euphemistically to be unforgiving; one can die under torture, in a concentration camp; one can die vaporized inside an atomic sun; one can die at the wheel of a Jaguar, or run over by one; one can die of hunger or indigestion; one can also die of a rifle shot, in the late afternoon, when it is still daylight and you don't think death is near. But the color of a man's skin has no significance whatsoever.

Martin Luther King was a man like any of us. He had the virtues we know of, and doubtless some defects that in no way diminish his virtues. He had work to do—and he was doing it. He was fighting against the currents of custom, habit, and prejudice, in them up to his neck. Until the rifle shot came to remind the absent-minded people we are that the color of a man's skin is very important indeed.

November 11: *The Old and the Young*

Some would say that cynicism is an illness afflicting the elderly, an ailment of one's final days, a sclerosis of the will. I wouldn't dare to say that this diagnosis is completely wrong, but what I would say is that it is too easy to dismiss our problems that way, as though the current state of the world were a mere consequence of the fact that old people are old . . . To this day the hopefulness of young people has never succeeded in making the world a better place, and old people's ever increasing acerbity has never been so bad that it has made it worse. Of course the world—poor old thing—isn't responsible for the ills it suffers. What we call the state of the world is the state of ourselves, wretched humanity, inevitably made up of old people who were once young, young people who will be old, and those who are no longer young but are not yet old. And the blame? I have heard it said that we are all to blame, that there is no one who can boast of being innocent, but it seems to me that such statements, which appear to distribute justice evenly, serve only to dilute and conceal in some imaginary collective guilt the responsibilities of those who really are to blame. Not for the state of the world but for the state of life.

I write this on a day on which hundreds of men, women and children have arrived in Spain and Italy on the fragile crafts they usually employ to reach the supposed paradises of a wealthy Europe. One of these boats reached the island of Hierro, in the Canaries, carrying a dead child, and some of the shipwrecked people said that during the journey twenty more of their fellow martyrs had died and been thrown into the sea . . . Just please don't talk to me about cynicism . . .

November 12: Dogmas

The most harmful dogmas are not really those that have been explicitly declared as such, as is the case with religious dogmas, because they appeal to faith, and faith doesn't know and cannot discuss itself. What is bad is the transformation into dogma of a secular system or theory that never aspired to be a dogma at all. Marx, for example, was not dogmatic, but straightaway there was no shortage of pseudo-Marxists to convert *Das Kapital* into a new Bible, exchanging active thought for sterile commentary or perverse interpretation. And you saw what happened. One day, if we are able to break free of ancient iron molds, to slough off an old skin that doesn't allow us to grow, we will meet Marx again; perhaps a Marxist re-reading of Marxism would help us to open up more generous pathways into the act of thinking. Then we would have to start by looking for an answer to the fundamental question: "Why do I think the way I think?" In other words, "What is ideology?" Such questions may seem to be of little importance, but I don't think there are any that matter more. . .

November 13: *R.C.P.*

The initials stand for Rádio Clube Português—Portuguese Radio Club—and I don't think there can be a single Portuguese person who doesn't know it. Today, November 13, the day I write these brief lines, the R.C.P. has decided to dedicate part of its broadcast to the première of *Blindness*, directed by Brazilian filmmaker Fernando Meirelles and based on my novel *Ensaio sobre a Cegueira* [*Essay on Blindness*, published in English as *Blindness*]. Pilar, who has only good ideas, thought we ought to pay a courtesy visit to the channel and to the presenters of *Janela Aberta*—"Open Window"—which is what the program in question is called. We went there in the greatest secrecy, sure of giving them a not unpleasant surprise. What we didn't expect was how much better than ours the surprise they gave us would be. The two presenters were blind—their eyes blindfolded with a black cloth. . . There are moments that manage to be both moving and pleasing, and this was one of them. I would like to record my gratitude and my profound recognition of the proof of friendship they gave us.

November 16: *Eighty-Six Years*

I'm told that the interviews were worth doing. I, as usual, tend to doubt this, perhaps because I'm tired of listening to myself. What might seem new to other people has with the passing of time turned into a reheated soup for me. Or, worse still, I'm left with a bitter taste in my mouth due to the certainty that the handful of sensible things I've said in my life have turned out after all to be of absolutely no consequence. And why should they be of consequence? What significance does the buzzing of bees inside the hive have? Do they use it to communicate with one another? Or is it a simple effect of nature, merely a consequence of being alive, with no pre-existing consciousness or intent, like an apple tree bearing apples without any concern for whether someone might come and eat them or not? And what about us? Do we talk for the same reason we perspire? Just because we do? Sweat evaporates, is washed away, disappears, sooner or later ends up in the clouds. And words? Where do they go? How many of them remain? And for how long? And what for, after all? I know, these are idle words, appropriate for someone turning eighty-six. Or perhaps not so idle when I think of my grandfather Jerónimo, who in his final hours went to bid farewell to the trees he had planted, embracing them and weeping because he knew he wouldn't see them again. It's a lesson worth learning. So I embrace the words I have written, I wish them long life, and resume my writing where I left off. There can be no other response.

November 18: *Alive, Very Much Alive*

I do try to be a practical kind of stoic, in my own way, but indifference as a condition for happiness has never been a part of my life, and if it's true that I stubbornly seek spiritual peace, it's also true that I have not liberated myself—nor do I mean to liberate myself—from passions. I try to get myself used to the idea (without too much drama) that not only must the body perish one day but that in a certain respect it is already, at every moment, perishing. What does this matter, however, if each gesture, each word, each emotion is capable of denying this mortality, also at every moment? The truth is, I feel myself alive, very much alive, whenever for one reason or other I have to talk about death . . .

November 19: *Flooding*

I have just come back from the Casa do Alentejo where I took part in an act of solidarity with the struggle of the Palestinian people for their complete sovereignty and freedom from the senseless acts and crimes perpetrated by Israel. I made a suggestion there— that from January 20, the date Barack Obama assumes power, the White House should be flooded with messages of support for the Palestinian people, demanding a rapid solution to the conflict. If Barack Obama wants to rid his country of the disgrace of racism, he should do the same in Israel. For sixty years the Palestinian people have been made to suffer in cold blood with the tacit or active complicity of the international community. It's time to put a stop to it.

November 20: *All the Names*

I've been signing copies of *A Viagem do Elefante* [*The Elephant's Journey*][1] at the publisher's for a good part of the morning. Most will remain in Portugal, as gifts for friends and colleagues, but others will travel to distant lands, such as Brazil, France, Italy, Spain, Hungary, Romania, and Sweden—where the recipients were Amadeu Batel, our compatriot and professor of Portuguese literature at Stockholm University, and the poet and novelist Kjell

---

1 Saramago's new novel. Portuguese edition published in 2008 by Caminho. English edition to be published by Houghton Mifflin Harcourt (US) and Harvill Secker (UK).

Espmark, a member of the Swedish Academy. As I was dedicating the book to Espmark I remembered what he told me and Pilar about the backstage goings-on over the prize that was awarded to me. *Ensaio sobre a Cegueira* [*Blindness*] had already been translated into Swedish and made a good impression on the members of the Academy, so good in fact that they had almost decided among themselves that the Nobel Prize that year, 1998, would be mine. It so happened, however, that the previous year I had published another book, *Todos os Nomes* [*All the Names*], which in principle, of course, shouldn't have posed any obstacle to the decision taken, apart from a question raised by the scruples of my judges: "And what if this new book is bad?" They charged Kjell Espmark to find an answer to this question, giving him the responsibility of reading the book in its original language. Espmark, who has a certain familiarity with Portuguese, fulfilled his mission with great discipline. With the help of a dictionary, at the height of August, when it would have been more appealing to sail among the islands that cluster around the Swedish coast, he read, word by word, the story of the clerk José and the woman whom he loved without ever having seen her. I passed my exam: the little book was no less good than *Blindness* after all. Phew.

November 22: *In Brazil*

We're traveling to Brazil,[2] where we are awaited by a program as heavily laden as a sky threatening rain. I trust, however, that some opportunity can be arranged so that this conversation doesn't need to be suspended for a week, which is how long my absence will last. Being in Brazil, we know there won't be any lack of material, so if there is a problem it will be a shortage of available time. We'll see. Wish us *bon voyage*, and from now on do please be so kind as to look after the elephant for us while we're away.

---

2   On a book tour for *A Viagem do Elefante*.

November 23: *Cattle*

It wasn't easy getting to Brazil. It wasn't even easy leaving the airport. Portela is crawling with people of both sexes who look at us with mistrust, as though we had a history of actual or potential terrorism written on our faces, denouncing us. These people are called security, which is quite ironical, since judging by my own experience and that of those I can see around me there are no travelers who feel even a tiny bit secure in their presence. We encountered our first problem when our hand luggage was being checked. As I am still on the rebound from an illness I suffered and from which, fortunately, I've been recovering, I have to take regular medication—every two weeks—that has to be accompanied by a medical statement when I pass through the airport. We presented this statement, stamped and signed just as the regulations demand, thinking that within a minute we'd be allowed through. But that was not what happened. The piece of paper was laboriously read through by "security" (a woman), who thought it best to call one of her superiors, who read the statement with furrowed brow, perhaps waiting for some revelation to appear to him between the lines. Then began a game of pushing and shoving. The "security" woman had already two or three times made the worrying pronouncement, "We will have to check," a statement backed up by her boss, who repeated it not twice or three times, but five or six times. What they had to check was right there before their eyes, a piece of paper and the medication; there was nothing else to see. It was an animated discussion, only brought to an end when I—impatient and irritated—said, "Well, if you've got to check, then check, and be done with it." The boss shook his head and replied, "I've checked already, but this bottle has got to stay." The bottle—if we can give the name to a little plastic yogurt jar—was taken off to join other dangerous explosives that had been previously apprehended. As we were leaving I couldn't help thinking that responsibility for airport security, at this rate, would yet end up being handed over to the Worshipful Company of Nightclub Bouncers . . .

The worst, however, was yet to come. For more than half an hour I don't know how many of us passengers were packed together, crammed like canned sardines in the bus that was meant to be taking us to the plane. For more than half an hour, so tightly packed we could hardly move, with the doors open so that the cold morning air could circulate at will. No explanation, no word of apology. We were treated like cattle. If the plane had crashed, one might very well have said that this bus ride was our trip to the slaughterhouse.

November 24: *Two Pieces of News*

In Brazil, between one interview and the next, I learned two pieces of news: one of them, the bad, terrible news, was that the storm that occasionally breaks over São Paulo, and a few raging minutes later leaves a clear sky and the feeling that nothing has happened, has caused at least fifty-nine deaths in the south, and left thousands of people without a home, without a roof over their heads to sleep tonight, without a place to live. We cannot be indifferent to stories like these, however many times we read them. Quite the contrary—each time we hear of some new natural disaster our pain and impatience increases. And we ask the question no one can answer, even though we know an answer exists: How long will we live, or how long will the poorest live, at the mercy of the rains, winds, and drought, when we know that a solution to all these phenomena can be found in the way our lives are arranged? How long will we avert our eyes, as though human beings didn't matter? These fifty-nine people who died in Santa Catarina, Brazil, the country where I am now, needn't have died such a death. This is something we all know.

The other piece of news is that the Spanish National Prize for Letters has been awarded to Juan Goytisolo, who today I recall from the time he was in Lanzarote, with Monique, with Gómez Aguilera, talking together about their books and the task of writing. Monique is no longer with us; she can't see this prize that is finally awarded to Goytisolo, so long after we read his first book, which then had just been published. Juan, I send you a hug and my congratulations.

November 25: *The Infinite Page of the Internet*

We have just come out of a press conference in São Paulo—a group interview, as they call it here.

I was surprised that several journalists wanted to ask me about my role as blogger, when we had a poster behind us for a superb exhibition, organized by the César Manrique Foundation in the Tomie Ohtake Institute, with the most important delegates and sponsors, and with the presentation of the new book on display. But many journalists were interested by my decision to write on "the infinite page of the Internet." Could it be, to put it more clearly, that it's here that we all most closely resemble one another? Is this the closest thing we have to citizen power? Are we more companionable when we write on the Internet? I have no answers; I'm merely stating the questions. And I enjoy writing here now. I don't know whether it is more democratic, I only know that I feel just the same as the young man with the wild hair and the round-rimmed glasses, in his early twenties, who was asking me the questions. For a blog, no doubt.

November 27: *A Day Well Lived*

We are still in Brazil, Pilar and I, and moved by the Santa Catarina tragedy, in which the number of dead and missing keeps going up, as do the human interest stories, of the desolation and despair of the survivors, that are coming to us from there. We crossed paths with President Lula, on his way to visit the area hit by the tragedy.

He has to bring a great deal of consolation in order to persuade people that the State is useful. Consolation in words and in deeds. We human beings need both of these. They tell us that people who work in companies are spontaneously organizing collections to help the victims. For those who, like us, haven't experienced the tragedy directly, gestures like these console us too; they make us believe that the young woman from the publisher's is concerned with the fate of people she has never met. This is an image of the world that is possible.

This afternoon I presented *A Viagem do Elefante* [*The Elephant's Journey*] at the Brazilian Academy of Letters. In his speech Alberto da Costa e Silva said that we are all libraries, because we keep what we read inside us like the best parts of ourselves. Alberto and I are old friends, which is why this former president of the Academy and former ambassador wanted to present my book as something with which he had a connection. Beforehand we had a meeting with members of the Academy, attended by generous friends like Cleonice Berardineli and Teresa Cristina Cerdeira da Silva, who are not members, though they are a part of the spiritual aristocracy, something that is truly necessary for social evolution. Before that we were with Chico Buarque, who is about to finish a new book. If it is anything like *Budapest*, we'll have quite a piece of work. Chico, the singer, the musician, the writer, is one of those all-round men who combine doing quality work with being good guys. Today was a worthwhile day. No doubt.

November 28: *Sex Education*

"Sexual exploitation is such an important subject for humanity that there can be no hypocrisy about it. We must convince the world's parents that sex education at home is as important as food on the table. If we don't teach sex education in schools, our adolescents will learn like animals out on the streets. We must eliminate religious hypocrisy, and that goes for all religions."

The words I quote above are those of Lula da Silva, president of Brazil. He was speaking at a global congress, the third that has been called to confront the problem of the sexual exploitation to which children and adolescents all over the world are subjected. The Queen of Sweden also made an appeal for action that will put an end to the delinquent behavior against young people that has taken over the Internet. Both spoke of these serious problems affecting a vulnerable portion of society, predominantly harming the child and adolescent populations in the poorest regions of the planet, where there is a lack of schools, the concept of the family simply doesn't exist, and people are ruled by a television that broadcasts violence and sex twenty-four hours a day. Who will hear the wise words spoken at the Congress against Sexual Exploitation?

Anyway, I wanted to talk about the presentation of *A Viagem do Elefante* in São Paulo, but this subject got in my way and it takes precedence. We'll leave the book for tomorrow.

November 30: *The Cultura Bookshop*

The last image we will take with us from Brazil is of a lovely bookshop, a cathedral for books—modern, efficient, beautiful. It is the Livraria Cultura—the Cultura Bookshop—in the Conjunto Nacional. It is a bookshop for buying books, of course, but also for appreciating the impressive sight of so many titles arranged in such an attractive way, as though it weren't a warehouse, as though what we are dealing with were a work of art. The Livraria Cultura is a work of art.

My editor, Luis Schwarcz from Companhia das Letras, knew that I would be moved by this marvel, which was why he brought me there. I was also quite moved by the Companhia bookshop, seeing those glowing shelves with essential texts, with timeless classics displayed just as new books are displayed elsewhere. And all together offered up to the reader, who is left with the difficult but interesting dilemma of not knowing what to choose.

A good send-off from São Paulo. Last night, before having dinner at the house of Tomie Ohtake, we went to see the "Consistency of Dreams" exhibition. We were the last of the 700 people to pass through in the course of the day to see the exhibition that the César Manrique Foundation, under Fernando Gómez Aguilera, put together about the author of *A Viagem do Elefante*, which has already been seen in Lanzarote and Lisbon. Aguilera should be pleased: his own work is just as familiar on its own continent, just as interesting, as precise as a watch, as beautiful as the Livraria Cultura. Sometimes pieces of good news just keep accumulating. We put our faith in them.

December 2008

December 1: *Differences*

I have already spoken here of my trip to Brazil, bearing witness to the happy hours we experienced, to the words we heard and spoke, to old friendships and new, and to the painful echoes of the tragedy of Santa Catarina, those torrential rains, those hills turned to mud that buried more than a hundred defenseless people, as is the norm with natural disasters, which seem to prefer the poorest of the poor as their victims. Now we're back in Lisbon, and this would seem to be the right moment for a general stock-taking, a summary of events, except that the description of my feelings—which I think I've revealed amply in my life—requires, this time, only the use of a comprehensive and concise formula: "It all went fine." If I have any more books in me, I could not wish a better welcome for them than the welcome received by this *Elephant's Journey* that took us to Brazil.

Yesterday I posted a few admiring phrases here about the magnificent set-up of the Cultura bookshop in São Paulo. I would like to return to the subject, first to reiterate, as it so richly deserves, the dazzling impression it made on us, Pilar and me, but also for some rather less positive considerations, the result of an inevitable comparison between a vigor that was not merely commercial, because it entailed the good humor of the many buyers present, and the incurable gloom that turns our own bookshops gray, contaminated by the low standards and inadequate professional training of most of those who work there. The bookselling industry of our sister country is a serious and well structured thing, thanks not only to its own merits—which are many—but also to a level of support from the state that is inconceivable to us. The Brazilian government is a major purchaser of books, a sort of public patron always ready to loosen its purse strings when it comes to stocking libraries, stimulating publishing activity, and organizing campaigns to encourage reading that are characterized, as I have had the opportunity to establish for myself, by the effectiveness of their promotional strategies. All in contrast to what happens in here in Portugal, which in many respects remains as yet unexploited, waiting for some sign, for a plan of action, and also, if I might be excused the commercialism, for a check. Money, as the popular wisdom goes, is what you need if you want to buy melons. And also books, and other spiritual goods, Mr. Prime Minister, and you have been rather distracted from these cultural matters. So much the worse for us.

December 3: *Solomon returns to Belém*

This afternoon the elephant Solomon will return to Belém. That is to say, the literary character (for that is the way that Fate arranges such matters) will be presented at the place from which the real elephant set off in the sixteenth century. The real Solomon traveled from there to Vienna, stopping in Castelo Rodrigo, Valladolid, Rosas, Genoa, Padua, and other places before crossing the Alps and ending his days at Maximilian's court.

The writer António Mega Ferreira and the teacher and writer Manuel Maria Carrilho will be responsible for leading the conversation, which may have a book as its main subject, but I wouldn't be at all surprised if certain other subjects were broached that concern the three of us because they are, as some journalists say, on the current affairs agenda. Yes, I wouldn't mind one bit if the presentation of this elephant could serve as an opportunity to talk about the world, this world that is splitting at so many seams because, from the time of the elephant Solomon until now, even the best of seams wasn't about to hold together. In order to avoid the night drawing in.

December 4: *For Anyone Who Might Be Interested*

I presented *The Elephant's Journey* and took advantage of the opportunity to say that my mind is caught up with a new book. Phew!

December 4: *Saviano*

Many years ago, in Naples, wandering down one of those streets where anything might happen, my curiosity was awakened by a café that looked for all the world as though it had opened its doors only a few days earlier. The woodwork was light, the chrome plating shone, the floor was clean—in short, a feast not only for the eyes but also the nose and the palate, as the excellent coffee they served me proved. The employee asked me where I was from. I replied from Portugal, and he, with all the naturalness of one offering a useful piece of information, said, "This place is Camorra." Surprised, all I let out of my mouth was an "Oh?" that didn't commit me at all but that served to try and disguise the disquiet that suddenly was rumbling in the pit of my stomach. The person I had in front of me might be a simple employee with no special responsibilities for his bosses' criminal activities, but common sense demanded I view him with caution and be suspicious of any out-of-place friendliness, now that I could not pass for a casual customer. I was unable to understand how an apparently incriminating revelation could have been offered with the friendliest of smiles. I paid, left, and out on the street I hurried my pace as though a band of hired assassins armed to the teeth were sent to pursue me. After turning three or four corners, I began to calm down. The café employee might be a criminal, but he had no reason to wish any harm to me. He was clearly satisfied with just telling me something that I, as an inhabitant of this planet, should be duty bound to know: that Naples, all of it, is in the hands of the Camorra, that the beauty of the bay was a deceptive disguise and the tarantella a funeral march.

Years went by, but the episode remained in my memory. And it comes back to me now, as though I'd experienced it yesterday: that light woodwork, the shine of the chrome plating, the complicit smile of the employee, who was no employee but the manager, a man trusted by the Camorra, a Camorrista himself. I think of Roberto Saviano, receiving a death threat for having written a book denouncing a criminal organization capable of kidnapping an entire city and those who live in it. I think of Roberto Saviano, whose head they would have on a plate, and I wonder whether one day we will wake up from the nightmare that is life for so many people, persecuted for telling the truth, the whole truth, and nothing but the truth. I feel humble, almost insignificant, faced with the dignity and the courage of the writer and journalist Roberto Saviano, the man who has mastered the art of living.

December 9: *Santa Fe Street*

The street does exist, in Santiago de Chile. It was there that Pinochet's agents surrounded a single-story house that was the home (or rather the refuge) of Carmen Castillo and her companion in life and political activity, Miguel Enríquez, main leader of the MIR, the Movement of the Revolutionary Left, which had supported and cooperated with Salvador Allende. Now the party was the object of persecution by the military power that had betrayed democracy and was preparing itself to establish one of the fiercest dictatorships that South America would ever have the misfortune to know. Miguel Enríquez was killed, and Carmen

Castillo, who was pregnant, was gravely wounded. Many years later Carmen would record and reconstruct those days in a documentary of striking sincerity and realism that we have been privileged to watch tonight at the King cinema. A documentary that, thanks to the wisdom and sensitivity of its creator, manages also to be cinema of the highest quality. More later.

December 10: *Tribute*

Today's gathering is in the Casa do Alentejo, at six in the evening. As the title suggests, it is a tribute. A tribute to whom? To no one in particular, for it will consider Portuguese letters in their entirety—from A to Z, as it were—commemorating them in a program of songs and readings presented by twenty writers, actors and journalists, who have generously put their time and talent at the disposal of an idea that was born at the José Saramago Foundation. The day chosen—today, December 10, 2008—recalls the awarding of the Nobel Prize to a Portuguese writer who in his acceptance speech expressed his understanding that he should share the distinction not just with all the writers who were his contemporaries, without exception, but also all those who came before us, those who, as Camões said, have freed themselves from the tyranny of death. The following authors will be read or sung: Antero de Quental, Padre António Vieira, Vitorino Nemésio, José Cardoso Pires, Ruy Belo, Sophia de Mello Breyner, Pedro Homem de Mello, Miguel Torga, Eça de Queiroz, Natália Correia, David Mourão-Ferreira, Ary dos Santos, Camilo Castelo Branco, Manuel da Fonseca, Almada Negreiros, José Gomes Ferreira, Teixeira de Pascoaes, Raul Brandão, Fernando Pessoa, Jorge de Sena, Aquilino Ribeiro, Almeida Garrett, Luís de Camões, Carlos de Oliveira and Fernando Namora. A real parade of honor, which should be honored by everyone.

December 11: *Baltasar Garzón (1)*

In spite of the wild weather, cold and with intermittent showers, the cinema was full. Carmen Castillo had worried that the length of her film, two and a half hours, would end up discouraging the audience, but that wasn't the case. Not a single person got up to leave, and at the end, with the spectators lost in the power of the images and the chilling testimonies of the members of the MIR who survived the Chilean dictatorship, Carmen received a standing ovation. Those of us from the Foundation were proud of that audience. I'd had confidence in them, but the reality exceeded my most optimistic predictions.

As I write, more than two hundred thousand copies of the Universal Declaration of Human Rights are circulating in the hands of readers of two newspapers, Lisbon's *Diário de Notícias* and Oporto's *Jornal de Notícias*. And today, December 11, it will be the turn of Baltasar Garzón, who is coming specially from Madrid to talk about human rights, about Chile and Guantánamo. Like the tribute to Portuguese letters that took place so successfully yesterday evening, the Garzón lecture will be held at the Casa do Alentejo, at 6 p.m. It's a good opportunity to learn. Yes, to learn.

December 12: *Baltasar Garzón (2)*

Judge Baltasar Garzón bestowed on Lisbon a lesson in what the law is, or rather, what it should be. The truth is that in the strictest sense what he spoke about at the event organized by the Foundation was justice. And common sense: there are crimes that cannot go unpunished, victims who must have satisfaction, tribunals which must pull up the carpets to see what lies beneath the horrors. Because often, beneath the horrors, there are economic interests, and clearly identifiable criminals, actual people or groups who cannot be ignored by states that claim to be subject to the rule of law. Who knows whether those who are responsible for crimes against humanity, which is the only way I can describe this international financial and economic crisis, might not end up being prosecuted, just like Pinochet or Videla or other terrible dictators who spread such pain? Who knows?

Judge Baltasar Garzón made us understand the importance of not slipping into baseness even once in order not to be base forever. He who tramples on human rights even one time, in Guantánamo for instance, throws years of law and legality overboard. We must not be complicit in the chaos with which the Bush administration has infected half the world. Neither as governments, nor as citizens.

A large and attentive audience followed the judge's points respectfully and thoughtfully. And applauded, like people who have heard not revealed truths but an effective voice that the world needs if it is not to lapse into condoning abject behavior.

The Foundation is satisfied: we have done what we could to remind people that there is a Universal Declaration of Human Rights, that it is not being respected, and that citizens must demand that it does not turn into merely a dead letter. Baltasar Garzón has played his part and we can only be pleased that this was made so clear in Lisbon this evening.

December 15: *Borges*

Maria Kodama has returned to Portugal, to be present on the occasion of the inauguration of a monument to Jorge Luis Borges. There were plenty of people in the Arco do Cego park, where the memorial was set. An orchestral group played the Argentine anthem, and then not the Portuguese anthem but the Maria da Fonte anthem, a musical expression of the revolution that was given this name around 1846–1847 and that is played at civil and military ceremonies to this day.

The monument is a simple one, a vertical block of the finest-quality granite, with an open space containing a golden hand, a model taken directly from a mold of Borges's right hand, holding a pen. It is simple, evocative, and far preferable to a bust or a statue, in which we would soon tire of seeking out resemblances. I improvised a few words about the author of *Ficciones*, whom I still consider the inventor of virtual literature, that literature of his that seems to have detached itself from reality in order better to reveal its invisible mysteries. It was a good start to the afternoon. And Maria Kodama was happy.

December 16: *The Final Blow*

Laughter is a spontaneous thing. Seeing the president of the United States shrinking behind the microphone while a shoe flies over his head is an excellent bit of exercise for those facial muscles responsible for laughter. This man, famous for his abysmal ignorance and constant linguistic absurdities, has made us laugh many times over the past eight years. This man, famous too for other less attractive qualities, such as his entrenched paranoia, has afforded us a thousand reasons to despise him, him and his acolytes, accomplices in falsehood and intrigue, whose perverted minds turned international politics into a tragic farce and made simple dignity the target of pure derision. If the truth be told, in spite of the distressing spectacle our world presents on a daily basis, that world did not deserve a Bush. We have experienced him, and we have suffered through him to such a degree that the victory of Barack Obama has been considered by many people to be a kind of divine justice. Belated, as justice tends to be, but definitive. But in the end we still needed that final blow, still needed those shoes that a journalist from Iraqi television hurled at the lying, shameless façade he saw in front of him, a blow that could be taken in two ways: either those shoes ought to have had feet inside them and the target of the blow should have been that rounded part of the body where a man's back assumes a different contour and a different name, or Mutazem al Kaidi (may his name survive for posterity) found a more bruising and effective way of expressing his scorn: through ridicule. A couple of kicks wouldn't have come amiss, but ridicule lasts forever. My vote goes to ridicule.

December 17: *Words*

It is not possible to have a press conference without words— usually lots of them, sometimes too many. Pilar insists on suggesting that I give brief replies, pithy formulas that encapsulate the long speeches that would be out of place there. She is right, but it's not in my nature. I think each word needs at least one other word to help explain it along. Things have reached the point where, because I have been doing this for a while, I've begun to anticipate the questions that I will be asked, a procedure made easier by the advance knowledge that I have accumulated about the sorts of subjects journalists tend to be most interested in. The fun starts with the freedom I allow myself when I begin one of these discourses. Without having to worry about the precise thematic framing that each question will necessarily establish, whether it means to or not, I release the first word, and the second, and the third, like birds whose cage door has just been opened, not really knowing, or really not knowing at all, where they will take me. In this way speaking becomes an adventure, communicating is transformed into the methodical search for a path that leads to whoever is listening, and I am always aware that no communication is definitive and instantaneous, that it is often necessary to retrace one's steps in order to clarify what has been expressed only summarily. But the most interesting part of all this is discovering that speech, rather than being limited to illuminating and making visible what I thought I personally knew about my work, invariably ends up revealing what was hidden, what was only intuited or foreseen, and which suddenly becomes straightforward evidence with which I'm the first to surprise myself, like someone who has been in the dark and has just opened his eyes to a sudden light. In short, I learn as I go along, through the words I speak. That is a good conclusion, perhaps the best possible one, for this discussion. Which turned out to be a short one after all.

December 18: *Publishers*

Voltaire had no literary agent. He didn't have one, and nor did any writer of his time or for a long time afterward. The literary agent simply did not exist. The business—if we want to call it that—functioned with just two interlocutors, author and publisher. The author had the work, the publisher the means of publishing it, with no intermediary between one and the other. It was a time of innocence. I don't mean by this that the literary agent has been, and continues to be, the tempting serpent born to pervert the harmonies of a paradise that, in reality, never existed. But, whether directly or indirectly, the literary agent was the egg laid by a publishing industry that had begun to concern itself more with the discovery of a chain of bestsellers than with the publication and distribution of works of merit. Writers, naïve people on the whole, who are easily fooled by a literary agent of the jackal or shark variety, run after promises of bulky advances and stellar promotions as though their lives depended on it. But things are not like that. An advance is simply a payment on account, and as for promotions, we must all know from experience how far reality almost always falls short of expectations.

These thoughts are no more than a modest gloss on the excellent lecture given by Basílio Baltasar in Mexico in late November, under the title "The Long-anticipated Death of the Publisher," following an interview given to *El País* by the famous literary agent Andrew Wylie. I say famous, and he is, though not always for the best reasons. I wouldn't dare, nor would it be appropriate here, to summarize Basílio Baltasar's trenchant analyses, which take as their starting point the foolish statement of the aforementioned Wylie that "The publisher is nothing, nothing," which reminds me of the words of Roland Barthes when he announced the death of the author. . . Well, the author didn't die, after all, and the resurgence of the publisher who loves his work is in the publisher's own hands, if he or she wishes it so. And in the hands of the writers, to whom I enthusiastically commend Basílio Baltasar's lecture, which ought to be published, along with the debate that followed it.

December 22: *Gaza*

As everyone knows, UN stands for the United Nations, which is, in reality, nothing or very little. What would the Palestinians in Gaza have to say to that, the people whose food is running out, or has run out already? Because that's the way the Israeli block-aders decided things should be, since they are apparently determined to condemn to starvation the 750,000 people recognized as refugees there. These no longer even have bread—the flour has been used up, and the oil, lentils, and sugar are all going the same way. Since December 9, the lorries of the UN agencies, loaded up with food, have been waiting for the Israeli army to allow them to enter the Gaza strip, an authorization which will be denied once again, or which will be delayed until the last gasp of the frustrated, famished, and desperate Palestinians. United Nations? United? Counting on international complicity or cowardice, Israel laughs at recommendations, decisions, and protests, does what it chooses, when it chooses, and how it chooses. This goes so far as preventing the entry of books and musical instruments, as though these were products that would put Israel's security at risk. If ridicule could kill, there wouldn't be a single Israeli politician left standing, nor a single Israeli soldier, those specialists in cruelty, those graduates in hatred who look down at the world from the height of insolence that is at the root of their education. We understand the Biblical god better when we see his followers. Jehovah, or Yahweh, or whatever you call him, is a ferocious and bitter god whom the Israelis maintain as a permanent presence.

December 23: *One Year On*

I "died" on the night of December 22, 2007, at four o'clock in the morning, not to be "resuscitated" till nine hours later. A complete organ collapse, a ceasing of bodily function, brought me to the final threshold of life, where it is already too late for good-byes. I don't remember a thing. Pilar was there, and my sister-in-law Maria was there, too, both of them standing before an inert body, which was bereft of any strength and from which the spirit seemed to be absent, which had more of the irrecoverable corpse about it than of a living being. They tell me today what those hours were like. Ana, my granddaughter, arrived the same afternoon, Violante the next. Their father and grandfather was still, like the pale flame of a candle that their own breath threatened to extinguish. I learned later that my body was going to be displayed in the library, surrounded by books and—if I might put it like this—other flowers too. I escaped. A year of slow, incredibly slow recovery, as my doctors told me it would be, gave me back my health, my energy, my agility of thought. That universal medicine called work was also restored to me. Heading towards life, not death, I have made my own *Elephant's Journey*, and here I am. At your service.

December 24: *Christmas*

> Christmas. In the country, snow.
> In the cozy homes once more
> A feeling that today preserves
> Feelings that have gone before.
>
> The heart that challenged all the world,
> And that family—so real!
> Thus my thought, profound, gives birth
> To this longing that I feel.

And how free and white it is
The landscape that is strange to me,
Seen from out the window glass
Of the home I'll never see!

—Fernando Pessoa

December 25: *Supper*

Many years back, as far back as 1993, I wrote a few words in the *Lanzarote Notebooks* that delighted some theologians from this part of Iberia, in particular Juan José Tamayo, who has since generously bestowed his friendship on me. These were the words: "God is the silence of the universe, and man is the cry that gives meaning to that silence." It is clear that this idea is not badly formulated, with its *quantum satis* of poetry, its slightly provocative intention, and the implication that atheists are very well able to explore the tricky pathways of theology, even if in the most elementary way. On this day when the birth of Christ is celebrated, another idea has come to me, one that is perhaps even more provocative, indeed revolutionary, which can be expressed in a very few words. These are the words. If it is true that Jesus at the last supper said to his disciples, referring to the bread and the wine on the table, "This is my body, this is my blood," then it would be legitimate to conclude that the countless suppers, the Pantagruelian feasts, the Homeric orgies of feasting that thousands and millions of stomachs have to digest in order to escape the dangers of a fatal blockage, will be no more than the multiple copy—simultaneously actual and symbolic—of the last supper: believers feed on their god, devour him, digest him, eliminate him, until next Christmas, until the next Christmas supper, following the ritual of a material and mystical hunger that is always unsatisfied. Now let's see what the theologians have to say.

December 29: *Siblings-in-law*

They are perfect. Well, almost. They talk loud and tirelessly, they are in love with discussion for discussion's sake, they are often sectarian, violent of speech, though more in style than in substance. The women, of whom there are five, make so much noise, even louder than the men, of whom there are ten. For these men, and women, no subject will ever have been sufficiently discussed. They never give up. The Granada accent frequently makes what they say incomprehensible. It doesn't matter. Whatever doubts I may have, they claim to be able to understand one another perfectly. They have a very distinctive sense of humor that often goes right past me and not infrequently has me asking myself what the joke was. The boyfriends and girlfriends, the husbands and wives, a group in which I am included, watch, stupefied, and since we cannot beat them, we end up joining in the chorus, except in the rare instance when I prefer to maintain a discreet silence. In twenty years I've never seen one of these arguments lead to anyone getting angry, or to any row requiring family counseling and reconciliation. However much it might have rained and thundered earlier, the sky always ends up cloudless. They may not be perfect, but, yes, good people.

December 30: *Book*

I am preoccupied with a new book. When I let this piece of news slip out in the middle of a conversation, the inevitable question I'm asked (my nephew Olmo asked it yesterday) is "What's it going to be called?" The most comfortable solution for me would be to answer that I don't have a title yet, that only when I get to the end will I decide between the possible alternatives that occurred to me (assuming some actually have) during the work. Comfortable, certainly, but false. The truth is that even before the first line of the book was written I already knew; I had known for almost three years, since the idea first came to me, what it was going to be called. So, someone will ask, why the secrecy? Because the word of the title (it's just one word) will tell the whole story all on its own. I'm in the habit of saying that anyone who doesn't have the patience to read my books can at least cast their eyes over the epigraphs and they'll learn everything there. I don't know whether the book I'm working on will have an epigraph. Perhaps not. The title will be enough.

December 31: *Israel*

It is not a very good omen that the future president of the United States keeps repeating again and again, without a quiver in his voice, that he will maintain the "special relationship" with Israel that unites the two countries, in particular the unconditional support that the White House has offered for the repressive policies (repressive is putting it mildly) with which the Israeli government (and why not also the governed?) have done nothing but martyr the Palestinian people by every possible means. If Barack Obama isn't disgusted by the idea of taking tea with executioners and war criminals, *bon appetit* to him, but then he cannot count on the approval of honest people. Others among his fellow presidents have done the same before him without needing further justification than this "special relationship" that has covered up so many ignominies hatched by the two countries against the national rights of the Palestinians.

Throughout his electoral campaign, Barack Obama, whether through personal experience or political strategy, gave the impression of himself as a diligent father. This leads me to suggest that tonight he tell his daughters a story before they go to sleep, the story of a boat that was transporting four tonnes of medication to assuage the terrible sanitary situation of the people of Gaza, and how this boat, whose name was Dignity, was destroyed in an attack by the Israeli naval forces on the pretext that it had no authorization to dock on its coast. (In my ignorance, I was under the impression that the coast of Gaza was Palestinian. . .) And he should not be surprised if one of his daughters, or the two in unison, should say to him "Don't go on, Daddy, we already know what a special relationship is: it means being partners in crime."

January 2009

January 5: *Reckoning Up*

Has it been worth it? Were these comments, these opinions, these criticisms worth it? Is the world better than it was before? And what about me, how am I now? Is this what I expected? Am I satisfied with my work? Answering yes to all of these questions, or even to some of them, would clearly demonstrate an unforgivable mental blindness. And to reply "no" without any exceptions, what would that suggest? An excess of modesty? Of resignation? Or merely the awareness that no human accomplishment is ever more than the pale shadow of what was imagined? They say that Michelangelo, having finished the Moses that you can see in the church of San Pietro in Vincoli in Rome, struck the statue's knee with his hammer and shouted, "Speak!" Needless to say, Moses did not speak. Moses never speaks. Likewise what I have been writing here over the past months does not contain any more words, nor any more eloquent words, than it was possible to write—precisely the words that the author would like to ask, in a murmur, "Speak, please, tell me who you are, what you are for, if there's something you are for at all." They remain silent, they do not reply. So what to do? Interrogating words is the destiny of anyone who writes. An article? A story? A book? Well, so be it; we already know that Moses will not answer.

January 6: *The Irresponsible Sarkozy*

I've never thought much of this gentleman, and I think that from today I will start to think even less of him, if that's possible. And that should not be so, not if—as the Internet has just informed me—the abovementioned Mr. Sarkozy is on a peace mission to the tortured lands of Palestine, a praiseworthy effort that at first sight deserves commendation and wishes for success. He would be getting all these from me, had he not yet again used the old strategy of two weights and two measures. In a move of remarkable political hypocrisy, Sarkozy is accusing Hamas of acting irresponsibly and unforgivably by launching rockets into Israeli territory. Now, I'm not one to absolve Hamas for such acts, and according to what I read they are being punished at each step by the almost complete ineffectiveness of these war maneuvers, which have achieved little more than damaging a few houses and knocking down a few walls. Since bad words cannot hurt him, Mr. Sarkozy should denounce Hamas. But on one condition. That his righteous admonitions should equally be applied to the horrific war crimes that have been committed by the Israeli army and air force, on an unimaginable scale, against the civilian population of the Gaza Strip. For this shame Mr. Sarkozy seems not to have found adequate phrases in his Larousse. Poor France.

January 7: *"No nos abandones"*

"Do not abandon us." I have given the title in Spanish, because that was how the words were said. This piece could also be called "The silences of Marcos," a title that explains everything. Today's text refers to the mythical—albeit completely real—subcomandante. There are few people I have admired as much in my life, and very few from whom I expected so much. I never told him, for the simple reason that some feelings one prefers not to mention: they are things one feels and that stay that way. A matter of bashfulness, it would seem. When the Zapatistas came out of the Lacandon jungle, having crossed half of Mexico to reach Zócalo Square, I was there, one of a million people. I experienced the thrill, the pulse of hope running through my whole body, the desire for change and the desire to make myself something better, less selfish, more capable of giving myself up to it. Marcos spoke, he named each of the ethnic groups of Chiapas, and as each name was spoken it was as though the ashes of millions of indigenous Indians had detached themselves from their tombs and been reincarnated. I'm not writing literature, which comes easily, I'm trying—awkwardly—to put into words something that no words can express: the moment when the human turns superhuman, and then, in one step, reverts to its most extreme humanity.

The following day, on the campus of a modest university, there was a rally that brought together thousands of people, and there was talk of the present and the future of Chiapas, of the exemplary struggle of the Indian communities that I dreamed I would one day see extended across all of America (those among you of a nervous disposition can relax; it didn't happen). On the platform, among others, were Carlos Monsivais, Elena Poniatowska, Manuel Vásquez Montalbán, myself. We all spoke, but the person everyone wanted to hear was Marcos. He spoke briefly, but intensely, almost unbearably, at the edge of each person's emotional capacity. When it was all over I went to hug Marcos and it was then that he said in my ear, in a low whisper, "No nos abandones." I replied in the same tone: "I'd have to abandon myself for that to happen." I never saw him again, to this day.

I thought, and said as much, that Marcos should have spoken at the Congress. Following a decision from high command, the speaker was Comandante Esther, and she did admirably. She moved all of Mexico, but I repeat, to my mind the person who should have spoken was Marcos. The political significance of a speech from him would have been the most effective way of bringing the Zapatista march to its culmination. That was what I believed, and what I still believe. Time passed, the course of the revolutionary process changed, Marcos came out of the Lacandon jungle. In recent years he has maintained a complete silence, leaving us orphaned of those words that only he would know how to say or write. We miss him. On January 1 in Oventic there was a gathering to celebrate and recall the start of the revolution, the taking of San Cristóbal de las Casas, the highs and lows of a difficult journey. Marcos didn't go to Oventic—he didn't even send a message, not a word. I didn't understand, and I continue not to understand. A few days ago Marcos announced a new political strategy for the year that has just come in. Let us hope so, if the strategies of the old year have lost all virtue. Let us hope, above all, that he doesn't fall silent again. What right do I have to say that? The simple right of someone who never abandoned them. Yes, someone who never abandoned them.

January 8: *From David's Stones to Goliath's Tanks*

This article was first published a few years ago. Its backdrop was the second Palestinian intifada, in 2000. I have dared to think that it has not aged too badly, and that its "resurrection" is justified by the criminal actions of Israel against the population of Gaza. So here it goes.

FROM DAVID'S STONES TO GOLIATH'S TANKS

Certain authorities on Biblical matters claim that the First Book of Samuel was written during the age of Solomon, or immediately after it—in any case, before the capture of Babylon. Other no less competent scholars argue that not only the First Book but also the Second Book was written after the exile from Babylon, the composition of both obeying what is called the historical-political-religious structure of the Deuteronomic order, which is the alliance of God with his people, the people's infidelity, God's punishment, the people's supplication, God's forgiveness. If these venerable

scriptures do come from the time of Solomon, we can say that they
have now been around for some three thousand years, in round
numbers. If the writers undertook their work only after the return
of the Jews from exile, then we would have to take some five
hundred years off that number, give or take a month.

This preoccupation with temporal precision has only one intention, which is to offer up the notion that the famous Biblical legend
of the fight (which ended up not taking place) between little David
and the Philistine giant Goliath has been badly told to children for
at least twenty or thirty centuries. Over time the various parties
interested in the subject have developed—with the uncritical agreement of more than a hundred generations of believers, Jewish
and Christian alike—a whole misleading mystification about the
inequality of strength that separated the fragile physical constitution
of the fair, delicate David from the bestial four-meter-tall Goliath.
Such inequality, which was apparently huge, was compensated for,
and then turned to the advantage of the Israelite, by the fact that
David was a cunning young man and Goliath a stupid mass of flesh;
and so cunning was the former that before confronting the Philistine
he picked up five smooth stones from the bank of a nearby brook and
put them in his shepherd's bag, and so stupid was the latter that he did
not realize that David was armed with a pistol. But it wasn't a pistol,
the lovers of sovereign mythical truths will protest indignantly, it
was just a slingshot, a very humble shepherd's slingshot, which the
servants of Abraham had already been using since time immemorial
to protect their flocks. Yes, the truth is it didn't look like a pistol: it
had no barrel, it had no grip, it had no trigger, it had no cartridges—
all it had was two thin, strong pieces of string tied at the ends to
a bit of flexible leather within the curve of which David's expert
hand placed a stone which was launched from a distance, swift and
powerful as a bullet, at Goliath's head, knocking him down, leaving him at the mercy of the blade of his own sword, already seized
by the adept stone-slinger. It wasn't because the Israelite was most
cunning that he managed to kill the Philistine and to hand victory

to the army of Samuel and the living God, it was simply because he had a long-range weapon with him and he knew how to use it. The modest, quite unimaginative historical truth teaches us only that Goliath didn't even get a chance to lay hands on David, while the mythical truth, from an expert spinner of fantasies, has for thirty centuries been cradling us in the fantastical tale of the triumph of the little shepherd over the bestiality of a gigantic warrior whose heavy bronze helmet, breastplate, leg armor and shield turned out to be useless. As far as we are able to conclude from the way this edifying story played itself out, David, in the many battles that made him king of Judah and of Jerusalem and extended his power as far as the right bank of the Euphrates, never used a slingshot and stones again.

Nor does he use them now. Over the past fifty years David's strength and size have grown to such a degree that it is no longer possible to see any difference between him and the lofty Goliath, so one might say—without any harm coming to the dazzling clarity of the facts—that he has become a new Goliath. David, today, is Goliath, but a Goliath who has stopped carrying heavy and ultimately useless weapons of bronze. That fair-haired David of yesteryear flies over the occupied Palestinian territories in a helicopter and fires missiles at unarmed targets; that delicate David of yore now crews the most powerful tanks in the world and crushes and destroys everything he finds in his path; that lyrical David who sang Bathsheba's praises, now made flesh in the gargantuan figure of a war criminal called Ariel Sharon, launches the "poetic" message that it is first necessary to crush the Palestinians in order afterward to negotiate with what is left of them. It is this, in short, that has constituted Israeli political strategy since 1948, with only slight tactical variations. Intoxicated by the messianic idea of a Greater Israel that will finally realize the dreams of the most radical Zionism; contaminated by the monstrous and deep-rooted "certainty" that in this catastrophic, absurd world there is a people chosen by God, and that they are therefore automatically justified and authorized—in the name, too, of past horrors and

present fears—in any of their actions that result from an obsessive, emotional, and pathologically exclusivist racism; educated
and trained in the idea that any suffering they have inflicted, are
inflicting, or will inflict on others, in particular on the Palestinians,
will always be less than what they suffered in the Holocaust, Jews
scratch at their own injury interminably so that it doesn't stop
bleeding, to make it incurable, and they parade it before the world
like a banner. Israel has made the terrible words of Jehovah in
Deuteronomy theirs: "Vengeance is mine, I shall repay." Israel
wants us to feel guilty, all of us, directly or indirectly, for the
horrors of the Holocaust, Israel wants us to renounce the most
basic critical judgment and transform ourselves into the docile
echo of their will, Israel wants us to recognize de jure what for
them is already de facto: their absolute impunity. From the point
of view of the Jews, Israel can never be brought to judgment
since they have been tortured, gassed, and burned at Auschwitz.
I wonder whether those Jews who died in the Nazi concentration
camps, the ones who were butchered in the pogroms, the ones who
were left to rot in the ghettos, I wonder whether that huge unfortunate mass of people wouldn't be ashamed at the dreadful acts their
descendents have perpetrated. I wonder whether the fact of their
having suffered so much shouldn't be the best reason not to make
others suffer.

The stones of David have changed hands, and it is now the
Palestinians throwing them. Goliath is on the other side, armed
and kitted out like no soldier ever before seen in the history of
warfare, with the exception, of course, of their friend in North
America. Yes, of course, the horrible killing of civilians by suicide
bombers. . . horrible, yes, undoubtedly, worthy of condemnation,
yes, undoubtedly, but Israel still has a lot to learn if it is unable to
understand the reasons that might lead a human being to want to
turn himself into a human bomb.

January 11: *Together with Gaza*

Public demonstrations are not appreciated by those in power, who not infrequently ban or suppress them. Fortunately this is not the case in Spain, where some of the largest demonstrations in Europe have taken to the streets. For this we should honor the inhabitants of a country where international solidarity has never been just an empty phrase and who will certainly be expressing this in the mass action scheduled for Sunday in Madrid. The immediate target of this demonstration is the indiscriminate, criminal military action, an offence against all fundamental human rights, carried out by the Israeli government against the population of Gaza, who are subject to a relentless blockade and deprived of the essentials for life, from food to medical assistance. The immediate target, but not the only one. Let every demonstrator bear in mind that the violence, humiliation, and scorn that the Palestinians have been victims of from the Israelis has been going on for sixty years without interruption. And let there burst forth from their voices, the voices of the crowd who I'm sure will be there, outrage at the slow but systematic genocide that Israel has been carrying out against the suffering Palestinian people. And let those voices, heard right across Europe, also reach the Gaza Strip and the whole West Bank. Nothing less than this is expected of us by those who suffer every day and every night in those parts. Endlessly.

January 12: *Let's Suppose*

Let's suppose that in the thirties, when the Nazis began their Jew hunts, the German people had come out into the streets, in impressive demonstrations that would go down in history, to demand that their government end the persecution and promulgate laws that protected any minority, whether Jews, communists, gypsies or homosexuals. Let's imagine that in support of this dignified and brave act by the men and women of the land of Goethe, the people of Europe had paraded down the avenues and squares of their cities and joined their voices to the chorus of protests in Berlin, in Munich, in Cologne, in Frankfurt. We already know that none of this happened, nor could have happened. Whether from indifference, apathy, or tactical or open complicity with Hitler, the German people—with only extremely rare exceptions—did not take a step, did not make a gesture, did not say a word to save those who would be butchered in the concentration camps and crematoriums, and across the rest of Europe, for one reason or other (other nascent fascisms, for example) an assumed connivance with the Nazi killers meant that any attempts to protest were disciplined or punished.

It's different today. We have freedom of expression, freedom to demonstrate, and I don't know how many other freedoms. We can go out into the streets in our thousands or our millions, our safety always assured by the constitutions that govern us, and we can demand an end to the suffering in Gaza or the restitution to the Palestinians of their sovereignty and reparation for the moral and material injuries they have suffered over sixty years, with no worse consequences than the insults or provocations of the Israeli army. My imagined demonstrations of the thirties would have been suppressed with violence, in some cases fiercely, while ours would at least be able to count on the indulgence of media coverage— immediately followed by the process of forgetting to act. German Nazism would have refused to retreat from its course, and everything would have happened just as it did and as history recorded. In turn the Israeli army, which the philosopher Yeshayahu Leibowitz accused in 1982 of having a Judeo-Nazi mentality, as it fulfils the orders of its successive governments and commanders, is faithfully following the genocidal doctrine of the people who tortured, gassed and burned their ancestors. It is even fair to say that in some respects the disciples have surpassed their masters. As for us, we will continue to protest.

January 13: *Ángel González*

A year ago, on January 12, to be exact, Ángel González died in a Madrid hospital. Being hospitalized myself in Lanzarote for an illness not unlike that which took him, I answered a telephone call from a newspaper that wanted to publish a few words on the unhappy news. In words that my interlocutor must have been barely able to hear, so intense was my emotion, I said that I had lost a friend who was also one of the greatest of Spain's poets. In his memory I leave you today with one of his poems.

SO IT SEEMS

Accused of realism by my critics,
My relatives, meanwhile, ascribe
The contrary defect to me;
I have, they say,
No sense of reality.
For them I am, no doubt, a grim spectacle:
Textual analysts, relatives from the country,
I have, it seems, cheated them all—
What are we to do with him!

Let me quote some examples:
Some of my devoted aunts cannot contain themselves,
And cry just to look at me.
Others, much shyer, make me rice pudding,
Like when I was small,
And smile contritely, and say to me:
So tall,
If your father could see you. . .
And stop, not knowing what else to say.

And yet I do know
That their ambiguous gestures
Disguise
A true and incurable compassion
That shines damply in their gaze
And in their rabbity pious false teeth.

And it is not only them.

At night
My old aunt Clotilde returns from her grave
To waggle her fingers before my face like twigs
And repeats, in admonition,
You can't live on beauty! What do you think life is?

In her turn,
My departed mother, her voice thin and sad,
Foretells a sad end to my existence:
Lunatic asylums, sanatoria, baldness, gonorrhea.

I don't know what to say to them, and they
Return to their silence.
The same silence, just like before.
Like when I was small.
It seems
Death has not passed between us.

January 14: *Presidents*

One, Bush, is leaving and never should have been in power; another, Obama, is now set to arrive and we hope he will not disillusion us; another, Bartlet, I have no doubt will remain with us for some time. This is the person to whom Pilar and I have been devoting some time these days as we enjoy the final season of *The

West Wing, which in Portugal they prefer to call *The President's Men*, an eminently *machista* title, given that some of the most important characters in the show are women. Jed Bartlet, played by Martin Sheen (remember *Apocalypse Now?*) is the name of the president we have followed with an undiminished interest, both because of the tension of the dramatic conflicts and for a few didactic elements constantly present in the American way of doing politics, both good and dreadful. Bartlet has arrived at the end of his second term, and so is on his way out. We are in the middle of a presidential campaign, a campaign with its share of low blows, but one that (we already know) will end with a victory for the better of the candidates, a Hispanic man with clear ideas and impeccable ethics called Matthew Santos. It is, of course, impossible to resist thinking of Barack Obama. Could the writers of the story have had the gift of prophecy? Because between a Hispanic man and a black man there is no great difference.

January 15: *Stonings and Other Horrors*

The news burns. The Mufti of Saudi Arabia, the country's highest religious authority, has just issued a *fatwa* that allows—"allows" is a euphemism, the precise word should be "imposes"—marriage on ten-year-old girls. This aforementioned Mufti (I must remember him in my prayers) explains why: because this is a "just" decision for women, as opposed to the *fatwa* previously in force, which had set fifteen years as the minimum age for marriage, which Abdul-Azeez aal ash-Shaikh (that is his name) considered "unjust." As to the reasons for this use of "just" and "unjust," we get not a word; he doesn't even tell us if the ten-year-old girls were consulted. It is true that democracy in Saudi Arabia is conspicuous by its absence, but in the case of something so sensitive one might have made an exception. Anyway, pedophiles must be happy: pederasty is legal in Saudi Arabia. Now to some more news that burns. In Iran two men were stoned for adultery, and in Pakistan five women were buried alive for going through civil marriage with men of their choice . . . I'm stopping here. I can't take any more.

January 19: *The Other Crisis*

The financial crisis, the economic crisis, the political crisis, the religious crisis, the environmental crisis, the energy crisis; if I haven't mentioned them all, I think I have named the most important ones. Yet one is missing, one that to my mind is hugely important. I'm referring to the moral crisis that is ravaging the world, and if I may I shall give a few examples. A moral crisis is what the Israeli government is suffering, for without it there is no way to explain the cruelty of its actions in Gaza; a moral crisis is what has been infecting the minds of the governments of Ukraine and Russia, pitilessly condemning half a continent to freeze to death; a moral crisis is what the European Union is experiencing, incapable as it is of developing and enacting a coherent foreign policy that is faithful to certain basic ethical principles; a moral crisis is what the people who took advantage of the corrupting gifts of a criminal capitalism are going through, and they now complain of a disaster they should have predicted. These are only a few examples. I am well aware that talking about morals and morality these days is inviting the derision of cynics, opportunists, and those who are just smart. But I have said what I have said, sure that there must be some reason in my words. Let each man put his hand on his heart and tell us what he finds there.

January 20: Obama

They killed Martin Luther King. Forty thousand police officers keep watch in Washington to ensure that the same does not happen to Barack Obama today. I say it won't happen, as though the power of protecting against the worst misfortunes lay in my hands. It would be like killing the same dream twice. Perhaps we are all believers in this new political faith that has burst onto the United States like a benevolent tsunami carrying all before it, separating the wheat from the chaff and the straw from the grain; perhaps we do still believe in miracles after all, in something that comes from outside to save us at the last moment, saving us among other things from this other tsunami that is currently devastating the world. Camus used to say that if someone wants to be recognized, he has only to say who he is. I am not such an optimist, as in my opinion the main problem lies precisely in the definition of who we are, the means of achieving it. However, whether just by chance or by design, Obama has told us so much about himself in his various speeches and interviews, and with such conviction and apparent sincerity, that we all feel we know him intimately, and that we have known him forever. The president of the United States who assumes his office today will solve or attempt to solve the enormous problems that are awaiting him; perhaps he will succeed and perhaps not, and he will undoubtedly fall short sometimes and we will have to forgive him, because to err is human, as experience has taught us to our cost. What we would never be able to forgive is if he were to deny, twist, or falsify a single word of what he has spoken or written. He may not manage to bring peace to the Middle East, for example, but we will not allow him to cover up the failure with a misleading speech. We know all about misleading speeches, Mr. President; think about what you're getting yourself into.

January 21: *Where?*

Where did this man come from? I'm not asking you where he was born, who his parents were, what he studied, what kind of life he planned for himself and his family. We know all this more or less; I have his autobiography with me, a serious, sincere book, and intelligently written, too. When I ask where Barack Obama came from I am expressing my own perplexity at this time in which we live—cynical, despairing, grave, terrible in a thousand ways— having created a person (he is a man, it could have been a woman) who raises his voice to speak of values, of personal and collective responsibility, of respect for work, and also for those who have come before us. These concepts that were once the cement for the best human cohabitation have long suffered the scorn of the powerful, of those same people who, starting from today (I'm sure of it), will quickly dress themselves in the new style and cry out in every kind of voice, "Me too, me too." In his speech, Barack Obama gave us some reasons (*the* reasons) for not allowing ourselves to be deceived. The world can be better than this version that we currently seem condemned to. Basically, what Obama told us is that a different world is possible. Many of us have already been saying this for a long time. Perhaps this is a good opportunity for us to try and agree on how. It would be a start.

January 22: *Israel, Again*

The process of the violent extortion of the Palestinian people's basic rights and territory by Israel has gone ahead unchecked, with the complicity or indifference of what is mistakenly called the international community. The Israeli writer David Grossman, whose always cautious criticisms of the government of his country have lately been stepped up a notch, wrote an article published some time back in which he said that Israel does not know compassion. We knew that already. With the Torah for a backdrop, there is new meaning given to that terrible, unforgettable image of a Jewish soldier smashing the bones in the hand of a young Palestinian captured during the first Intifada for throwing stones at Israeli tanks. It's lucky that he didn't cut it off. Nothing and nobody, not even the international organizations whose duty it is, such as the UN, has managed to halt the more than repressive—criminal—actions of successive Israeli governments and their armed forces against the Palestinian people. Based on what has happened in Gaza, it would appear that the situation is not getting any better. Quite the contrary. Faced with heroic Palestinian resistance, the Israeli government altered some of its initial strategies, believing that any means could and should be used, even the cruelest and most arbitrary, from selective assassinations to indiscriminate bombings, to bend and humiliate the now legendary courage of the Palestinian people. Every day has been adding to the unending tally of their dead, and every day revives the immediate response of those still living.

January 23: *What?*

The questions "Who are you?" and "Who am I?" have easy answers: the person who is asked, or asks himself, tells the story of his life and thus introduces himself to other people. The question that doesn't have such an easy answer is formulated differently: "What am I?" Not "who," but "what." Whoever asks himself this question has to confront a blank page, and, what's worse, there is not a single word he can write on it.

January 26: *Clinton?*

Which Clinton? The husband, who has now passed into history? Or the wife, whose own story, in my opinion, is still just beginning, however influential a senator she may have been? Let us stay with the wife. Invited by Barack Obama to be Secretary of State, she will have her first great opportunity to show the world and herself what she's really worth. She would have had an opportunity too, of course, and a greater one, had she been elected president of the United States. In any case, as they say where I come from, if you don't have a dog, hunt with a cat, and I think we'd all agree that the US Secretary of State is, though feline, not a cat, but a tiger. Though she has never struck me as a particularly nice person, I wish Hillary Diane Rodham great triumphs, the first of which will be to live up to the level of her responsibilities and the dignity that is the foundation of her office.

All that is merely an introduction to the subject I have decided to consider today. Attentive readers will have noticed that when I gave the full name of the Secretary of State I wrote Hillary Diane Rodham. It was no accident. I did so in order to emphasize that the surname Clinton was not given to her at birth, to show that her surname is not Clinton, and the fact that she adopted it, whether from social convention or political convenience, has not altered the truth of things at all: her name is Hillary Diane Rodham, or, if you want to abbreviate it, Hillary Rodham, which is much more attractive than the worn, tired "Clinton." Neither she nor he knows me, and I'm sure they've never read a single line that I've written, but let me offer a little piece of advice—not to the ex-president, who never paid much attention to advice, especially when it was good. I am addressing the Secretary of State. Drop the surname Clinton, which has started to look like a frayed old coat with the elbows torn, and take back your surname, Rodham, which I presume was your father's. If he is still alive, can you imagine how proud he will be? Be a good daughter, give this piece of happiness to your family. And, along the way, give this pleasure to all the women who think the obligation to wear a husband's surname was and continues to be yet another way—and not the least important way—of diminishing their personal identities and emphasizing the submission that has always been expected of women.

January 27: *Rodham*

There were no consequences attending my boldness yesterday, apart from the (un)expected interest awakened by my posted suggestion that Hillary Clinton go back to her real surname. There were no diplomatic protests, the Secretary of State didn't release a statement, nor does it seem that there were any references to what I wrote in the *New York Times*. Tomorrow I'll change the subject. Meantime, however, I will rest, and contemplate.

January 28: *Gervasio Sánchez*

My eyes have not been of much use to me. I see the letters as I tap them out there, one after another, on the white page of the computer screen, forming words that, good or bad, express certain opinions to whoever is reading me, certain ideas I call my own, which I might rhetorically call visions of the world if only the world allowed itself to be known by so little. Much of what I see, I see only because others have seen it before me. I'm pained by the regret of having so rarely been the person who actually did the seeing in my life. I don't usually live inside a protective bubble, but I'm aware of being surrounded by people determined to save me from shocks that they say, and they may be right, might have a negative impact on my work. I don't know. What I do know is that the wall that I sometimes feel surrounds me, which is actually much more fragile than it seems, is often violently assailed by the brutal attacks of reality. The recent book that the photographer Gervasio Sánchez named *Sarajevo* is a case in point. I would like to express my profound gratitude for being allowed to see through his eyes, since my own have been of so little use to me. And I thank him, too, for the personal and professional loyalty that led him to write that "war cannot be told." So that those of us who write are left without any illusions.

January 29: *Testimony*

Things seem to be well under way. The president of the United States, who goes by the name not of Messiah but Barack Obama, today signed the Fair Pay Act into law. The person directly responsible for this document was a woman, a worker who, on discovering that her whole life she had been earning less precisely because she was a woman, filed a complaint against the company she worked for and won her suit. As though she were in a relay race, this white woman, called Lilly Ledbetter, handed her testimony on to the next runner, a black man with a Muslim name, the 44th president of that country in North America. Suddenly the world seems cleaner to me, more promising. Please, don't deny me this one hope.

February 2009

February 2: *Bread*

Did the superlatively dignified notary of Badalona ever read *Les Misérables*, or does he belong to that portion of humanity that believes that life is learned and led only according to the law? The question is—obviously—rhetorical, and I only raised it to afford myself a way into the topic. Thus the reader will already know that the aforementioned notary could, with complete justice, be one of the characters described in Victor Hugo's novel, that is, the public prosecutor. The book's protagonist, Jean Valjean (do you recognize this name, Senhor Inspector?), was accused of having caused to be stolen (or of having himself stolen) a loaf of bread, a crime that cost him almost a lifetime in solitary confinement, thanks to a succession of sentences imposed to punish his repeated attempts at escape, some more successful than others. Jean Valjean suffered from a disease that affects prison populations in particular, which one might call an anxiety—or a longing—for liberty. The book is hefty, among those that today we would describe as over-endowed with pages, and most certainly would not be of interest to the Senhor Inspector, who most probably is not the right age to appreciate *Les Misérables*. This novel is to be read in one's youth, before cynicism sets in; there are few adults who would be interested in the poverty and antiheroic adventures of Jean Valjean. For all this, there is always the possibility that I could be mistaken:

maybe the Senhor Inspector has after all read *Les Misérables*. . .
Should that be the case, please allow me a question: How was it
that he then dared (if the verb seems a little strong to you, please
select your preferred alternative) to demand a year and a half in
jail for the beggar who, in Badalona, attempted to steal a baguette,
and I say "attempted" advisedly, since he only succeeded in steal-
ing half of it? How come? Was it because the inspector had only
a code in place of a brain inside his skull? Kindly explain it to me,
please, so that I can immediately begin preparing my defense, just
in case one day I find myself up before someone like him.

February 3: *Davos*

I have read that this year's gathering at Davos was not exactly a
success. A lot of people didn't turn up; the shadow of the crisis
pitilessly froze the smiles on the faces of those who did; the debates
lacked any real interest, possibly because no one there really knew
what to say, fearful that the hard facts to come the following
day would make their analyses and proposals appear ridiculous,
however much effort they poured into engendering them, which
in the end came up to even the most modest expectations only
by mere accident. Above all, there was much talk of the disturbing dearth of ideas, and participants went so far as to admit that
the "spirit of Davos" was dead. Personally, I never myself saw
any sign of a "spirit" putting in an appearance, or anything even
remotely resembling one. As to the alleged lack of ideas, I'm
surprised that reference is being made to such a thing only now,
since no ideas—or what, with all due respect, we are pleased to call
ideas—ever came out of there that anyone could point to. For over
thirty years, Davos has been the neocon academy par excellence,
and, as far as I can recall, not a single voice was raised inside that
heavenly Swiss hotel to point out how dangerous were the paths
taken by the economy and the financial services. The winds were
getting up, but not one of them wanted to notice that storms were

on the way. And now they tell us they are running out of ideas. Let us watch and see if ideas arise, now their one line of thought has run out of lies to tell us.

February 4: *Bankers*

What can be done about the bankers? They tell us that the founders of the banking system, back in the sixteenth and seventeenth centuries, at least in Central Europe, were in general Calvinists, folk with an exigent moral code who, at least for a while, had the laudable scruple to labor honestly at their profession. That period must have been short, given the infinite power of money to corrupt. Gradually, the banks changed a great deal, and always for the worse. Now, in the midst of an economic crisis affecting financial systems around the world, we are beginning to experience the uncomfortable sensation that those who are going to come off best from the financial storms are precisely our Senhores Bankers. Everywhere governments, following the logic of the absurd, rushed to rescue the banks from losses for which, for the most part, those self-same bankers were responsible. Millions of millions left state coffers (or the accounts of the bankers' clients) in order to keep hundreds of major banks afloat and to allow them to resume one of their principal functions, that of providing credit. It would seem there are serious signs that bankers had their wits about them, abusively assuming that the money was theirs simply because it happened to be in their grasp and, as if all this weren't already more than enough, reacting coldheartedly to pressure from their governments to put the cash rapidly into circulation, the one way to save thousands of businesses from failure and millions of workers from unemployment. It is now clear that bankers are not men to be trusted, the proof being the disdain with which they bite the hand that feeds them.

February 5: *Adolf Eichmann*

At the start of the 1960s, when I worked at a publisher's in Lisbon, I edited a book with the title *Seis milhoes de mortos* (*Six Million Dead*), which told the story of Adolf Eichmann, the principal executor of the plan to exterminate the Jews (six million of them), which he systematically carried through to the bitter and almost scientific end, in the Nazi concentration camps. Critical as I have always been of the oppression and repression of the Palestinian people by the Israeli state, my main argument in condemning them was and continues to be on a moral plane: the unspeakable sufferings inflicted on the Jews throughout history, and most especially as part of what is called the final solution, ought to afford the Israelis of today (or of the past sixty years, to be precise) the best possible reason not to commit their very own tyrannies on Palestinian land. What Israel needs above all else is a moral revolution. Firm in this conviction, I will never deny the Holocaust. I only wish to extend the concept to the outrage, humiliation, and violation of every kind to which the Palestinian people have been subjected. That is, after all, my right for as long as the facts bear me out as they do. I am a free writer who expresses himself as freely regarding our world as it permits. I do not have available to me as much information on this subject as the pope—or the Catholic Church in general—is able to access. What I know of these matters from the early 1960s onwards is adequate for my purposes. All the same, it seems to me highly reprehensible the Vatican should behave so ambiguously over the question of the bishops who have sworn obedience to the Lefebvrists, formerly excommunicated but now cleansed of their sins by papal fiat. Ratzinger was never a man with whom I shared any intellectual sympathies. I view him as someone who makes great efforts to disguise, even to hide, what he actually thinks. This is hardly unusual behavior on the part of church congregations, but when it becomes that of a pope, even an atheist such as I should have the right to demand directness, coherence, and a critical conscience. A self-critical one wouldn't go amiss, either.

February 6: *Sampaio*

It was a pleasure to see him. He remains the same sober, intelligent, and sensitive man as ever. Twenty years ago we campaigned together in the nongovernmental elections, which we succeeded first in winning and then in celebrating. He won the position of president of the Lisbon town council, an office he went on to exercise with consummate competence and innovation, while I went on to perform the luckless task of being president of a regional town hall of poor repute. We courageously went up and down the streets, squares, and market places of Lisbon asking for votes even though—I suspect out of modesty—we did so as unobtrusively as possible. As has already been mentioned, we won, although the real winner was the city of Lisbon, which should be proud of itself for making Sampaio its representative at the highest level of the National Council Chamber. That president in turn became president of the republic for two terms, and left his mark as a personality born to civilized dialogue, to a free solicitation of open consensus, never overlooking the fact that politics, or service to the community, should be a loyal and coherent service, otherwise it risks becoming the mere instrument of personal and partisan interests, not necessarily of the cleanest reputation. We promised to meet again when we had greater leisure, a mutual promise that I hope to see fully accomplished in the near future, despite the intense activity around the project called Alianca de Civilizacões (Alliance of Civilizations), of which he is the chief representative. You know that with Jorge Sampaio there are no false words, and we know we can trust in his words because they are an accurate depiction of what he thinks.

February 9: *Vaticanadas*

Or Vaticanisms. I cannot bear to see those cardinals and bishops decked out with a luxury that would scandalize poor Jesus of Nazareth, humbly dressed in his seamless tunic of the cheapest fabric. It matters not how inconsequential such a thing might appear, though it is hard not to be reminded of the crazy parade of ecclesiastical fashions that Fellini brilliantly inserted into his *8½* for his and our delectation. Those gentlemen appear to believe they are cloaked in power, a power that has only persisted thanks to our tolerance. They call themselves the representatives of God on earth (not that they have either seen Him or presented the least proof of His existence), but pass through the world sweating hypocrisy from every pore. Whether or not they always lie, every word they either speak or write has behind it another word that negates or delimits, corrupts or perverts it. Many of us were more or less used to all this before growing up to become either indifferent or, worse still, contemptuous of it. It has become commonplace to say that Mass and church attendances are rapidly falling, but permit me to suggest that numbers are also falling among those who, while not necessarily believers themselves, used to go into a church to enjoy its architectural beauty and that of its paintings and sculptures—in sum, a setting of which the falsity of the doctrine that sustains it is hardly worthy.

Cardinals and bishops, and naturally also the pope who governs them, are now getting off lightly. They live as parasites on civil society and are not obliged to account for themselves. Throughout the lengthy but implacable sinking of this Titanic that is the Catholic Church, the pope and his acolytes, steeped in nostalgia for the time when they wielded real power, thanks to a criminal complicity between throne and altar, are now attempting by whatever means, not excluding moral blackmail, to insinuate themselves into various governments, in particular those that for social and historical reasons remain reluctant to abandon the submissiveness that persists in all their dealings with Vatican institutions. This type of (religious?) intimidation makes me sad when it threatens to paralyze the Spanish government, which has always had to confront not only papal emissaries but also their very own domestic "popes." And there's something more: as a person, an intellectual, and a citizen, I am deeply offended by the way the pope and his cohorts disregard Rodríguez Zapatero's government, which the Spanish people wholeheartedly elected. It would appear that someone urgently needs to throw a shoe at one of these cardinals.

February 10: *Sigifredo*

Sigifredo López is the name of a Colombian member of parliament held hostage by the FARC[1] for over seven years, and who has just regained his freedom thanks to the courage and persistence of, among others, Señora Piedad Córdoba, director of the social and humanitarian movement Colombians for Peace. Thanks also to an unforeseeable set of circumstances, Sigifredo López was the sole survivor of a group of eleven kidnapped MPs, ten of whom were recently murdered by the terrorist organization. He managed to escape and now is at liberty. At a press conference just held in the city of Cali, he thanked Piedad Córdoba in terms that moved all who heard him, and his powerful words and images reached out to us here. It's not for me to boast of my emotional control. I cry easily, and it has nothing to do with my age. But on this occasion I was obliged to break with custom when Sigifredo, in order to express his infinite gratitude to Piedad Córdoba, compared her to the wife of the doctor in my *Ensaio sobre a cegueira*. Kindly put yourselves in my place: thousands of kilometers between me and those words and images, and poor me, dissolved in floods of tears,

---

1 The guerrilla movement Fuerzas Armadas Revolucionarias de Colombia, which has intermittently controlled whole regions of the Colombian countryside.

and with no other recourse than to take refuge on Pilar's shoulder and let them flow freely. My entire existence as a man and a writer was justified by that moment. Thank you, Sigifredo.

February 11: *Atheists*

Let us face facts. Some years ago (already a great many) the famous Swiss theologian Hans Küng wrote this maxim: "Religions never served to bring people closer together." No truer word was ever spoken. That is not to say (it would be absurd even to think so) that you haven't the right to adopt whatever religion most appeals to you, from the best-known to the least-heard-of, or to follow its precepts and dogmas (whatever they might be), without questioning a recourse to faith, which is its own supreme justification and by definition (as we know all too well) entirely closed to the most elementary powers of reasoning. It is indeed possible that faith moves mountains, even without the confirmation that something similar ever actually occurred, for God has never appeared disposed to experiment in that kind of way, or to employ his powers in such a geological undertaking. What we do know is that religions not only fail to bring people closer together, but actually exist—these religions—in a state of mutual enmity, despite all the pseudoecumenical speeches which the rank opportunism of one lot or another deems profitable for occasional and generally fleeting tactical and strategic reasons. Things have been this way ever since the world has been the world, and there is no clear prospect that it might change to any degree. Apart, that is, from the obvious notion that the planet would be a far more peaceful place if we were all atheists. Of course, human nature being the way it is, there is no lack of other motives for every kind of disagreement, but at least we would be free of the infantile and ridiculous notion of believing that our god is the best of any number of others on offer, and that Heaven awaits us in a five-star hotel. More even than this, I believe we would start reinventing philosophy.

February 12: *As We Usually Say*

As we usually say to someone who is feeling confused, "Learn to know yourself"—as if self-knowledge were not the fifth most difficult operation of human arithmetic to acquire. In the same way, we generally remind someone who is feeling apathetic, "To want is to get"—just as if the world's beastly realities did not have more fun with their daily inversion of the relative position of the two verbs. Similarly, it is common to say to someone indecisive, "Begin at the beginning," as if this beginning were the obvious starting point of a knotted ball of yarn, and we could unravel it until the very end was as clearly in view. As if between the former and the latter—the beginning and the end—we had a smooth and continuous line between our fingers, with no knots to unravel or disentangle, something that would indeed be unthinkable in the life of a ball of yarn. And, if the reader will permit me another phrase written to inverted effect, in the yarns of our lives.

February 13: *Chinese Feathers*

It is an ancient culinary practice of the Western world to toss a live lobster into boiling water and cook it in a pot. Apparently, if an already dead lobster were conveyed to the pan, the ultimate flavor would change, and for the worse. There are those who insist that the bright red color the crustacean acquires on cooking is exclusively due to the exceptionally high water temperature. I don't know about this; I speak only of what I have heard, since I am incapable even of boiling an egg. One day I watched a documentary about what hens are fed on and how slowly they are brought to be killed and the methods used, and it almost made me vomit. On another occasion I cannot expunge from my memory, I read a magazine article about the use of rabbits in the cosmetics industry, which informed me that, in order that no irritation might be caused to my eyes by the contents of my shampoo bottle, its formula was

first squirted into the eyes of these small animals, the way the
black-hearted Dr. Death injected petrol into his victims' hearts.
Today a brief insert in my newspaper informs me that in China,
bird feathers, the kind used for stuffing pillows, are plucked from
live birds, before being cleaned, disinfected, and exported to bring
pleasure to civilized Western societies, who know what is best for
us and what is in the latest fashion. I make no comment, for there
is no need: these feathers speak for themselves.

February 16: *Domestic Abuse*

I am generally described as pessimistic. In spite of how I might
formerly have appeared, and the emphasis I usually accord my
radical skepticism as to the possibility of any effective and substantive improvement in our species regarding what used to be known
as moral progress, I would actually prefer to be optimistic, even
if only to retain a hope that the sun, having risen every day up
until today, will also rise tomorrow. And so it will, but there will
also be a day when it no longer rises. These opening reflections
are prompted by a consideration of the subject of domestic abuse,
the insane ill treatment of a woman by a man, whether he is her
husband, fiancé, or lover. Woman, subjugated throughout history
to male power, became reduced to a thing without greater prestige
than a servant—a man's servant, in charge of nothing more than
the responsibility of restoring a man, exhausted from his physical
labor, to sufficient strength to return to work again. Even today,
when she has access to every place outside the home, is free of all
constraints, and engages in activities that men once deemed exclusively masculine, it would appear, though we still do not wish
to confront the fact, that the overwhelming majority of women
continue to live inside a system of relationships that could well
belong to the Middle Ages. They are beaten, brutalized, sexually
exploited, enslaved to traditions, customs, and obligations that
they never chose and that continue to maintain them in submission

to male tyranny. And, when the hour arrives, they risk death by murder.

Schools affect to ignore that reality, which is hardly surprising, since we know that the teaching capacity of our educational system is a shadow of what it was. The family, the perfect home to every contradiction, the cradle of all egotism, an institution in permanent failure, is undergoing the gravest crisis in its entire history. The state starts from a first principle that all of us will die sooner or later, and that women cannot be treated as an exception. To some delirious imaginations, to die at the hands of your husband, fiancé, or lover, whether by gun or knife, might just be a better proof of mutual love than any other: him killing and her dying. In the darkest recesses of the human mind, all is indeed possible.

What can be done? Others may know better than we do, but may not say so. Since the fragile society in which we live would be scandalized at the introduction of measures to inflict permanent social exile for this type of crime, at the very least prison terms should be increased to the maximum, with no possibility of sentence reduction for good behavior. Good behavior? Please don't make me laugh.

February 17: *Death at Our Front Door*

As luck would have it, the door of the house on Lanzarote was on its way to becoming the entrance to their new home. They were only twenty yards away from the shore, at Costa Teguise, and at the sight no doubt merry smiles and words of joy passed between them at having finally reached safe haven, when a sudden squall overturned their raft. They had crossed over fifty miles from the African coast and probably met their death that mere twenty yards from salvation. Of the more than thirty immigrants—mainly youngsters and teenagers—whose extreme need forced them to brave the dangers of the deep, twenty-four drowned, including a pregnant woman and several small children. Six were saved, thanks to the courage and self-sacrifice of two surfers, who plunged into the water and rescued them from certain death.

This is, in the most simple and direct words I can find, the account of what happened here. I don't know what more I can say. Today I lack the words and am overwhelmed by the emotion. How long can such a situation go on?

February 18: *What Is to Be Done About the Italians?*

I recognize that such a question could sound somewhat offensive to sensitive ears. What does it mean? It is simply an appeal to the entire population, and begs them to account for the use of their vote to crown, at every available opportunity, the increasingly flagrant right-wing party whose head is Berlusconi, who has been granted the powers of absolute lord and master of Italy and of millions of Italians. The truth also being, as I may have already indicated, that the most offended party in all this is me. Yes, specifically me. My love for Italy is offended, along with my love for Italian culture and Italian history. Even my tenacious hope that the nightmare will somehow end and Italy will return to the exalted spirit inspired by Verdi, who was, in his time, its best manifestation, is offended. And to those intending to accuse me of gratuitously mixing music and politics, I say that every cultured and honorable Italian understands not only that I am right, but also the grounds on which I am right.

The news of Walter Veltroni's sacking has just reached us here. Welcome news indeed, since his Democratic Party began as the caricature of a party and has ended, lacking either a manifesto or a program, as a dead weight on the political scene. The hopes we had vested in him were undermined by his ideological vagueness and the weakness of his personality. Veltroni is mainly, although not uniquely, responsible for the debilitation of the left-wing alternative of which he purported to be the savior. May he rest in peace.

Yet not all is lost. Or so the writer Andrea Camilleri and the philosopher Paolo Flores d'Arcais have just told us in an article recently published in *El País*. There is work to do, alongside the millions of Italians who have already lost patience at seeing their country daily held up to public ridicule. The small party headed by Antonio di Pietro, the former magistrate in the Clean Hands[2] campaign, could turn the emetic situation of present-day Italy into an awakening collective catharsis ready to be harnessed to civic action for the betterment of Italian society. It is high time. Let us hope it really is.

February 19: *Susi*

If I could, I would close all the zoos in the world. If I could, I would also forbid the use of circus animals. I can't be the only person to think as I do, but I would willingly risk the protests, outrage, and the ire of the majority who still enjoy seeing animals behind bars or in cages where they cannot move about according to their nature. This is what it's like in zoos. Even more depressing than these kind of parks are the circus spectacles which serve to make animals into objects of ridicule, with pathetic small dogs dressed in skirts; seals obliged to applaud with their flippers; horses to wear feathers in their bridles; monkeys to ride bicycles; lions to jump through hoops; mules trained to chase black-clothed dwarfs; elephants forced to balance unsteadily on metal balls. "How much fun it all looks, and the children adore it," say their parents, who to complete their children's education should also bring them to the training (or torture?) sessions to witness the agonies inflicted on these poor animals, the hapless victims of human cruelty. Parents also used to say that visits to the zoo were equally instructive. Perhaps they were in the past, however much I doubt it. But they are hardly so today, thanks to the numerous documentaries about animals' lives and habitats continually available on television. If education is what it's about, let them be better educated this way.

---

2   With an anti-Mafia platform.

Ask me the reason for the above and I will tell you right away. At Barcelona Zoo there is a lonely female elephant, dying painfully of various ailments, mostly intestinal infections, which sooner or later attack animals deprived of their freedom. The additional emotional pain she suffers isn't hard to imagine, and is intensified by the recent death of her sister elephant, who with Susi (for that is the name given to this sad and lonely survivor) shared a miserably restricted space. The floor Susi walks on is made of concrete, absolutely the worst material for the sensitive feet of these creatures, who perhaps retain a vestigial memory of the secure ground of the African savannah underfoot. I am already well aware that the world has more acute problems to worry about than the well-being of a cow elephant, but the fine reputation Barcelona enjoys entails certain obligations, and whether or not my assertion seems just a personal eccentricity, I say that this happens to be one of them. Taking proper care of Susi would involve awarding her a more dignified end to a life than that of seeking refuge in such a depressingly confined space, or of having to tread on a concrete floor that is a very hell to her. To whom should I speak? To the director of the Barcelona Zoo? To the town hall? Or to the Generalitat of Catalonia?

February 20: *Paco*

Ibañez, of course. Who else? I can recognize his voice in any place or at any time it reaches my ears. I first came to know his voice at the start of the 1970s, when a friend sent one of his records to me in Paris, a piece of now ancient vinyl that years of technological improvements have rendered long since out of fashion, but which I retain as a treasure without price. I am not exaggerating: at that period of political oppression at home in Portugal, the record appeared to me as made of magic, its sounds almost transcendent, bringing me the sonorous glories of the best of Spanish poetry, and that voice (Paco's unmistakable voice) was its perfect vehicle, the vehicle par excellence of the most profound human fraternity. Today, as I was at work in my library, Pilar put on his last recording of the Andalusian poets. I stopped what I was writing and surrendered myself to the pleasures of the moment and of the memory of that initial instant of discovery when I first heard him. With age (which has to have something—for once something good—to do with it), Paco's voice has gained a particular velvety quality, fresh powers of expression, and a warmth that envelops your heart. Tomorrow, Saturday, Paco Ibañez will sing at Argèles-sur-Mer, on the coast of Provence, in homage to the memory of the Spanish Republicans, among them his father, who suffered torments, humiliations, ill treatment of every kind, in one of the concentration camps the French built to incarcerate the refugee Republicans. To them *la douce France* was as bitter as their worst enemies. May Paco's voice soften the echoes of those sufferings; may it be capable of opening up paths of genuine fraternity in the spirits of those who hear it. It is something we all really need.

February 22: *Letter to Antonio Machado*

Antonio Machado died seventy years ago today. Beside his resting place in the cemetery at Collioure there is a letter box that daily receives mail addressed to him, written by people filled with a tireless love that refuses to accept that the poet of *Campos de Castilla* could be dead. They are right, for few people are as alive as he. With the text below, composed for the fiftieth anniversary of Machado's death, and for the International Congress that took place in Turin, organized by Pablo Luis Avila and Giancarlo Depretis, I took my modest place in the queue. One more letter to Antonio Machado. I remember, as clearly as if it were today, that man called Antonio Machado. At the time I was fourteen years old and going to school to acquire skills that would later be of little use to me. Spain was at war. The combatants on one side were called the reds, and the other side, according to the generosity that was their hallmark, chose a color like that of the skies when the weather is good. The dictator of my

country so loved this blue army that he ordered the newspapers to
publish reports couched in such terms as to convince the naïve that
every combat ended in the victory of his friends. I had a map where
I planted little flags of glossy paper stuck to pins. That was the front
line. This proved that I knew Antonio Machado without even needing to read him, something we have to forgive, given my extreme
youth at the time. One day, when I thought I might be discovered
by the officers of the Portuguese armed forces responsible for press
censorship, I threw out the map with the little flags on it. I unthink-
ingly allowed myself to be led by a sort of rashness, a youthful impatience, that Antonio Machado had done nothing to deserve and of
which I repent today. And so the years rolled on. At what point I
don't recall, but at some point I learned that this man was a poet, and
I felt so excited by this that, without any hope of vainglorious future
reward, I set to reading everything he had written. At precisely that
moment, I also learned that he had just died, so naturally I went to
place a flag at Collioure. If I am correct, it is high time for us to
plant this flag in the heart of Spain. However, we can leave his bones
precisely where they are.

February 24: *The Left*

We are correct, and being correct helps those who propose to
construct a better world before it is too late. However, either we
don't know how to communicate to others the substance of our ideas,
or we come up against a wall of suspicion, or of ideological preconceptions or social or class prejudice that, if it doesn't succeed in stopping us completely, ends—in the worst-case scenario—by arousing
in many of us all kinds of doubts and worries, which can themselves
prove paralyzing. If one day the world is to succeed in becoming a
better place, I know it will only result through our own actions. Let
us become more conscious and proud of our part in history, for there
are instances in which humility is our worst counsel. Let us be heard
saying the word *left* aloud and loudly. Let others hear and take note.

I have written these reflections for an election pamphlet for the
United Left of Euzkadi,[3] but I have written it while thinking also
of the left in my own country, of the left in general. Despite what
the world is going through, the left continues not to raise its head.
As if it had no right to.

February 25: *Forms of Justice*

On July 22, 2005, a Brazilian citizen, Jean-Charles de Menezes, by
profession an electrician, was murdered at a tube station in London by
officers of the Metropolitan Police, who took him—or so they say—
for a terrorist. He got into a tube compartment, sat down quietly, and
it would seem he even had time to open the free newspaper he had
picked up at the station, when the police burst in and dragged him
onto the platform.[4] Then they knocked him to the ground and fired on
him ten times, with seven shots to the head. From day one, Scotland
Yard has done nothing but create obstacles to a proper investigation.
There was no judgment given. The prosecution prevented the police
from being implicated and the judge forbade the jury to return a guilty
verdict. You will therefore be ready, if one day you see a white wig
appear before you—just like in the movies—to kindly tell the wearer
what honest people like you think of this form of justice.

February 26: *Water Dog*

When Camões appeared in these parts around fourteen years ago,
with the black coat and white tie that so distinguish him from all
other examples of the canine species, all those of the human variety in the house pronounced on the newcomer's presumed breed:

---

3   The Basque country.
4   Jean-Charles de Menezes was in fact put down on the floor of the train
carriage and shot seven times at point-blank range. All the witnesses present on
the crowded tube train insisted in their evidence that no police warning had been
given before the plainclothes officers shot him dead.

he was a poodle. I was alone in insisting that he was not a French poodle but a Portuguese water dog. Since I am not particularly a dog expert it would hardly be surprising if I had got it wrong, but when the rest of them declared him to be a poodle, I remained firm in my convictions. Over time, the matter ceased to be of interest: poodle or water dog, former companion to Pepe and Greta (who have already ascended to Dog Heaven), he became merely Camões. Dogs live too short a time for the amount of love they bestow on us, and Camões, this last repository of the love we have lavished on all three, has already lived for fourteen years, and the ailments of old age have begun to bother him. Nothing too serious, as it happens, but yesterday he gave us a shock: Camões was running a fever, he was droopy, he huddled in corners, and from time to time let out a high, weird wail. Strangest of all, despite seeming devoid of all strength, he went down to the end of the garden and started scrabbling in the soil, excavating a pit, which in Pilar's imagination was the most sinister symptom of all. Happily, the bad phase has passed, at least for the time being. The vet couldn't find anything seriously wrong, and Camões, as if to placate us, has recovered his agility, his appetite, and his characteristic good humor, and now walks about joyful as a flower with his lady friend Bol, who spends a fair amount of time at our home.

By coincidence, it was today that news came that the dog promised by Obama to his daughters was to be just such another Portuguese water dog. No doubt this has to be a significant diplomatic triumph for Portugal, from which our country should draw maximum benefit in terms of our bilateral relations with the United States, so unexpectedly facilitated by one of our most obviously direct representatives—I would even be tempted to say our ambassador—to the White House. New times are on their way. I am absolutely certain that now, were Pilar and I to return to the United States, the border police would no longer impound our computers in order to take copies of the hard drives.

March 2009

March 2: *Gonçalo M. Tavares*

Among the new generation of Portuguese romantic novelists, meaning those aged between approximately thirty and forty, we have Gonçalo M. Tavares, one of the most distinguished and original writers. Author of an impressively extensive body of work, in the main the outcome of long and meticulous labor undertaken away from the world's gaze, the writer of *O Senhor Valéry* [*Mr. Valéry*], a small book that spent many months on my bedside table, burst onto the Portuguese literary scene armed with a wholly unique imagination that broke every link with what was current in imaginative fiction. Besides this, he is the master of a very particular use of language, a vernacular that he deploys in such a manner that it is no exaggeration to say—with no trace of scorn for the excellent young novelists whose talents we enjoy nowadays—that he has become the benchmark, and there is now a pre-Gonçalo and a post-Gonçalo in fiction writing. I consider that this is the greatest praise I can offer him. I have made a prophecy that he will receive the Nobel Prize thirty years hence, or even before, and I think I will be proved right. My one regret is that I won't be around to offer him a congratulatory hug when this happens.

March 3: *Elections*

As always, some won and others lost. These election campaigns are so monotonous and repetitive and—perhaps their greatest sin—utterly predictable. It is the same here as anywhere else. Once the votes were counted, some laughed while others cried. The victors are generous, greeting citizens on all sides, including the defeated, and this despite the lack of effusion, caused by the pain of losing, on the part of the latter. The winners do not give thanks to God, for nowadays it's old-fashioned to do so, yet they will kiss a bishop's hand at the first opportunity.

March 4: *To Observe and to Restore*[1]

If you can see, look.
If you can look, observe.

So I wrote in *Blindness*[2] some years ago. Today, in Spain, at the launch of the film based on my novel, I found this refrain on the bags provided by the bookshop Ocho y Medio, and again on the dust jacket of Fernando Meirelles's book, *Diario de Rodaje*,[3] which the same bookshop-publisher has issued in a beautiful new edition. It is my custom sometimes to say, "Read the epigraphs in my novels and you already know the rest." Seeing this one today, I don't know why, I had a sudden insight as to the urgency of restoring sight and fighting blindness. Can it be because I have just seen these words written on a book in which they are not written? Or is it because in today's world it has become necessary to fight shadows? I don't know. But if you can see, observe.

---

1   In Portuguese the infinitive *reparar* means to repair/restore/compensate/admit/notice/observe/criticize. [Translator's note—and a translator's nightmare.]
2   In the opening epigraph.
3   *The Motorcycle Diaries* of Che Guevara, subject of a film directed by Meirelles. The cinema bookshop and publisher is called Ocho y Medio (8½) after the title of Fellini's seminal film.

March 5: *To Restore and to Observe Once More*

Yesterday, in the course of a conversation with Luis Vásquez, a particularly dear friend and the healer of my various ills, we discussed Fernando Meirelles's film, which is now showing in Madrid and which we were unable to attend, Pilar and I, as we had intended, because a sudden cold obliged me to retreat to bed, or to retire between the sheets, as they elegantly used to say in not-so-distant times. Our talk began by considering the public's reaction to the screening: greatly positive, according to Luis and other trustworthy commentators, whose impressions, relayed to us, proved them worthy of the faith we had put in them. After this, we naturally began discussing the book itself, and Luis requested that we examine the epigraph on the frontispiece (*If you can see, look* / *If you can look, observe*), since, in his opinion, the action of looking was previous to that of seeing, and the first injunction could have been omitted without prejudicing the meaning of the epigraph as a whole. I could not avoid conceding the correctness of his opinion, but I knew that I had had other reasons in mind, for example the process of vision as it passes through three tenses, sequential yet somehow autonomous, that can be expressed as follows: it is possible to see without looking at anything; and it is possible to look without observing, depending on the degree of attention we afford to each stage of the process. We are all familiar with the way a person will look at his watch and then, if someone asks him the time no more than a second later, has to consult it all over again. That was when the light bulb went on in my mind, regarding the first origin of this famous epigraph. When I was a child, the words *to observe* (or *to restore*, as in sight) meant little to me, assuming I was even familiar with them. They only became an object of predominant interest the day one of my uncles (I think it must have been Francisco Dinis, of whom I wrote in my *Pequenas Memorias*)[4] called my attention to the particular way bulls almost

---

4   *Small Memories*, translated by Margaret Jull Costa (Harvill Secker, 2009).

always had, I was given to understand, of holding their heads up. My uncle used to tell me, "He sees you, and when he has seen you, he looks at you, and this time there's something different about it: he *observes* you." This was the story I recounted to Luis, who imme- diately conceded the argument, not so much—I'd guess—because I had really succeeded in convincing him, but because his memory was jogged into recalling a similar situation. There had been just such another bull that had looked at him in the same way, with the same raised tilt of the head, and a look that was not merely seeing, but also observing. Finally, we were in agreement.

March 9: *The Eighth of March*

On tonight's television news, I have just seen demonstrations by women across the world, and I'm asking myself once again what kind of a vile world we inhabit, in which half the population has to go out into the streets in order to claim a right that obviously ought to belong to everyone. . .

Official information has reached me of serious institutions that admit their women employees are paid 16 percent less for doing exactly the same job as men, and doubtless this statistic has been falsified to avoid the shame of a still higher differential. They say that administrative policies always work better when they are composed by women, but company boards do not dare to recom- mend that 40 percent, or more likely 50 percent, of their members should be women, so that, when the coming collapse arrives, as it has in Iceland, these women can be called on to take over running the banks and the country. They say furthermore that in Lima, in order to avoid corruption in the transport system, they are going to employ women guards, since experience shows that they do not accept payoffs, nor do they ask for bribes. We know that soci- ety could not function without women's work, and that without women's conversation, as I wrote a while ago, the planet would leave its orbit, and that neither the home nor those who inhabit it would enjoy the same quality of life without them, however frequently men pass women by without noticing what they do, or in spite of noticing still fail to take note of what it means to be half of a couple—even though the male half no longer serves as a role model.

I continue watching the women demonstrating on the street. They know what they want, which is not to be humiliated, objectified, despised or, finally, murdered. They want to be properly esteemed in their working lives, for their work, not for the everyday abuse they put up with.

I'm told my strongest characters are women, and I believe it. Sometimes I consider the women I have described set examples that I myself would like to follow. Sometimes they are no more than examples, sometimes they don't really exist, but of one thing I am certain: with women like these, we would not have had this chaos in the world, because they would always have remembered what it means to be human.

March 10: *Douro-Duero*

More than thirty years ago, when I was still an intrepid young writer filled with hopes, on the brink of entering my sixth decade, I wandered to the lands of Mirando do Douro, the point of departure for the unforgettable adventure that was going to form the elaborate account of my *Journey to Portugal*.[5] This title was no accident. It was intended to make the reader understand, from the first page onward, that the book's theme was a journey *to* somewhere, in this case, to Portugal. To reinforce my intended meaning, I left this native country of mine via Monção and spent a week traveling through Galicia and León until, with my sight finally cleared of more familiar images, I went forward to my encounter with the land of my birth. I remember pausing in the middle of

5   Op cit. Section 1, p. 5ff.

the bridge between the two river banks—on one side the Douro, and the other the Duero—and trying in vain, or pretending to try, to find the fine line of the frontier that while appearing to divide in fact ultimately unites our two countries. It then struck me that a good way of opening my book would be to start with a gloss of the famous *Saint Anthony's Sermon to the Fishes*, by Father Antonio Vieira, who addresses the fish that swim in the waters of the Douro, asking them whose side they think they are on, thus expressing (in however obvious a manner) the innocent dream of friendship, companionship, and mutual collaboration between Spain and Portugal. I did not entirely fall into the trap of making such a utopian proposal. In that same part of the river, surrounded by the same indivisible water, representatives of 175 river communities just came together, from both banks, to discuss the creation of a joint endeavor able to coordinate programs of development and propose viable plans for the future. Perhaps none of those present heard my rendition of Father Antonio Vieira's sermon, but the spirit of the place called to them across thirty years, and they came. Welcome, one and all.

March 11: *Common Sense*

The global media all carried the news: Obama proclaims an end to the ideological barriers to the progress of research into the many diseases that spell true martyrdom for individual human beings. Some reports highlight President Obama's decision to base scientific decisions on science, on the reports of experts with credentials and experience rather than according to their political and ideological affiliations. In more or less these words, Obama says that to suppress or alter scientific discoveries or conclusions or to promote technologies based on ideas or beliefs is a sin against honesty. For others, however, the real mortal sin is the investigation of stem cells, which is why the Vatican daily, *L'Osservatore Romano*, sought to remind us all that human dignity should be accorded at every stage of human existence, whatever that may mean, while bishops in the United States commented that this was a sad victory of politics over science and ethics, which is really something beyond meaning, since it plays with all kinds of variables, including those of dogma, faith and mystery, all too much at this late hour.

So, while we are in the realms of religion, I ought to confess that what I would have enjoyed reading today would have been an account of the symptoms of happiness on the part of legions of people afflicted with diseases such as Alzheimer's, Parkinson's or diabetes. What a great day for them, and what a great day for common sense.

March 12: *Kissing the Names*

When Argentina inaugurated the memorial to the victims of military dictatorship, the mothers who were our guides showed us— one could almost say with the pride with which mothers customarily refer to their sons—"Look here, this is my son's name, there is Juan Gelman's,[6] this one is of a nephew of mine. . ." They were just names inscribed in stone, names that had been kissed a thousand times, and I, too, kissed them, as in Madrid people kissed the names of the victims of the worst atrocity committed in contemporary Europe, on March 11, now five years ago, a day we can scarcely forget, since the terror went so deep, right into the heart of Spanish society. Surely we do this in order to ensure that we never again forget the reasons for that attack and, once and for all, the method used: terror, their only means of argument. May they be cursed.

Today one could see the mothers embracing, the victims looking at one another, perhaps wishing not to see the others actually

---

6   Young Argentine poet, who went into exile when General Videla seized power in 1976.

there but to see some of those disappeared. I remembered that a while back we heard of the lacerating beauty of this image. Pilar asked me to recall the memory, with my hugs for the victims and my kiss on the inscribed names also inscribed in my memory.

In Spain, to act in solidarity (*solidarizarse*) is a verb daily conjugated in three tenses: present, past, and future. A memory of past solidarity reinforces the solidarity demanded by the present, and both together pave the way for future solidarity to return and show itself in its fullest glory. March 11 was not only a day of pain and tears but also a day on which the Spanish people's spirit of solidarity touched the sublime, with a dignity that moved me profoundly and that even now touches me whenever I remember it. Beauty doesn't merely belong to the category of what we call aesthetic, it can equally be found in moral undertakings. This is why I've said that rarely, anywhere in the world, has the countenance of a people wounded by tragedy been endowed with such beauty.

March 13: *Democracy from a Taxi*

The eminent Italian statesman who goes by the name of Silvio Berlusconi, also known by the nickname Il Cavaliere, has just finished mulling over in his exquisitely privileged brain an idea that places him definitively at the head of the squad of great political thinkers. What he wants is to avoid long, monotonous, and time-consuming parliamentary debates and to facilitate processes in both the senate and chamber of deputies, since the leaders of the parliament have now assumed the powers of the members, at a stroke doing away with the dead weight of however many hundreds of deputies and senators, who in most cases never actually open their mouths during the passing of legislation except to yawn. I have to admit this is fine by me. The deputies of the principal parties, let us say three or four of them, get together in a taxi on the way to a restaurant, where, sitting around a well-laden table, they take the pertinent decisions. Behind them will arrive, traveling by bicycle, the deputies of the smaller parties, who proceed to eat outside on the balcony, or else in a canteen in the immediate vicinity. Nothing more inherently democratic than this. En route they can even begin to discuss removing these impotent, arrogant, and pretentious structures we call parliaments and congresses, sources of incessant discussion and colossal expense, never approved of by the people. As one reduction succeeds the next, I can tell you that soon we will arrive at the condition of the ancient Greeks. Of course, this time we will also have got rid of the Greeks. Clearly this is not a Cavaliere to be taken seriously. No, but the danger is that we'll end up not taking seriously the people who elected him.

March 15: *Madam President*

This blog is nearing the end of its first six months' work. Other blogs and years will follow, assuming the Fates permit. Today, which happens to be her birthday, my theme is Pilar. Nothing surprising there for anyone who wishes to be reminded of all that I have spoken and written about her for the near quarter-century we have spent together. This time, however, I want to bear witness, more than ever, to what she means to me, not simply for being the woman I love (for this needs to be confessed as we recite the beads on our personal rosary), but also for her intelligence, her creative ability, her sensitivity, and also her tenacity. Thanks to her, the life of this writer has fulfilled its potential to be something even more important than that of a reasonably successful author, a life of continual human ascendance. It lacked only one thing, even though such a lack was unimaginable to me: the conception and creation of something that transcended the sphere of my professional activities or that could offer itself as its natural continuation. That was how our Foundation came to be born, entirely due to Pilar's labor, and its future would have been inconceivable, in my view, without her presence, her actions, her particular genius. I leave the destiny of this work she created, its progress and development, in her hands. Nobody could ever be more worthy than she of such a task. This Foundation is a mirror in which we can see ourselves, but the hand holding up the mirror, the firm hand that holds it steady, is Pilar's. I trust her in a way I could no one else. I am almost tempted to say: this is my will and testament. Let us not be afraid, however. I am not about to die, Madam President will not permit it. I have already escaped death once thanks to her, and it is now the life of the Foundation that she needs to protect and defend. Against everyone and everything, and if need be, without pity.

March 23: *Funes and Funes*

It is now many years since we broke a journey from Canada to Cuba with stops in Costa Rica and El Salvador. It is concerning the latter that I would like to speak today. As always happens on my travels, I gave a number of interviews, the most significant of which was with Martin Funes, now El Salvador's president-elect. I hadn't met him before, and it was an unexpected pleasure to encounter a competent journalist who had not been charged with convincing a newly arrived author of the virtues of a system based on the most ferocious repression, nor was directly responsible, as governor of the armed forces, for the abuses, arbitrary acts, and crimes committed by the state and by the most powerful landowning families, who were absolute lords over the state economy. Instead he was a well-informed and cultured conversationalist, not only on the subject of the long martyrdom suffered by the people of his country, but also on the potential problems of a change, which was as yet still not clearly visible on the social or political horizon of Salvadorean society. We did not see one another again, but ever since—including through periods that have proved personally and politically hard for them both—Pilar has maintained an assiduous correspondence with Vanda Pignato, Mauricio's wife. One that as of now is likely only to increase in intensity.

The other Funes, who appears in one of Borges's book titles, is a man endowed with a memory that can absorb everything, and can register facts and images, all he reads and feels, down to the dawning light of day and a ripple on the surface of a lake. I just wish to ask the new president of El Salvador not to forget a single one of the words he spoke on the night of his triumph, in front of thousands of men and women who finally saw their hopes being realized. Do not deceive them, Senhor Presidente:[7] the political history of South America is filled with frustration and deception, wearying entire populations with lies and trickery, and it is high time to change all this. In Daniel Ortega, we already have a man of this ilk.

March 24: *Here Comes the Wolf!*

History, most often handed down by the grandfather of the family, was an infallible resource for the night workers in our province, not just as basic entertainment for innocent children, but also as a fundamental element in a sound education system—the precursor, in some sense, of what a witness swears in avowing to tell only the truth, the whole truth, and nothing but the truth. The only doubt I have regarding this comparison arises from my lack of regular experience of the jury system, and my lack of curiosity as to the variety of demonstrations of human nature—a deficiency that scarcely tempts me to stick my nose into other people's business, even the business of the greatest criminal of the century. Now, a story once relayed by a grandfather, perhaps to while away the lonely night hours up on the mountainside, was about the day a young shepherd suddenly decided to cry, "Wolf! Here comes the wolf!" so loudly that all the villagers came out in droves, equipped with clubs, cudgels and the odd blunderbuss from the war before

7 *Señor Presidente* is the title of a famous book by the Guatemalan Nobel Prize–winner Miguel Angel Asturias, and tells of the rise, fall, and intervening evil practices of just such a politician.

last, to defend the boy and his sheep. There was no wolf, however, and the lad said it "must have run away when it heard all the shouting." This was not the truth, but a lie carried off with an air of conviction. Satisfied with the outcome of his deception, our young shepherd decided to repeat the experiment, and, once again, the village rallied in force to his cries. There was nothing to be seen of the wolf and not a whiff of its scent. The third time, however, nobody was willing to set foot out of doors: it was clear the lad's mouth was as full of lies as teeth, so let him yell, he would soon grow tired of it. The wolf carried off as many sheep as he wanted, while the lad looked on helplessly at the catastrophe from his retreat up a tree. While this may not be our chosen theme today, it is important to remind ourselves of the number of occasions on which we ourselves also cry wolf. There were also many more who denied the wolf was coming before it indeed descended upon us, and when in the end it did, I saw and traced the word on its collar: *crisis*.

Let's take a look at what will happen following the recent news that many, many Portuguese have decided to learn Spanish, and are taking the decision very much to heart. I am afraid that those patriots who rush to the defense of every national custom are starting to cry out that they have spotted a wolf over there. I grant that they have spotted *something*, and this is the reason for the need for the people of our peninsula, some from here and others from there, to approach closer to one another. History, when it so wishes, can push hellishly hard.

March 25: *Tomorrow Is the Millennium*

A few days ago I read an article by Nicolas Ridoux, author of Menos é mais. Introdução à filosofia do decrescimento *(Less Is More: Introduction to the Philosophy of Decline). It made me remember how some years back, on the eve of the millennium we are now living in, I took part at a meeting in Oviedo where certain writers were proposing that we draw up aims and objectives for the new millennium. It seemed to me somewhat ambitious to be discussing impromptu an entire millennium, so I proposed that we should defer discussion until the following day. I remember making specific suggestions, one of which is now being put forward by Ridoux in the body of his* Menos é mais. *I searched my computer hard drive, and decided to retrieve some of what I wrote that day, at a time when it now seems more relevant than ever.*

Regarding visions of the future, I consider that it would be preferable to concern ourselves with no more than tomorrow, when, we trust, we may still be alive. In reality, if in a year as remote as 999, in one or another part of Europe, the few sages and many theologians around then had set themselves to divining what the world would be like a thousand years later, I am sure they would have been wrong about everything. Yet there is one matter on which I think they might have been more or less correct: that there would be little fundamental difference between the confused human being of today, who neither knows nor cares to inquire where he is going, and the terrified people of past centuries, who believed that the end of the world was at hand. By comparison, I think we could well foresee a far greater number of all sorts of differences between the kind of people we are today and those to come, perhaps not even in a thousand but in only a hundred years. In other words: it may be that we have more in common with those who lived on our planet a millennium ago than with those who will live on it a hundred years hence . . . And now the world is really about to end, whereas a thousand years ago it was still flourishing.

On the subject of whether the world is or is not ending, of whether the sun will rise tomorrow or not, why not put ourselves to considering tomorrow, the one day on which we know we will be lucky to be alive? Instead of however many gratuitously ambitious proposals for and about the third millennium, which itself will more than likely reduce all such recommendations to dust, why should we not decide to put forward a few simple ideas, along with a number of projects comprehensible to most reasonably intelligent people. If there are no better proposals, I would like to start by suggesting we do the following: a) allow development not from the front but from the rear, meaning those growing masses of the population left behind by current models of development, who should now become the front line; b) create a new sense of human duty, making it entirely interdependent with the exercise of human rights; c) live simply, like foragers, given that the patrimony and products, the goods and fruits of the planet are not inexhaustible; d) resolve the contradiction between the assertion that we are all increasingly close to one another and the evidence that we are daily feeling more and more isolated; e) reduce the difference between those who know much and those who know little, which is presently increasing from one day to the next.

I think that our tomorrows will depend on the answers we give to these questions, and most of all our days after tomorrow. For the whole century to come. Not to mention the next millennium.

Therefore, let us return to philosophy.

March 26: *A Question of Color*

The text of a dialogue in a TV car ad. A six- or possibly seven-year-old girl sitting in the front passenger seat of a car asks her father, who is driving, "Daddy, did you know that Irene, my school classmate, is black?" Her father answers, "Yes, of course. . ." and the girl replies to him, "I didn't. . ." If these few words are not exactly a blow to the solar plexus, they could certainly be called something else: a fillip to the mind. The rumor goes that this little piece of dialogue was no more than the creative outpouring of a marketing man of genius, but here at my side is my niece Julia, no more than five years old, who when asked whether black people live in Tías—the region where I reside—replied that she didn't know. And Julia is Chinese.

It is a commonplace to say that truth comes from the mouths of babes and sucklings. However, according to the above examples, this appears not to be the case, since Irene really is black and there are plenty of black women in Tías. The problem is that, contrary to what is generally supposed, and however hard they try to convince us of the opposite, absolute truths do not exist: truths are plural, and only a lie is global. The two children did not see black women: they saw human beings, other people just the same as themselves, so the truth that emerged from their mouths was simply *another*.

But Mr. Sarkozy happens not to think just like them. Now he's come up with the idea of demanding that an ethnic census be conducted, designed to provide an "X-ray" (his expression) of French society to show where each and every immigrant is living, supposedly in order to bring them out of their invisibility and prove how well the anti-discrimination policies are working. According to a widely held opinion, the road to hell is paved with good intentions. That is where I believe France will go if this initiative wins out. It is not hard to imagine (the past provides a wealth of examples) how the census could be used to demonstrate a perverse need for new and more refined forms of discrimination. I am seriously thinking of asking Julia's parents to take her to Paris as an adviser to Mr. Sarkozy . . .

March 27: *A Sack of Cats*

There will be no lack of advice: beware, the European Union could turn into a sack of cats, at risk as much of turning dangerous as turning ridiculous. It is impossible for the same old national egotisms, for the politicians' eternal personal ambitions, for mental corruption (this at least) that from the very start always contaminates every attempt at collective organization unless it is governed by principles of intellectual honesty and mutual respect—I repeat, it is impossible for such a combination of extremely negative features not to end up by turning the European Union into the most grotesque caricature. This is what has now happened with the intervention of the Czech minister Mirek Topolanek, elected rotating president of the European Union for a six-month period and—a disconcerting paradox, this—resigning his office as prime minister of his country, which he used to inveigh against the president of the United States in the most vulgar terms, accusing him of setting the economy on 'the road to Hell' (or, in a toned-down version, 'to disaster'), thereby revealing clearly the nature of his hopes and allegiances: a return to old-school radical liberalism and the rejection of any measures in favor of accepting, however superficially, the attempts of the social democrats to become involved. As we see, Mr. Topolanek is a sound hope for humanity.

By coincidence, a couple of days ago, Rodríguez Zapatero, president of the Spanish government, found himself under close fire from the whole lineup of his parliamentary opponents, not for the imminent withdrawal of Spanish troops, since this had been already planned more than a year ago, but for his failure to conform to the most elementary requirements in notifying the NATO alliance or the United States administration in advance. But the question that presents itself to me now is the following: What does the European Parliament plan on doing to make it clear to Mr. Topolanek that, along with being a reactionary, he is also an ill-bred and rude man?

March 30: *Raposa do Sol*

Over there and far from here, the sun rises differently. The Indians on the indigenous reserve at Raposa do Sol, in the state of Roraima up in northern Brazil, say as much. They are those whom their country's federal high court has only just recognized, definitively approving their full ownership and unrestricted use of the thousand square kilometers that make up the reserve. The ruling allowed for no margin of doubt: all non-Indians were obliged to leave Raposa do Sol immediately, along with the rice companies that for years had invaded the territory, installing themselves there in defiance of indigenous rights. Back in 2005, President Lula had determined to grant the land to the indigenous peoples and to oblige the rice companies to leave, but the Roraima state authorities favored the rice companies, and went to the high court in order to have the presidential decree declared unconstitutional. Four years later, the high court has reached a decision and drawn a line under the proceedings. Not everything in the garden is coming up roses. In the end, the class struggle, so extensively discussed in the relatively recent past and which seemed to be consigned to the dustbin of history, still exists. With the tunnel vision we Europeans have of Latin American problems, we tend to overlook differences there and reduce their affairs to a state of simplicity that is not and never was. In Raposa do Sol, there are rich members of the indigenous community who have made common cause with the non-indigenous and the rice companies. Today's celebrations were for the others, the poor ones.

Down here in the Marvelous City[8] there is samba and carnival, but the local situation is no better. The latest idea is to fence in the shantytowns, the *favelas,* with a concrete wall three meters high. We have already had the Berlin Wall, we have all the walls imposed on Palestine, and now it seems to be Rio's turn. Meanwhile, organized crime stalks every street, its tentacles reaching vertically and horizontally to penetrate the state apparatus and society in general. Corruption appears to be invincible. So what is to be done?

March 31: *Fractal Geometry*

Just as Molière's M. Jourdain wrote in prose without realizing it, there was a moment in my life when, without my actually noting the phenomenon, I found myself deeply involved in something as mysterious as fractal geometry, of which, with apologies for my ignorance, I had absolutely no prior knowledge. It happened

---

8   *A Cidade Maravilhosa* = Rio do Janeiro.

sometime in 1999, when a Spanish geometrician Juan Manuel García-Ruiz, wrote to direct my attention to an example of fractal geometry presented in my book *Todos os Nomes* (*All the Names*). The passage in question reads as follows:

"Seen from the air, the General Cemetery looks like an enormous felled tree, with a short, fat trunk, made up of the nucleus of the original graves, from which four stout branches reach out, all from the same growing point, but which, later, in successive bifurcations, extend as far as you can see, forming, in the words of an inspired poet, a leafy crown in which life and death are mingled, just as in real trees birds and foliage mingle.'

I have not been thinking of changing my job, but all my friends observed a new sense of conviction in my spirits, a kind of conversion on the road to Damascus.

For those few days I was rubbing shoulders with no lesser a company than the best geometricians of the world. The point they had attained after so much hard effort, I realized I had reached through a sudden flash of scientific intuition, a realization from which, to tell you the truth, I still haven't recovered, despite the amount of time that has gone by. Now, ten years later, I felt the same emotion when I saw the cover of a book titled *Armonía Fractal* [*Fractal Harmony*], of which Juan Manuel is the author, together with his colleague, Hector Garrido. The illustrations are in many instances quite extraordinary, the text of a scientific precision in no way incompatible with the beauty of its form and concepts. Buy it and give yourself a treat. It comes highly recommended from an authoritative source . . .

9   Translation of *All the Names* by Margaret Jull Costa (Harvill, 1999, p. 186).

April 2009

April 1: *Mahmoud Darwish*

This coming August 9 will be the first anniversary of the death of
the great Palestinian poet Mahmoud Darwish. Were our world a
little more sensitive and intelligent, and more aware of the nearly
sublime grandeur of the individual lives it produces, his name
would now be as widely known and admired as was, for example, that of Pablo Neruda during his lifetime. Rooted in life, in
the sufferings and the eternal longings of the Palestinian people,
Darwish's poems have a formal beauty that often skirts transcendent moments of the ineffable with a few simple words, like a diary
where one can trace step by step, teardrop by teardrop, the catas-
trophes—but also the profound, if scarce, moments of joy—a
people who have undergone a martyrdom for the past sixty years
to which there is still no end in sight. To read Mahmoud Darwish,
besides being an unforgettable aesthetic experience, is to embark
on a Via Dolorosa along the broken roads of injustice and igno-
miny, through the Palestinian lands that have suffered cruelly at
Israeli hands. Israel is the hangman here, described by the Israeli
writer David Grossman, at the moment of truth, as a stranger to
all compassion.

Today in the library, I read Mahmoud Darwish's poems for a
documentary to be screened in Ramallah on the anniversary of his
death. I have been invited to go and read them there, but we have

yet to see whether it will be possible for me to undertake such a long journey, one that will certainly not please the Israeli police. Once there, I would recall where it happened: the fraternal embrace we gave each other seven years ago; the words we exchanged and which we will never be able to repeat. Sometimes life extends a hand from one person to another. So it was in my encounter with Mahmoud Darwish.

April 2: *G20*

On the subject of the chimera that is the G20, just three questions:
    Why?
    What for?
    For whom?

April 3: *Santa Maria de Iquique*

Santa Maria is the name of the school, so it is natural to assume that the saint so described, up in the heavens, did nothing to intervene in the situation as a matter of principle and in accordance with the powers awarded her. The name of the place is Iquique, once a vitally important seaport in northern Chile, a region rich in saltpeter, that mixture of sodium nitrate and potassium nitrate that comes straight out of hell, a thought doubtless shared by the thousands of men—in Chile and in neighboring countries—who worked to extract it. We are now back in 1907. As inevitable as destiny, since she is the logical ruler of capital, the merciless overexploitation of the labor of this poor people was reaching unbearable extremes. A strike was their understandable response. From the mining communities in the mountains there began to descend first hundreds and then thousands of workers, who gathered together in the Santa Maria school in Iquique. After a period of days during which the strikers attempted, without success, to negotiate, the national government—under pressure from foreign capitalists—decided to put an end to the dispute by whatever means. On December 21 more than three thousand people—not only miners, but also old people, women, and children—were criminally slaughtered by the armed forces massed to suppress them. There is no lack of blackened pages in Chile's history books. This is one of the most tragic, and the most absurd, among them.

Decades later, the Chilean composer Luis Advis, a self-taught musician of immense talent, composed and wrote the libretto for the *Cantata to Santa Maria* for a group called Quilapayún. First performed before an audience in the early 1970s, even today it remains among the best examples of the New Chilean Song tradition, and of the New Song movement in South America. I have with me the DVD, ninety minutes of music led by the magical instrument that is the Andean flute and sung by the magnificent voices of the choir. I also appear in it. A few days before I was admitted to hospital, in November 2007, they came to record me making a statement on their behalf. I inform viewers that I am not José Saramago but his ghost. There are no more shocking images of me than these here, taken at that time. I would almost like to ask for them to be erased, but that living shade is after all still alive, and the living are not to be denied. In any case, out of respect for three thousand dead, modesty forbids me to enlarge upon my personal suffering. Let us leave it at that.

April 6: *The Fob Watch*

One of my newest friends has just made me the present of a watch. Not any old kind of a watch, but an Omega. He had promised me that he would move heaven and earth to obtain one for me, and he kept his word. You might say that the fulfillment of this promise should not have been a major challenge: surely it was enough to go into the nearest watch shop and choose one from among the many models on offer, from the most classical to the most modern taste, including all kinds of variations the purchaser would never even have thought of. The matter seems straightforward, but the reader was tempted by the prospect of finding an Omega made in 1922, the year of my birth. Try it out yourself, in any modern watch shop, and then tell me what happened. "Probably," the shop assistant was thinking, "this gentleman has more than one screw loose."

My watch is one of those ones with a winder, and needs to be wound up on a daily basis to recharge its energy. It has a sober aspect that derives, I believe, from the substance of which it is made: silver. Its face is an example of clarity to console the contemplative heart. And the mechanism is protected by two lids, one a hermetic seal that defies penetration by even the tiniest dust particle. The worst I can say of it is that the watch began by causing a crisis of conscience. The first question that occurred to me was, "Where shall I put it? Do I sentence it to being locked forever in the bottom of a drawer?" No, I could never be accused of having such a hard heart. "So, shall I then use it?" I already possess a watch, a wristwatch obviously, and it would be ridiculous to go about wearing both, not to mention that the ideal place for a fob watch is in the waistcoat pocket intended for it, only who today sports a waistcoat? In the end I decided to treat it like a small domestic pet. It spends its days placed on a little table beside my workstation, and considers itself to be a happy watch indeed. And, to consolidate our relationship, I have decided it will accompany me on my travels. It deserves this at least. It has a slight tendency to gain time, but this is the sole fault I have been able to find with it. Better that way than to lose time.

The friend who gave me this present is called Jose Miguel Correia and lives in Santarém.

April 7: *Further Reading on the Crisis*

Traditional values called for the construction of vast surfaces called cathedrals; modern imperatives require the construction of other vast surfaces called commercial centers. The commercial center is not merely the new church, it is also the new university. It occupies an important place in the formation of our new human mindset. Do away with the idea of a square, a garden, or a street by way of a public space where people can meet. The shopping center is the only place of safety created by that new mindset, fearful of being excluded, fearful of expulsion from the paradise of consumption, and, by way of extension, from the shopping mall cathedral.

And what do we fear now? The crisis.

Will we return to the town square or the university? Or return to philosophy?

April 8: *To Read*

This thing that is called my style demonstrates great admiration and respect for the language spoken in Portugal during the sixteenth and seventeenth centuries. Let us open the book of Father Antonio Vieira's Sermons and confirm that everything he wrote was as full of flavor and meter as if these qualities were not external but intrinsic to the language.

We are not altogether certain as to how people spoke at that time, but we know how they wrote. The language of the day was in a state of continual flux. We might choose to compare it to a river, a weighty mass of water, sliding along with great force, brilliance and rhythm, even if at times its course is interrupted by roaring cascades.

The holidays are upon us, the perfect occasion to immerse yourself in that river of language as written by Father Vieira. I'm not in the business of dispensing advice to anyone, but I can freely admit that I intend diving into his best prose, so deep I may disappear one of these days. Anyone else like to join me?

April 13: *L'Aquila*

I read a news report on the earthquake in the Abruzzi, where desperate, powerless survivors are asking themselves why the fates chose them and their lands to be the site of such a tremendous catastrophe. It is a question to which there can never be an answer, but which we invariably ask whenever unhappiness knocks at the door, as if somewhere in the universe there were someone responsible for our misfortunes. Mostly there is little time to do more than look death in the face, or perhaps not even that much, as the bomb explodes ten short paces ahead, when the kayak suddenly breaks into pieces within reach of the coast, or a flood sweeps away houses and bridges as if they hardly counted as obstacles, or when mudslips or landslides bury entire communities. We all ask ourselves, Why us? Why me? And answer comes there none. Jacques Brel also asked: "Pourquoi moi? Pourquoi maintenant?"—and died. It was his fate, we say, and the word *resurrection* wasn't written in it. It is as well to know that, since, to tell the truth, the world is not made for resurrections. That is all we need to know.

April 14: *Bo*

Let us congratulate him, our very own water dog, for being in the White House. I don't know how they will pronounce the name they have given him, but I hope they do so in the French fashion, as if there were a circumflex over the letter *o*, which would make it sound nothing less than beautiful. By this time his portrait will have traveled around the world, and the Great Danes and Pomeranians will be biting their lips with envy while the Portuguese breed already referred to celebrates his success with expressions of entirely justified patriotic pride. In any case, let me say that I have a serious reservation to put to you: it is that of never having heard of a water dog with a garland of flowers hung around his neck, as if he were a hula-dancer. At only six months old, Bo is not as yet fully aware of the respect due to the canine line into which he had the good fortune to be born. Were the White House to wish it, we might consider a short loan (not a long one, since then we would miss him ourselves) of our dear Camões, to serve as mentor to the presidential puppy, and to teach him the manners that he ought to display at all times, worthy of a dog dignified by true Portuguese descent. *Portugal oblige.*

April 15: *Colombia in Lanzarote*

The nation came to me in the person of one of its most dignified representatives: the citizen and former member of parliament Sigifredo López Tobón, freed two months ago from a captivity that lasted almost seven years, where he endured the toughest conditions in the Colombian jungle, compounded by the inhumane treatment the FARC guerrillas impose on their captives. Sigifredo López was one of a group of twelve deputies kidnapped by the Colombian guerrilla movement; the other eleven had been recently executed. Sigifredo escaped by chance, after being kept in isolation for an act of insubordination. Though the man has every reason to loathe this world and its executioners, he does not raise his voice to recount his personal sufferings (to which he appears to attach minimal importance), yet he cannot suppress a shiver as he describes the horrific actions of the FARC—the murders and tortures, including those visited on twenty-two soldiers who lived chained to trees for more than twelve years. . .

The hall at the César Manrique Foundation didn't have a single empty seat left in it; there was standing room only. For nearly two hours we were in a constant state of heightened emotion impossible to translate into words. There were some who cried, from the unbearable shock of the monstrous revelations disclosed to us but also (at least in my case) at the infinite sadness of being made the way we are, for which there is neither remedy nor salvation. Could anyone have imagined that the paramilitaries killed, and continue to kill, their fellow men by cutting off their limbs with a chainsaw?

April 16: *Delusions of Grandeur*

The matter is serious, more than serious. I have recently heard that Portugal has a surfeit of motorways, no fewer than nine, measuring a total of some 350 miles. If we pause to consider how much it actually costs to construct even one mile of these sumptuous means of vehicular transportation, along which the user can enjoy almost all the commodities available in domestic life, we must inevitably conclude that someone has been fiddling the bills, or at least has been using them to deceive us.

According to the law, or what seems to pass for the law in this instance, the opening of a motorway requires a degree of accurate forecasting as to the quantity of traffic anticipated, in order for us not to fall into the trap of making jokes like "here he comes, there he goes," as in the case, for example, of the one (not the joke, the road) linking Lisbon with Elvas, evoking a nostalgia for the times when the route followed a more modest national policy and transported multitudes to Pousada to eat salt cod cooked in the local Bras style. *Mutatis mutandis*: with or without salt cod, this situation persists along the eight remaining motorways.

When they told King João V how much the bells he wanted to have installed at Mafra would cost, he could not contain himself and, in the ridiculous prose style of the *nouveau riche* he said, "Cheap at the price. Buy me two." Not so long ago, when Portugal was in charge of organizing the European Football Championship, which they then disgracefully failed to win, someone must have thought to mention that we really needed to build a whole quantity of stadia, since we were really rather short of them. I can picture the dialogue: "How many would you like?" inquires the fashionable big shot. "I think that three or four ought to be enough," answers the technician. "What do you mean, three or four?" the dignitary splutters indignantly. "We need ten or twelve at least, and we'll look right idiots if we don't draw down sufficient European funds to scrape the bottom of the barrel." Yet again, either someone was bamboozled over the final bill, or bamboozled us about it.

The figures stack up when we count the number of the poor in Portugal. There are two million of them, according to the latest reckoning. That is to say, one more monument to our historic delusions of grandeur. . . I can hear those bells ringing now.

April 17: *Together with Dario Fo*

A number of people met with Dario Fo in the auditorium of the Caja Granada to participate in the ceremonial granting of the Prize for International Cooperation, which, if I am not mistaken, the very same Caja has awarded for the past ten years, and which this year was due to be shared between Fo and myself. I should have been there, too, in order—as the highly embossed invitation put it—to participate in the joys and embraces of such a moment. Sadly, I was unable to make the journey, but thanks to modern communications I was almost transported there in real time for the unfolding of this occasion where, at my own request, most kindly satisfied, I was represented by the rector of the University of Granada. In some sense, Dario Fo and I had been invited there to represent the Festival of the Sete Sóis–Sete Luas, of which we are proud to be the honorary presidents. The tradition throughout the history of this prize, which gives it such value, is that the prize-winner renounces the award in favor of a cultural or social institution, and we donated ours to the festival itself, which will use the funds toward the construction of a cultural center on the Ribeira Grande in the Cape Verde Islands—that charming country, as I described it in my pre-recorded contribution. After all this, I think I can say that all of us, including this absent party, emerged from the awards ceremony of the Caja Granada Prize for International Cooperation pretty much delighted.

April 20: *Showing Off*

Words such as discretion, reserve, restraint, modesty, and decency can always be found in the dictionary. I am afraid, however, that some of them will come, sooner or later, to meet the sad fate of words such as *esgártulo*[1] removed, as so many have been, from the lexicon of the National Academy because of a clear and persistent lack of usage that rendered them a dead weight upon its erudite columns. *Esgártulo* is not a word I can recall ever having mentioned, still less written. By contrast, the word *reserved*, although it follows the pattern and fits the list above in slowly losing currency when applied to a person, will yet be granted a long and useful life as a word used by booking agencies and box offices, a word without which such basic services as airlines would be unable to function. This without our even needing to have recourse to that special variety of reserve, the mental discipline invented by the Jesuits as a conclusive justification for preaching one thing before doing just the opposite, an exercise that spread and flourished until it was diffused throughout human society, to the point where it became a condition for survival.

Far be it from me to moralize, for were I to do so, I would only waste time—mine and, I suspect, that of some of my readers. We know full well that the flesh is weak: how much more so, then, is the spirit, however much one boasts of all its supposed strengths, since the human being is the terrain par excellence where all possible and pleasant temptations meet, those that men's flesh is naturally heir to and those he has been inventing and refining across centuries and millennia. Make the most of it. Let he who has resisted all temptation cast the first stone. The whole thing began with the shedding of garments, in favor of ever lighter and briefer ones, made of fabrics of increasing transparency, at each stage revealing

---

1 The translators believe this word means "life imprisonment," but, as it has been removed from the lexicon, they cannot be certain.

more square centimeters of skin before finally giving way to bare nakedness, the total nudity openly displayed on certain designated beaches. Nothing to worry about in that. At its heart, as I have written elsewhere, there is actually something rather innocent about this. Adam and Eve also went about naked and, contrary to what the Bible tells us, were well aware of the fact.

In order for this dominant universal spectacle to have its effect in both focusing and distracting the world's attention, we apparently didn't foresee that we would give birth to a society of exhibitionists. The division between actors and spectators is over: the spectator attends not only to hear and see, but also to be seen and heard. The power of television, to give but one example, is in large part fed by this unsavory symbiosis via its so-called reality shows, on which the guests, and this is what I am obliged to pay for, discourse at length on the miseries of their lives, describing the betrayals and evils they have suffered, their own and others' scurrilous behavior, including, should it be deemed necessary to the spectacle, that of their nearest and dearest. Without holding anything back—without reserve, without shame, decency, or modesty. There will be no lack of viewers who thank God for it, saying that it is high time to abandon that old-fashioned vocabulary, to open doors and pry inside private homes, however malodorous. Some people, let there be no doubt about it, go to the extent of insisting that this is one of the key benefits of living in a democracy. It is permitted to say everything, on condition that what really matters remains hidden. Shamelessly so.

April 21: *Nightshirt (Camisola)*

When I left hospital today, fresh as a rose, I brought two sources of satisfaction home with me. One was that of finding myself finally free from an impertinent attack of bronchitis that for months on end, through various highs and lows, had refused to depart and was now obliged to resign itself to going in search of another host.

(May it not find one.) The second source was of a different order. It so happened that in this little hospital on the isle of Lanzarote—and this is something that will no doubt surprise all my readers—at least seventeen or eighteen Portuguese nurses are employed, the majority of them from the region of Minho. It also so happened that in order to be discharged, I had to undergo an X-ray of my thorax, that it might be decisively recorded that the patient was, as they say, fit and able to leave. I was wearing what today we usually call a jersey, and when asked to undress, I'd removed and put it on the back of a chair. The nurse, a Portuguese from Felgueiras, had to check that the plates were clear, and in order to do so, was obliged to go into the next room. As he did so he said to me: "São só dois minutos, depois dou-lhe a camisola." ("It'll just be a couple of minutes, then I'll bring you your nightshirt").

I think I was trembling. I had not heard the word *camisola* for a good thirty years, maybe longer, and here, in Lanzarote, 1,750 miles away from my homeland, a young nurse from Felgueiras, without any idea of what he was saying, was telling me that the Portuguese language was still in existence. Blessed be bronchitis.

April 22: *On the Impossibility of Such a Portrait*

This text was the foreword I wrote for the catalog of an exhibition of portraits of Fernando Pessoa, held at the Calouste Gulbenkian Foundation in the early 1980s, I think probably in 1985. Since it does not seem to be out of place in a blog such as this, I'm posting it here.[2]

What kind of a self-portrait would Fernando Pessoa have painted if instead of a poet he had been an artist or—better still—a portrait painter? Standing full-face in front of the mirror,

---

2 *Fernando Pessoa: A Galaxy of Poets, 1888–1935*, Servicio Internacional da Fundacão Calouste Gulbenkian (Lisbon: 1985).

or, possibly, in half-profile, studying himself obliquely in three-quarter view, like someone hidden from himself but taking a peep, wondering which expression to adopt and for how long? His own resemblance at different ages, if we follow the likenesses in the various photographs we still have of him, as well as in the succession of blurred images from birth to death, following his habitual walks every afternoon, night, and morning, beginning at the Largo de São Carlos and ending at the hospital of São Luis? And what of Alvaro de Campos,[3] the Glasgow-trained naval engineer? Or of Alberto Caeiro, lacking both an education and a profession, who died of tuberculosis in the flower of his youth? Or of Ricardo Reis, the expatriate doctor of whom all trace was lost, despite vague recent reports, clearly apocryphal in intent?[4] Or again of Bernardo Soares, assistant to the chief librarian in the lower town of Lisbon? What about all the rest, like Guedes or Moura, invoked no doubt on innumerable, probable, or possible occasions? Would he show himself with his hat on his head? With his legs crossed? With a cigarette held between his fingers? Wearing his spectacles? With his gabardine raincoat on, or just hung over his shoulders? Might he employ a disguise, for example removing the moustache and revealing the skin beneath, suddenly naked and cold? Would he surround himself with symbols, codes from the Kabbalah, signs of the Zodiac, seagulls over the Tejo River, stone quays, blue horses and yellow jockeys, premonitory tombs? Or, instead of this burst of eloquence, would he sit before the easel with its blank canvas unable to raise an arm, either to attack it or defend himself against it, waiting for another painter to come and paint the impossible portrait? Of whom? Or of what?

Out of an individual named Fernando Pessoa emerges the proof

---

3   This, and the names that follow, are Pessoa's famous heteronyms, which recur in his work.

4   Saramago's novel *The Year of the Death of Ricardo Reis* was published in English in 1991.

of something we already know about Camões. Ten thousand portraits—sketched, painted, modeled—in the end rendered Luís Vaz invisible. Even what little remains is superfluous: a drooping eyelid, a beard, a crown of laurels. It is easy to see Fernando Pessoa embarked on the same path to invisibility and, considering the current multiplicity of portraits of this artist, inspired by our rapacious appetite for representation and facilitated by all of our new technologies, this man of heteronyms, already voluntarily confused with the creatures of his imagination, will enter into total darkness in far less time than the man with but a single image, although with just as many voices. Perhaps it will prove to be— who knows?—the perfect destiny for a poet, to lose the substance that fills the contour of his face, the worn-out gaze and wrinkled skin dissolving into space and time, swallowed up between the lines of what he was able to write; as if from that undefined, featureless face there remains something more to be drawn, surely one day even the tiniest new addition will not be found there. The poet shall be no more than a memory embedded in memories, so that some adolescent can tell us that he has all the dreams of the world within him, as if he were the first person ever to have dreams and announce the fact. There are reasons to think that language, all of it, is a work of poetry.

Meanwhile, the artist is continuing to paint the portrait of Fernando Pessoa. He is still near the start of his task, he is unsure as yet of which expression to select. All that can be seen is the finest brushstroke of green, when it so happens a dog of this color emerges, to accompany the yellow jockey and the blue horse, assuming the green is a physical or chemical result of the conjunction of the jockey and his horse, itself a matter of professionalism and taste. But the artist's greatest doubt does not concern his choice of colors; that's a difficulty long since resolved once and for all by the Impressionists, for only the men of antiquity—those from way back when—failed to realize that one color contains all the rest. No, the artist's greatest doubt is (and has to be) whether or not to adopt a reverential attitude—whether to paint this Virgin as St. Luke described her, on her knees, or whether to treat this man as a pathetic, homeless creature, ridiculous in the eyes of even the hotel maids, who wrote absurd love letters and who, if he had allowed himself to do so, would have laughed out loud as he painted himself. The painted green line, therefore, is no more than the jockey's yellow leg on the horse's blue flank. Until the conductor raises his baton, the music cannot surge forth, languorous or melancholy, nor can a shop assistant begin to smile at the childhood memories of the artist. There is a kind of innocent ambiguity about this green leg, with its capacity to transform itself into a green dog. The painter lets himself be drawn by an association of ideas: to him the leg and the dog are merely heteronyms of green, and so many more incredible things than this have proved possible, there's nothing strange in that. Nobody can know what thoughts pass through the head of an artist as he paints. The portrait is done, and will be linked to the ten thousand or more earlier representations. It can be a devout genuflection or a sardonic smile, it doesn't matter which, for each one of these colors, all of these brushstrokes, each superimposed upon the other, approximates an instant of invisibility, of that absolute blackness incapable of reflecting the tiniest particle of light, not even the fugitive brilliance of the sun, which, in a confrontation with that blackness would last but the blink of an eye before it vanished forever. Poised between reverence and irreverence, at some indeterminate point perhaps the man who was Fernando Pessoa will appear. Only perhaps, because not even this much is certain. Albert Camus did not think twice when he wrote: "If someone wishes to be recognized, it is enough for him to say who he is." In most instances, the worst that can happen to one daring such a venture is being able to provide only the name given on their birth certificate.

In Fernando Pessoa's case, not even this was an option. For him, it was not enough to simultaneously go by the names of Caeiro and Reis, but in addition he added on those of Campos and

Soares. Now that he is no longer a poet but a painter, and is about to produce his own self-portrait, what face should he paint? What name will he use to sign the canvas with? Will he place it on the left or the right side of his painting? For every painting is a mirror, but of what, of whom, and for whom? At last his arm is raised, his hand firmly holds the slender wooden wand, let us say about the length of a pencil, but we have cause for suspicion: it is not dipped in green, blue, or yellow paint; in fact, no color, no paint can be seen. This is the absolute blackness with which Fernando Pessoa, thanks to the work of his own hands, renders himself invisible.

Still painters will always continue painting.

April 24: *Eduardo Galeano*

There was great excitement in newspaper columns and on radio and television across the world when Hugo Chávez approached Barack Obama with a book in his hand. It was obvious, any person endowed with minimum common sense would have thought, that this was not a well-chosen moment to request an autograph from the president of the United States, there in the midst of a summit meeting. However, as it transpired, this was not what Chávez was up to. Instead, he was making a delicately timed offer, from one head of state to another, of nothing more than a copy of *The Open Veins of Latin America* by Eduardo Galeano. Clearly this had to be a gesture of some significance. Chávez will have been thinking, "This man Obama knows nothing of us, he was hardly born when this book appeared, but Galeano can still teach him something." Let us hope that this will be so. The most interesting part about the incident, however, is that afterward not only did *Open Veins* immediately sell out on Amazon, passing in an instant from an extremely modest position at the bottom of the sales list to rank in the glorious heights with new best-sellers—rising from something like fifty-thousandth place to number two—but that simultaneously there appeared all these negative criticisms that seemed to chime in unison (this was particularly noticeable in the gutter press), all engaged in a debunking of Galeano's work, leavened by the occasional bare hint of approval, but mostly insisting that in addition to being marred by feeble analyses based on shaky foundations and by marked ideological preconceptions, the book was also entirely out of sync with present-day reality. While it is true that *The Open Veins of Latin America* was first published in 1971— almost forty years ago—it is also the case that unless the author had been some sort of Nostradamus, only by some Herculean feat of imagination could he have managed to anticipate the realities of life in 2009, so entirely different has this year turned out from even the most recent intervening years. Leaving aside the bad faith of these irresponsible critics, their accusations sound as ridiculous as saying that *The True Conquest of New Spain* written by Bernal Díaz del Castillo in the seventeenth century abounds in badly-phrased analyses heavily underlined by ideological prejudice. The truth is that whoever wants to be informed about what has happened in America, that whole transcontinental stretch of America[5] from the fifteenth century onward, can only stand to gain from reading Eduardo Galeano. The problem with these and other critics currently swarming around is that they themselves know so little history. For now, we only need to wait and watch to see how Barack Obama makes use of the lessons in *The Open Veins*. At least he certainly has the makings of a good pupil.

April 27: *Boys in Black*

A good friend of mine—the artist Sofia Gandarias—told me that when, some years ago, she was on a work trip to Sri Lanka (formerly known as Ceylon) she was surprised to find gangs of youths out on the streets all dressed in black. It didn't seem to her

---

5   Central and South America are, of course, America, too, and deeply resent North America's appropriation of their common name (taken from the early Italian cartographer, Amerigo Vespucci).

to be the distinctive clothing of a caste or a particular ethnic group, not least because there were no adults around dressing the same way. Inquiring of one youth and then of one adult after another, she finally ended up with the answer as to why they adopted this unusual form of dress. The families of these youths had been prevailed upon to hand their children over to Islamic militants who practiced the most extreme version of their faith, the *jihad* or holy war. Perhaps this was in order to someday see them converted into martyrs of the Islamic Revolution, in other words, to find them dressed in one last outfit, that of the explosive-packed jacket of the suicide bomber setting out to detonate himself in a marketplace, night club, or parking lot—anywhere the number of deaths would be maximized. I don't know whether these mothers and fathers were awarded financial compensation, or if they did this on the facile promise of their children's immediate entry into paradise to meet Allah. I also don't know whether these youths in their black tunics are still waiting for their designated moment to arrive, or are already no longer of this world. I don't know anything. And I am now going to end here. Not that words fail, but that the subject is repugnant to me.

April 28: *Memories*

We are the memory we retain; without memory, we would not know who we are. This sentence, which sprung into my mind many years ago, amid the ferment of the numerous conferences and interviews my work imposes upon me, not only immediately appeared to me as a revealed truth, meaning one of those that brooks no argument, but also as endowed with a formal equilibrium, a harmony within its elements that—or so I thought—would make it extremely easy for my listeners and readers to remember. As far as my pride goes, and I am pleased to add it doesn't go all that far, I am proud to be the author of this sentence. This, despite the fact that in my other ear modesty, with which I am equally well

endowed, whispers every now and then in all seriousness that what
I had said was as much a certainty as the sun rising in the east. In
other words, it was blatantly obvious.

Well, it would seem to be the case that even the most apparently
obvious things—as this one seemed to be—are subject to question at any given moment. This is so with our memory, which,
according to the most recent information, is purely and simply at
risk of disappearing—of joining, in a manner of speaking, the list
of species on the way to extinction. According to new sources of
information, published in scientific journals as respected as *Nature*
and *Learn Mem.*,[6] a molecule has been discovered, named ZIP (not
that the name does it justice), that is capable of blotting out all
memories, good or bad, happy or damaging, leaving the brain free
of the burden of the memory accumulated throughout however
long a lifetime. The newborn child has no memory, and now we,
too, can attain that state. It has been said by others that science
brings progress, which is in any case absurd—but I, for one, do
not want this kind of science. I have grown used to being what
memory has made me, and am not in the slightest bit discontented
with the result, even if my deeds have not always been the most
worthy. I am a creature of this planet like any other human being,
with qualities and defects, making both bad mistakes and good
decisions, so please let me be as I am. Together with my memory,
this is who I am. I do not want to forget any of it.

April 29: *Swine Flu (1)*

I know nothing of the subject, and the direct experience of having
lived with pigs during my childhood and adolescence is of no use
to me here. More than anything else, mine was a hybridized family
of humans and animals. But I read the newspapers attentively and
I hear or watch reports on radio and television, and thanks to a

---

6   Actual name *Learning and Memory*.

quantity of providential reading that has helped me the better to understand the background to the original causes of the so-called pandemic, perhaps I may here note some facts that will in turn serve to enlighten the reader. For some time our virology specialists have been convinced that the intensive agricultural systems of southern China have been the main cause of flu mutations, as often through seasonal drift as through episodes of genomic exchange. It is now six years since the journal *Science* published an important article in which it demonstrated that, after years of stability, the North American swine flu virus had taken a vertiginous evolutionary leap. The process of industrialization, by major companies, of pig production broke what had hitherto been China's natural monopoly on the evolution of the flu. In recent years, the pig sector of US agribusiness has been transformed into something more closely resembling the petrochemical industry than the rustic family farm that school textbooks so revel in describing.

In 1966, for example, the United States had 53 million pigs, distributed in around a million rural farms. Today, there are 65 million pigs concentrated in some 65,000 factory farms. This signifies a transition from the traditional pigsty to the gigantic fecal inferno of today, where, amid their own dung and an asphyxiating heat, capable of exchanging pathogenic agents at the speed of light, tens of millions of animals are heaped up, and the damage extends further than just their autoimmune systems.

This will not, no doubt, be found to be the sole cause of the new flu. However it is not one that should be ignored. I shall return to the subject.

April 30: *Swine Flu (2)*

Let us now continue. Last year, a committee assembled by the Pew Research Center published a statement on "animal production in industrial farms, where attention was drawn to the grave danger of the continued spread of the virus, a characteristic of oversized flocks and herds, increasing the chance that new viruses will appear through processes of mutation or reformulation, which can give rise to new viruses more efficient at transmitting themselves to humans." The committee was also alarmed by the fact that the promiscuous use of antibiotics in the pig factories—cheaper than those offered to humans—was in direct proportion to the surge of resistant staphylococcus infections, at the same time as the residual discharges from these increased the presence of *E-coli* and pfiesteria (the protozoa that killed millions of fishes and infected dozens of fishermen in the estuaries of North Carolina).

Whatever improvement to the environment is achieved thanks to studies of this new pathogenic threat, it will have to come through a confrontation with the monstrous power of the major bird and herd-animal business conglomerates such as Smithfield (pigs and cows) and Tyson Farms (hens). The research committee spoke of a systematic obstruction of its investigations on the part of major businesses, which included barely concealed threats to suppress the paychecks of any agricultural inspectors found to be cooperating with the committee. This is the result of having a highly globalized industry that enjoys wide political influence. It is what happened with the gigantic fowl factory called Charoen Pokphand, based in Bangkok, which was able to derail investigations into the part it played in the spread of avian flu across Southeast Asia. It now seems most likely that attempts to establish a cause for the overseas upsurge in swine flu came sharply up against the brick wall of the pork industry. This is not to say that the industry will never find itself singled out by the finger of blame: in Mexico it is already rumored that the epicenter of the swine flu outbreak was in the largest branch of Smithfield, down in Veracruz. But the most important aspect is always the forest, not the trees: in this case, the failed antipandemic strategy of the World Health Organization; the progressive deterioration of world public health; the gag applied by the giant transnational pharmaceutical companies on the most basic and vital medicines; and the planetary catastrophe that is pig production on an industrial scale, carried out with an utter disregard for the environment.

As has been seen, the infection goes further and is a lot more complex than the simple entry of a—presumably mortal—virus into the lungs of a citizen caught in a web of material interests unchecked by any scruples on the part of big business. All this is infecting all else. The first death—and that long ago—was the death of honor. Could one honestly imagine demanding honor from a transnational company? Who will save us now?

May 2009

May 1: *Javier Ortíz*

Yet one more has passed away. When circumstances found me on this African isle, alternating living here with lengthy stays in Lisbon, thanks to Pilar it did not take me long to get to know a group of journalists who greatly impressed me, in part by how different they were from those I had become accustomed to in my native country. Their names are Manuel Vincent, Raul del Pozo, Juan José Millás, and Javier Ortíz. Superb literary ability, rare acuity of perception, and a highly evolved sense of humor are some of the characteristics they have in common, with the exception of Javier Ortíz, who shared them, for he has recently died. Of the four, Javier was the most politically active. He was a man of the left who never concealed nor attenuated his ideas, and achieved the feat of maintaining the strongest ideological positions. While still working as a journalist for *El Mundo*, he was unique in refusing to make the least concession that might have stood him in good stead in his career, while at the same time daring to contradict the right-wing editorial line that *El Mundo*'s editor, Pedro J. Ramírez, adopted when he allowed the paper to fall into the loving arms of José Maria Aznar. Now he is dead, there is no longer any answer to the question we used to regularly ask: "What will Javier Ortíz make of it?"

Relations between us reached a particularly fortunate point when I gave him an interview that has just been published, along with interviews with Noam Chomsky, James Petras, Edward W. Said, Alberto Piris, and Antoni Segura, in a book Ortíz edited called *Palestina existe!* (*Palestine Exists!*) [published by Foca]. Since I had recently returned from Israel (where I left behind traces of a political scandal) and was on the point of departing for the United States, where I was going to launch a book and grant a number of other interviews, our own interview was entirely conducted by e-mail, while I flew over the Atlantic and then coast-to-coast across the North American continent. That was how I came to know the intelligence, the brilliant dialectic, and, best of all, the humane qualities of Javier Ortíz. Few people know that Javier wrote his own obituary, a supremely ironic and demystifying text that should have been published in every newspaper. It's a shame it wasn't. Now is the moment to beam a final smile to him, and the one I now wear on my face is intended in some small way to defy his death.

OBITUARY: JAVIER ORTÍZ, NEWSPAPER COLUMNIST

The writer and journalist Javier Ortíz died yesterday of a heart attack. It was something he himself, the author of these lines, knew full well would happen, which was how he could foresee it, there being nothing more inevitable than death from a heart attack. As long as you carry on breathing and your heart carries on beating, they don't pronounce you dead.

That is how we come to be where we are (well, he isn't, not any longer). Javier Ortíz was the sixth son of a schoolteacher from Irún, María Estévez Sáez, and an administrative manager from Madrid, Jose María Ortíz Crouselles. His grandparents were, respectively, a gentleman from Granada with the look of a policeman—justified in its way, given the fact he really was a policeman—and a cultured and alluring lady whose surname was Rosellón; and an honorable and discreet customs officer from Orense endowed with considerable skills as a calligrapher, and a widow from Haro, whose second marriage was with the aforementioned, Javier Estévez Cartelle, from whom the Christian name of the recently deceased was derived. If any of these forbears hold any interest at all for us, and clearly they do, it lies in the proof they furnish that, contrary to what others regularly avow, mixing races does not necessarily improve the line. (Please take note of the rich variety of forbears it took to arrive at the production of a short, bald Basque male.)

Javier Ortíz's childhood was spent in San Sebastián, a city he felt to be his natural environment, since he was born there. Basically he dedicated himself to the observation of what was going on around him, in particular to ladies' bosoms—now that he has died, we can disclose this innocent secret of his—and to the study of such abstruse topics as the coastal cities of Peru, which he remembered to his dying breath. The Jesuits strove to set him on the path of righteousness, but he learned early on that he was really a communist. This thoroughly messed up any chances of a religious vocation—for which until then he showed considerable promise—especially once he had noted with displeasure the interest that certain priests were taking in his private parts.

His first literary undertaking was published in the pages of a college newspaper, and was—curiously—a necrology, in which it was already clearly demonstrated that his career in journalism could well be reversible, a peculiar circumstance that few could have predicted, even in the highly unlikely event they'd have attempted to do so.

At the age of fifteen, wearied by human injustices—one of which was the obsessive male tendency to closely observe the female bosom—he determined to become a follower of Marx and Lenin. Over the ensuing years he was obliged to invoke them as an alibi for his behavior, even though this attracted the ire of certain hyperactive members of Franco's political police.

From then on, he dedicated himself with heartfelt enthusiasm to the noble genre of the pamphlet. Ceaselessly. Daily. Year after year. He kept changing addresses, not always as a matter or

in a manner of his own choosing—here we pause to give special
mention to his various spells in jail and in exile, first in Bordeaux,
then in Paris—which never dampened his unquenchable dedication to political agitation, which he claimed to have acquired,
however absurd this may seem—and in fact is—from his reading of *The Posthumous Papers of the Pickwick Club* by Don Carlos
Dickens and the *Aventuras, inventos y mixtificaciones de Silvestre
Padarox* [*Adventures, Inventions and Mystifications of Silvestre
Padarox*] by Don Pío de Baroja.

Bordeaux, Paris, Barcelona, including on the black [market] during
periods of acute penury. Sometimes he even worked for nothing but
Madrid, Bilbao, Alicante, Santander. . . he went to innumerable places
and holed up at innumerable watering holes without stopping writing for a moment, wherever he might roam. He wrote articles for
Zutik! Servir al Pueblo, Saída, Liberación—and *Mar* and *Mediterranean
Magazine*—and *El Mundo,* and a dozen or more books. and numerous radio broadcasts, and a few television ones. . . To keep writing, he
eventually wrote for everyone, out of friendship.

Profoundly moved by reading *Selections from the Reader's
Digest* and other US publications guided by their style of operation, I decided one day to calculate how many miles his writings
would cover, should he one day decide to hang them all in one
long line of 12-point printouts. The upshot result of my calculations was conclusive: they would go on forever.

In matters of the heart (in which it would be unfair to say he
lacked some degree of experience), he was equally capricious. He
used to say that the best, most caring and most noble women with
whom he shared his life (without dogmatically excluding any of
the others), were the first and last to appear in it. Even though his
favorite came in the middle: his daughter, Ane.

And all of this to end in something as vulgar as death. Thanks
to a heart attack, as already explained. Finally, another post left
vacant. That's something, at least.

*   *   *

Javier Ortíz, writer and columnist, born in Donostia (San Sebastian) on January 24, 1948, who died yesterday in Aigües (Alicante), after writing the above obituary.

May 2: *Expulsion*

I hope that very soon those who are attacking Vital Moreira will be identified. After all, who are they? What brought them to instigate proceedings so repulsive in every aspect? What partisan connections do they have? No doubt the most elucidating answer will be the one we are given to the latter question. They called Vital Moreira a traitor and this, like it or not, is obviously the umbilical cord tying the despicable episode of the May Day march to Vital Moreira's departure from the Communist Party twenty years ago. Right now we are witnessing something we are familiar with, all of us, a demonstration of the most blatant lack of sincerity, either in offering excuses or, if you are the offended party, demanding apologies from others. All of a sudden, no one is interested in knowing who his attackers were, those worthy successors to the celebrated blackjack wielders of yore, who played an important political role simply by flailing about with their truncheons. Not in the interests of starting an argument, but for reasons of mental hygiene, I would like to know what organic relationship exists (if exist it does) between the attackers and the party in which I have been an activist for the past forty years. Are they also activists? Or are they merely sympathizers or fellow travelers? If merely sympathizers, the party can do little about them, but if they are activists, of course it could. For example, it could expel them. What does the secretary general have to say to this idea? Or are they provocateurs from outside the political realm, driven to desperation by the sufferings of the current crisis and believing that their enemy is the PS [Socialist Party] and the independent candidate for the European elections? It's too easy to oversimplify matters, both on the streets and in the cabinet.

Although he was on the list of candidates, this winner of the Nobel Prize for Literature never did get to meet up with his friend Vital Moreira inside the European Parliament. One might say this was his fault, as he always wanted to work in ways outside the electoral mainstream, but it is also worth mentioning that never at any time was the least pressure put upon him to do anything more. Not even the assembly of the republic had the benefit of my brilliant oratorical gifts . . . I am not complaining, since it gave me more time for my books, but still, some explanation is required. I do hope that it wasn't because they also considered me a traitor, for I was clearly a disciplined militant, though I sometimes disagreed with my party's political decisions. For example, that we should present separate lists to the part of the parliament known as the Lisbon Chamber of Deputies, lists that we are to hand over to Santana Lopes, apparently in order to ensure that no one sullies the virginity of the municipal pact. One is tempted to say, "May God justify us," since we ourselves are incapable of doing so.

May 4: *Benedetti*

It was a major scare: Benedetti was in the hospital, where his condition was said to be grave. Ángel González had departed from us almost without warning, one cold morning in January, and now Mario Benedetti's life was in danger, there in his distant Montevideo, and when the news reached here, it filled us with unbearable concern. We felt there was absolutely nothing we could do. Send telegrams, in the old-fashioned way? Send messages via mutual friends? Recite a prayer for his swift recovery, though surely this would risk provoking the rage of our secular Mario? Pilar found the solution. After all, who was Mario Benedetti, really? Who had he been all his life. What was the most important to him of the many professions he exercised? He was a poet. So, said Pilar, let us lift his poems from where they cling to the page and create a cloud of words, of sounds and music, Benedetti's own words and sounds and music, which will cross the Atlantic Ocean and hover like a protective orchestra before the hospital window that must not be opened, cradling him in sleep and putting a smile on his waking face.

We owe something to his doctors, it has to be said, but we—all those around the world who offered our personal contribution by linking our multiple recitals of Benedetti's poems—played our part in his cure. Mario Benedetti is now better. So let us now read one of his poems.

May 5: *A House Saint*

The refrain says that house saints don't perform miracles, at least not before the Church decides, one day or another, to confirm that they do. If the Lord is responsible for them, the sole remaining problem lies in their documentation, in gathering sufficient evidence, and in proving their trustworthiness. It would seem that Nuno Álvares Pereira, recently regarded as one Blessed by Saint Mary of the Roman Catholic Church, performed one miracle in his lifetime, just one, but more than enough for him to be elevated to the highest place on the altar by Pope Ratzinger, for whom, it would seem, any old miracle will do. A woman who was frying a fish (was it really a fish?) was hit in the eye by a drop of boiling oil, which caused a wound—an ulcer, or something of the kind—and a degree of pain, along with the risk of losing her sight in that eye. The woman invoked the aid of the one Blessed by Saint Mary and the wound immediately healed. At least this is what can be deduced from the information accumulated by the Vatican Commission charged with verifying the suitability of candidates passing through the process of beatification. The result is that we will soon have one more Portuguese saint in the heavenly roster.

Nuno Álvares Pereira, the Constable of the land, was always a cornerstone of the Portuguese education system—starting with a child's very first days in primary school—when it came to forging the civic spirit and patriotic sentiment of our future citizens. These, after all, were the good old days. An invincible warrior (let us recall Atoleiros and Aljubarrota), a mirror of virtues, a sublime example of dedication to the homeland and absolute loyalty to the king, here in Portugal each and every deed performed by Nuno Álvares was to the greater astonishment of the universe; we had no need to await the arrival of the Fifth Empire as foretold by Father Antonio Vieira, or the fulfillment of the prophecies of the cobbler Bandarra. However, the life of this spotless young man disguised a spreading stain, from which we were accustomed piously to avert our eyes, whenever we didn't simply choose to keep looking in the opposite direction. Nuno Álvares Pereira was a wealthy, lavishly wealthy, man. Thanks to the grateful liberality of King João I for services rendered, he went on acquiring goods and territories throughout his life, to the point where he owned more lands than any other noble of his time, including—however extraordinary it may seem—the owner of the royal household himself. This situation persisted until the day when King João I finally comprehended that if things continued that way, he would soon end up without a country of his own. If this had happened in our day, he would simply have expropriated the properties, but in his time the best solution he could come up with was to buy back whatever he had given to Nuno Álvares Pereira and also to Martim Vásquez da Cunha; João Fernandes Pacheco; Pacheco's brother, Lobo Fernandes; Egas Coelho; João Gomes da Silva; and others. The Constable was well known for his contrariness. Finding himself obliged to go to Estremoz, he sent, as noted by Fernão Lopes, for "some people, even those who served in the war like others among his friends and his servants, some of whom were already there together with those of whom the count spoke, saying how the king[1] had for his part retracted some of the lands he had given him

---

1   The ironically named *el-Rei*.

in reward for his services, the count's cause being that his honor was directly attached to the amount of land he owned therefore he could not bear to find himself diminished by its reduction, so he wished to depart thence from the kingdom to seek his fortune, always and forever in the service of el-Rei . . ." He did not carry out this plan; the Tejo did not flow red with blood; Nuno Álvares Pereira did not even leave Portugal; but history was left with a mystery: What on earth was the Constable thinking of when he said that even during his "emigration" (where? why? with whom?) he would always remain in the king's service? Fernão Lopes has nothing more to tell us on the subject, and we find ourselves repelled by the notion that Nun'Álvares could have gone and offered his services to the Castilians. . . All the same, there's something suspicious in the fact that the pope should have announced his canonization under the name of *Nuno Álvarez*. . .[2]

May 7: *New Man*

Culturally, it is easier to mobilize men for war than for peace. Throughout history, men have been brought up to consider war the most effective means of resolving conflicts, and those in power have always made use of any brief interludes of peace to prepare for future wars. But wars have always been declared in the name of peace. The sons of the homeland are always to be sacrificed today in order to secure peace for tomorrow

This is said and written and believed to let it be known that man, however traditionally educated for war, nonetheless bears in his soul a perpetual longing for peace. This is why it is so often used as a means of moral blackmail by the lovers of war: no one—but no one—admits to making war for its own sake. Instead everyone—but everyone—claims to be waging war for peace. This is

---

2 Spelled the Spanish —i.e., Castilian—way (with a final z replacing the Portuguese s).

why every day, in every part of the world, men still go forth to war, even to wars that threaten the destruction of their own homes.

I mentioned culture. Perhaps it would be clearer were I to speak of cultural revolution, although we know this is really an outworn expression, frequently lost in plans that distort it, become consumed by contradictions, or led astray into adventures that end up serving interests that are radically opposed to it. Nevertheless, its stirrings have amounted to more than merely this. Spaces have been created, horizons expanded, even though it seemed to me that it was more than high time to realize and proclaim that the one cultural revolution truly worthy of the name would be a revolution for peace, capable of transforming a man trained for war into a man educated for peace, because peace requires a proper education. This indeed would comprise the great mental, and therefore cultural, revolution of humanity. And this would mean, finally, the advent of the much discussed new man.[3]

May 8: *The Fair*

This year I won't go to the Lisbon Book Fair, which is nothing like the one in Frankfurt, or the one in Guadalajara, or even the one in Madrid, since ours is held at an attractive venue, where there was once a hill, though these days less of one, now that rampaging urbanization has eaten away at its slopes. But you can still view the river at its base, and there is a fine panorama of our Piombaline city, which was set on becoming modern and rational, and did, so that it is easy to observe the presence of reason in its design, in spite of later planners who preferred darkness to light and almost put paid to it.

They tell me the weather was fine and that this year's fair was livelier, as if terrible things weren't happening in the outside world—crises, poverty, and depression. They say that people read more in times of crisis, and it seems that the accountants have confirmed this

---

3   Much discussed by Karl Marx and Ernesto "Che" Guevara, among others.

proposition. It pleases me to think that in times of crisis people want to know how we reached such a position, and that these thirsty readers approach books as if they were sources of fresh water.

I like the Lisbon Book Fair. I like spending hours sitting in a chair signing books and receiving all kinds of people, who often arrive with a gift, generally a discreet one. I like lifting my gaze and watching people circulate between the pavilions, perhaps trying to find the human beings contained within the pages of the books. I like the warmth of the early part of the afternoon and the freshness that follows: it feels as if a kind of lyricism runs over my body, and I—the least lyrical of men—become sentimental. I consider books to be good for our health, and also our spirits, and they help us to become poets or scientists, to understand the stars or else to discover them deep within the aspirations of certain characters, those who sometimes, on certain evenings, escape from the pages and walk among us humans, perhaps the most human of us all.

I deeply regret being unable to be at the Lisbon Book Fair this year.

May 11: *Tortures*

To my knowledge (however small that may be), no animal tortures another, least of all one of its own kind. It is equally true that a cat experiences pleasure and amuses itself no end in tormenting the rat that may have just fallen between its claws, and only finally devours the little beast after having chewed its flesh thoroughly, with a particularly feline form of maceration. But those who understand these things (I am unclear as to how far you can understand cats and rats) insist that felines, just like the most refined restaurateur in eternal pursuit of the coveted five stars, is merely seeking the best means of improving the flavor of a delicacy by means of an inexorably fierce bite through its gall bladder. Given nature's wealth of variety and diversity, anything is possible. Human nature, however, is less various and diverse, contrary to what is commonly assumed. Man has tortured in the past, still tortures today, and, let there be no doubt about it, will continue to torture down all the years to come, starting with the animals, all of them, whether domesticated or not, and continuing up to his own species, whose agonies afford him a particular delectation.

For those who insist on the existence of something that they dare—their eyes rolling heavenward—to call human kindness, the latest lesson was tough and eminently liable to cause them the loss of some of their dearest illusions. One of the most extreme cases of torture we could possibly imagine has recently been drawn to public attention. The torturer is brother to the emir of Abu Dhabi and president of the United Arab Emirates, one of the richest countries in the world and a major oil exporter. The unhappy torture victim was an Afghani businessman, accused of having lost a shipment of cereals valued at €4,000, which Sheikh Al Nayan (this being the name of the beast) had acquired.

What actually took place can be relayed in a few words, given that a full account would consume a book of a good many pages. The recording of a forty-five-minute video shows a man in a white djellaba beating the testicles of the victim with an electric prod (the kind used for prodding cattle), which he then proceeded to introduce into the man's anus. Next you can watch him emptying the contents of a cigarette lighter over the man's testicles and setting them alight, before pouring salt onto the open flesh-wound. As a finishing touch, he several times ran over the unfortunate man repeatedly with an all-terrain vehicle. On the video you can hear the sound of breaking bones. As you can see, yet one more brief chapter in the history of boundless human cruelty.

If Allah takes no account of his people, this will all end badly. We already have the Bible used as a manual for crime, and now it is the turn of the Koran, which Sheikh Al Nayan recites every day of his life.

May 12: *Courage*

Patricia Kolesnikov is an Argentine journalist—more a journalist than an Argentine in my opinion, but this is just a little literary conceit—who places her profession ahead of her nationality, as if substituting one world for another. Years ago a malignant tumor was discovered in her breast, and she confronted this with the courage of which only a woman is capable. I don't use these words to look fancy or obtain the indulgence of the other half of the human race. I mention this merely because it is what I think: in pain and suffering, women are far braver than we are. The child who cries and wails at having a grazed knee persists in the man, however many years have elapsed between, and however many more have yet to run, and the wailing has its effect: the woman puts the appropriate pacifier in his mouth, and if she doesn't succeed in quietening him altogether, at least she has tamped down his complaints, reducing noise levels to make them bearable to the ears and sensitivities of others. A suffering man courts attention; a suffering woman avoids it.

When her cancer was overcome, Patricia wrote a book, which she called *The Biography of My Cancer*. I didn't like this title and I told her as much, but she paid me no heed. In the book (also published in Portugal, by Caminho), she traces her incredibly difficult path without showing any degree of complacency and, perhaps to honor the words of those who insist on the existence of a peculiarly Jewish sense of humor (for Patricia is Jewish), she tells her tale, which in other hands could have been told seriously, disturbingly, even frighteningly, in a way that evokes many a complicit smile from the reader, a sudden giggle or an irrepressible guffaw. Read a little further on, and Patricia Kolesnikov has turned into the mistress of paradox and the blackest humor.

Patricia has just succeeded in recovering the rights to her work, and had the brainwave of putting it up on the Internet for the perusal, enjoyment, and edification of all. There it has been

read and appreciated. As of now, readers can additionally appreciate that I am her friend and write these amply justified words to
her, minimal according to the standards of what she deserves, but
which others (her readers) will multiply through their own respect
and admiration. Thanks to her courage.

May 13: *Corruption British Style*

You can read it but not believe it. It leaves one with an urgent
desire to launch a public subscription with the intention of collect-
ing some small change to assist the English MPs, Labor as well
as Conservative, get through to the end of the month with a few
pounds still in their pockets. It gives rise to the question "O British
Empire, where have you gone and where are you now?" They who
bossed about half the world in the not-so-distant past are now but
a short step from the streets, where they will extend their begging
hands and plead for alms from their voters. It is not that they don't
have enough to eat. From what little we know, there is no indication that any MP, male or female, has fainted from hunger in the
course of a debate. Matters haven't quite yet reached this pitch.
But what can we say about MP Cheryl Gillan, who passed on the
sum of 87 pence, the cost of two cans of dog food, to the state? Or
of MP David Willetts, who called a firm to change 28 light bulbs,
charging the bill to the state? Or Alan Duncan, who landscaped
his garden at the taxpayers' expense? The list of examples runs on
and on.

The Great British Scandal is acquiring such serious proportions
that Prime Minister Gordon Brown has found himself obliged to
beg pardon on behalf of the whole political class of the country,
across all the parties, all of them, for the gravity of the discredit and
damage done to the reputation of politicians who abused public
funds in order to cover their expenses as MPs. Really, something
needs to be done to pay for such a disgrace, in which it is hard not
to see signs of farce. For my part, I have come up with an idea: to

contract in a latter-day Robin Hood, one who can rob from the poor in order that the nation's representatives not lack cash for their minor expenses, which in many cases were not minor at all, as in the case of David Cameron, leader of the Conservative Party, who submitted to the government a bill for the €92,000 he spent on his second home. Believe me, a solution is in sight and Robin Hood would not be an unsuitable candidate to set forth to the rescue.

May 14: *Sofia Gandarias*

For an answer to the anguished, though rhetorically obvious, question "Where was God?" uttered by the pope at Auschwitz to the astonishment and scandal of the world of believers, go and see Sofia Gandarias's great exhibition, which responds with consummate simplicity: "God is not here." It is plain that God did not read Kafka—any more, it would seem, than Ratzinger did. Nor did either of them get around to reading Primo Levi, who is closer to our times, and who never once made use of allegories to describe the horror. If you will permit me to be so audacious, I would advise the pope to go and observe, with open eyes, Sofia's exhibition. Further, I recommend that he listen attentively to the explanations offered by a painter who, besides knowing a great deal about her art, knows just as much of the world and the life we have made for ourselves within it—believers and unbelievers alike; those who hope and those who lack all hope, and those in between, those who created an Auschwitz, and those who asked where God was in all this. It would be better to ask ourselves where we are, what is the incurable illness we suffer that prevents us from inventing a different way of life, with gods if you will, but without the least obligation to believe in them. The unique authentic freedom of a human being resides in the spirit, a spirit uncontaminated by irrational beliefs and superstitions, which, however poetic they may sometimes be, deform our perception of reality and offend the most elementary sense of reason.

I have followed Sofia Gandarias's work for many years. Her

capacity for her art astounds me—the strength of her vocation, the mastery with which she transfers visions from her inner world to her canvas, along with the memory of everything she has lived and learned, and the recollections of others that she has internalized and made her own, those of Kafka, Primo Levi, Roa Bastos, Borges, Rilke, Brecht, Hannah Arendt, and of the many more, in short, who peered so deeply into the well of the human spirit they felt in danger of falling.

May 15: *How Long?*

Some two thousand and fifty years ago, give or take a day or a few, an hour or two, our good man Cicero was indignantly protesting in the Roman senate, or possibly in the Forum. "How long, O Catiline, will you abuse our patience?" He posed this question repeatedly to the dishonest conspirator who wanted to assassinate him, and to abuse a power to which he had no right. History is so prodigious, so generous, that not only does she provide excellent lessons on reality through the accounts we inherit from the distant past for our better governance, but she does so with certain pithy words, certain pithy sentences that, for one reason or another, put down roots in popular and collective memory. The line I quoted above is as fresh and vibrant as if it had just been pronounced this instant, or at some historically similar instant. Cicero was a great orator, a tribune endowed with many gifts, yet it is curious to observe how in this case he preferred to use the most commonplace phrases, ones that could have emerged from the mouth of a mother reprimanding her restless child, with the one enormous difference that this son of Rome, the aforesaid Catiline, was a rogue of the worst order, both as a man and as a politician.

The history of Italy is enough to astonish anyone. It is like an enormously long rosary of geniuses, including painters, sculptors, and architects; musicians, philosophers, writers, and poets, some inspirational, others illusory, an endless list of sublime individuals who produced a large share of the best that humanity has ever thought, imagined or achieved. At the same time, they have never run short of Catilines, either, for not a single country is exempt from the leprosy of soul that affects men of that bent. The Catiline of present-day Italy goes by the name of Berlusconi. He has no need to seize power, for it is already his, and he has more than enough money to buy all the accomplices he could possibly need, including judges, members of parliament, deputies, and senators. He seems to have accomplished the feat of dividing the Italian population into two camps: those who wish to be like him and those who already are like him. He has now promulgated a new set of laws granting him absolute discretion to act against illegal immigration, laws that create vigilante patrols to collaborate with the police in the physical suppression of immigrants without identification papers and, to cap it all, prohibit the children of immigrant parents from being entered in the civil register. Catiline, the historical Catiline, could not have improved on this.

I mentioned above that the history of Italy is enough to surprise anyone. It might be thought surprising, for example, that no Italian voice (or at least none that has reached my ears) has repeated, with the slightest of amendments, the words of Cicero: "How long, Berlusconi, will you abuse our patience thus?" Try it: it could bring results, and Italy might once again surprise us all.

May 18: *Charlie*

One evening recently I watched some of the old Chaplin films on television. Two or three episodes were run from a lengthy film called *The Pilgrim*, set in the trenches of the First World War, which reprises one of his recurrent themes: a blameless Chaplin wanted by the police. I didn't actually smile once. Surprised at myself, as if I had failed in a solemn vow, I dedicated myself to the effort of attempting to recall, insofar as such a thing is feasible eighty years later, how many giggles and guffaws Charlie

had evoked in me when I was a six- or seven-year-old attending
one or other of our two popular cinemas in Lisbon. There was
not a lot to recall. At this period in my life my idols were two
Danish comedians, Pat and Patachon, who were for me the true
champions of laughter. Continuing with like contemplations
of my navel, ever a sound practice for someone disposed never
to change his home or his opinion, I reached the unexpected
conclusion that ultimately Chaplin was not a comedian but a
tragedian. Observe how all is sad, all is melancholy in his films.
The Chaplinesque mask itself, entirely black and white, with a
plaster of Paris skin, black eyebrows and moustache, eyes like
blobs of tar, a mask that would be in no way out of place among
the most classical statues of the tragic actor. And there's more
to it than all this. Chaplin's smile is not a happy smile: on the
contrary. I dare say, even knowing the risks involved, that it is
so disturbing that it would look better on the face of Dracula.
Were I a woman, I would flee a man who smiled that way at me.
Those incisors, too large and too regular and white, are fright-
ening. There is a grimace about the rigid set of the lips. I know
in advance how few of you will agree with me on this matter. It
so happened that, once people decided that Chaplin was a comic
actor, no one really looked him in the face again. Think again
and consider what I am saying to you. Look him in the face,
without preconceptions, and observe his features carefully, one
at a time, forgetting for a moment the dance of the fingertips,
then tell me what you see. Chaplin would have brought all his
films to tragedy if he could have.

May 19: *Poets and Poetry*

It won't happen to everyone, and it won't last forever, but occasionally what we are now witnessing does occur: when a poet suddenly
dies, a new poet appears, and all across the world poetry readers
are now declaring themselves to be devotees of Mario Benedetti,

offering up poems expressing their disconsolation. Perhaps such moments serve to recall a time in which poetry had a permanent place in the world, whereas today it's the economy that keeps us awake at night. So it is we see the establishment of a sudden new traffic in poetry that must have perplexed all official statisticians of prosody with short lines that actually say more than they seem to at first sight. Code-breakers do not have the resources to handle it. There are too many enigmas to decipher, too many embraces and too much music in those sentiments that want to say too much: the world cannot bear so much emotional intensity for more than a few days. All the same, without that poetry being expressed today, we would not be fully human. In a few words, this is what it is all about: Mario Benedetti died in Montevideo and the planet became smaller to accommodate the emotional response to this fact. All at once his books were opened and began to expand into verse— verses of farewell, verses of militancy, verses of love, all those constant features of Benedetti's life, along with his homeland, his friends, football, and a few low-life bars where he indulged in long drinking sessions on even longer nights.

Benedetti has died, the poet who knew how to get us to live our most intimate moments and expose our most deeply hidden anger. If we take his poems out into the street—side by side, for there are many more than just two of us—reading *Geografías* [*Geographies*], for example, we learn to love a small country in a large continent. Now, to judge by the letters arriving at the Foundation, we can recoup those loving moments from long ago, now brought back into the present. It is something else we owe to Benedetti, to the poet whose death leaves us heirs to an extraordinary life's work.

TANIA AND MARIO: FREEDOM[4]

It's not true that the whole world has already been discovered. The world is more than its geography, its valleys and mountains, rivers and lakes, vast oceans and plains, cities and streets, the deserts that watch time go by, and time that watches us all go by. The world is also the human voice, the miracle of the word repeated on a daily basis, like an aura of sound moving through space. Many of our voices sing out, yet only a few of us really know how to sing. The first time I heard Tania Libertad sing, the heights of emotion to which a bare human voice can carry us were revealed to me, as she stood facing the world alone, singing solo, without any form of instrumental accompaniment. Tania sang Rafael Alberti's *La Paloma* [*The Dove*] a capella, every note caressing a cord of my sensibilities on the way to enlightenment.

Now Tania Libertad sings Mario Benedetti, the great poet who could as well be called Mario Libertad. . .

They are two human voices, profoundly human voices, in which the music of poetry and poetry of music are reunited. The words are his and the voice hers.

Listening to them, we are closer to the world, to liberty, to our very selves.

May 20: *A Dream*

I never met the man in question, and never spoke to him. He had nothing to do with anything that interested me either closely or remotely, and, to put it in a nutshell, however many times during the passing years I must have heard or read his name, I had no idea whether he was dead or still alive. I am referring to the Portuguese editor Domingos Barreira, who visited me in my dreams last night.

---

4   These are the front cover notes to Tania Libertad's latest CD, *Ese Parentesis la Vida* (*Life in Parenthesis*).

As a matter of fact, I didn't get to see him, and if I had seen him, I would have had no idea what face to give him. What he did was send me his secretary bearing a note explaining that he would like to meet me, so that we could have a chat about the past together. What aspects of the past he wanted to discuss I never learned, because although he set our meeting for the following weekend, he made no mention of a place. And when I suddenly realized this, the secretary was no longer there and I saw the whole thing was impossible.

Now let the academic doctors come and explain this dream with no apparent cause or motive. Perhaps they would like to corroborate an idea of mine, which I was tempted to call a conviction, at a point last year when I suffered an illness that nearly carried me away. The experience jolted my brain, shaking up old memories before rearranging them in their proper order, so this, too, might have played a part in prompting such an unexpected dream. Unfortunately, the question "Why?" still remains unanswered. Too bad, for all the doctors of the Academy will never agree upon what to do with this page, beyond reading it.

May 21: *Bribery*

I had promised myself not to resume writing about this larger-than-life caricature of our times, but, once again, the facts have overcome my will. This time it's not a question of young girls, models, and dancers picked out by simply pointing a finger—or fingers—at the European Parliament, or of jewels offered as birthday presents to *ragazze*,[5] girls barely out of adolescence, who call the Italian prime minister Papi, a term whose precise meaning I cannot vouch for (my expertise is not specifically in the Italian spoken by local Lolitas), but which I know gains rewards even for those girls who have made the least possible effort in their exams. It

---

5   Italian for "young girls."

is even less a question of the much-gossiped-about divorce, which I personally very much doubt will go through, given the parties' weight of shared material interests. Meaning there's a considerable risk that the comedy (if indeed this is what it is) will end in a reconciliation canvassed by many hours of prime time TV transmission.

No, what dragged me out of my relative peace and quiet to address further matters relating to "il padrone"[6] Berlusconi was a sentence imposed by the Milanese Court of Justice condemning British lawyer David Mills (estranged husband of the present British Olympics Minister Tessa Jowell) to four and a half years in prison for corruption displayed in the course of a legal action. The sentence confirmed that Berlusc (that's how it came out, so that's how we shall let it stay) bribed the British lawyer in 1997 with no less a sum than $600,000 to reach a finding of false witness, with the object of "awarding impunity to Berlusconi and the Fininvest Group." Berlusc's response was entirely typical: "This sentence is absolutely scandalous, and flies in the face of reality." There was more: "There will be an appeal, there will be another judge. I feel quite calm about it." The reader will note the reference to "another judge," which— or at least this is how I read it—implies a barely concealed intended prejudicial action that I will allow myself to interpret in the following manner: "There will be another judge, whom I will attempt to bribe." As he has bribed others, I might add.

I would like to think that the end of Berlusc is approaching. But for this to happen, it is necessary for the Italian electorate to emerge from its collective apathy, whether involuntary or complicit, and take up Cicero's phrase, which I employed only a few days ago. Let them once and for all say what is being said everywhere else around the world: "You have abused us too long and too much, O Berlusc. There is the door, go through it and vanish!" And if the door were to lead into a prison, we could say that justice had been done. Finally.

---

6 Italian for "the owner/proprietor."

May 22: Grown-ups[7]

In Portuguese we say "persons of a certain age." Whenever possible, we find euphemisms to avoid the boring term *the old* and find one that could and should be taken as a vital affirmation ("I've lived and am still living!") but which is far too often thrown in the face of the old as a kind of moral disqualification. Meanwhile, in my country at least, we used to say (would we still say it now?) in a final, deadly riposte, "You're old hat!" to the elderly of my time when they reacted to anyone who dared call them old. So the old went on with their work, without paying further attention to the world's voices. Of course they were old, but they were not useless, not incapable of mending their own shoes or guiding the handle of the plough they used for their labors. And life used to be about something else, too: it was hard. And about something good, too: it was simple.

Nowadays, life continues to be hard, but it has lost its simplicity. It may possibly have been this perception, formulated in this or some other manner, that brought about the birth of the idea to create a university of the third age in Castilla–La Mancha, an organization of which I have the honor of being a patron. People for whom old age means having to retire from their jobs, what are they supposed to do next? And others for whom old age means the leisure to pursue fresh interests, up to then left unexplored, what to do with them? The answer to these questions was not slow in coming: create a university for the generation with white hair and wrinkled skin, a place where they can study and discover worlds of unknown or little-known learning. Each one of these people, each one of these women, each one of these men, can now say, each time they open a book or write an essay on any topic whatever, "I have not surrendered." At such a moment an aura of youth revives and illuminates their features, as if they were sitting beside their

---

7   This title is in Spanish: *Mayores*.

grandchildren, in spirit at least—or perhaps it is the children who find themselves seated beside their seniors. Understanding brings each one closer to the other and everyone closer to all.

Any age is a good age for learning. A lot of what I have learned came in my mature years, and today, at eighty-six years of age, I am still learning with the same appetite. I do not attend the University of the Third Age at Castilla–La Mancha (though I plan to visit someday), but I share the joy (I could as well say the happiness) of those who learn there, those whom I address with these modest words: *Dear Colleagues*.

May 25: *The Life Cycle of a Flower*

Back around the beginning of the 1970s, back when I was still barely starting out as a writer, a Lisbon publisher had the unusual idea of asking me to write a story for children. I was not at all sure I could comply in a dignified manner, so to amend my story of a flower who was on the point of death for the lack of a drop of water I had the floral narrator apologize for not knowing how to write stories for small persons and diplomatically invite them to rewrite the story in their own words. The young son of a friend of mine, to whom I had the effrontery to offer this little book, confirmed my suspicions without mincing his words. "Really," he told his mother, "he just doesn't know how to write stories for children." I took the hint and tried not to think too much about it, this frustrated attempt to join the ranks of the Brothers Grimm in a fairytale paradise. Time went on, I wrote other books that had better luck, and one day there came a telephone call from my editor, Zeferino Coelho, to let me know he was thinking of re-issuing my children's story. I told him he must be mistaken, because I had never written anything for children. It has to be said that at this stage I had completely forgotten the unhappy tale. Yet I can now confess that this was how the second life of *The Greatest Flower in the World* began, but this time I had the benefit of the incredible collages created by João Caetano for the new edition, which played a definitive role in achieving the book's new success. Thousands of new stories (yes, thousands, no exaggeration) were written in the primary schools of Portugal, Spain, and across half the world, thousands of versions in which thousands of children demonstrated their creative capacities, not just as small story-tellers, but also as budding illustrators. Finally, my friend's son was proved wrong: the story, one of a transparent simplicity, had found its readers. But matters did not rest there. A few years ago, Juan Pablo Etcheverry and Chelo Loureiro, who live in Galicia and work in films, contacted me with their plans for making an animated film of my *Flower*, for which Emilio Aragón had already composed the music. It seemed an interesting idea to me, so I gave them the permission they sought, and once sufficient time had gone by and—it has to be admitted—after numerous sacrifices and difficulties, the film was screened for the first time. I appear in it myself, wearing the sort of hat that goes with being well advanced in years. The rest of the film is fifteen minutes of the best in animation, and has recently been applauded by the public in cinemas and at film festivals in, for example, Japan and Alaska. And it has even just been awarded the Festival of Ecological Cinema Prize in Tenerife, happily re-established after a forced suspension lasting some years. Chelo found out where we lived and brought us the prize—a sculpture in the form of a plant, which seems to want to climb to the sun and which, most probably, will continue its life at the Casa dos Bicos[8] in Lisbon. There it will demonstrate how in this world of ours everything is linked to everything else: dream, creativity, work. It defines what has value to us: our work.

May 26: *Weapons*

Arms sales, thanks to the flexibility of laws within national boundaries or else simply to blatant smuggling, are hardly in crisis—I

---

8   Where the José Saramago Foundation is housed.

mean the much-discussed and deeply suffered crisis to which the
physical and moral destruction of much of the population of our
planet bears witness but which as yet doesn't touch everyone.
Around the globe, the unemployed can be counted in millions,
thousands of businesses declare themselves bankrupt and close
their doors on a daily basis, but there is still no sign that even one
armaments factory has closed down. To work in an arms factory is
a life insurance policy. We already know that armies always need
arms, for they are forever replacing the weapons they have with
newer and deadlier ones—that's what it's all about—for the old
arsenals, useful in their time, no longer fulfill the requirements of
modern days. It should be obvious that the governments of arms-
exporting countries ought to strictly control the production and
sale of the weapons their industries supply. Put simply, some don't
bother, and others look the other way. I am talking of governments because it is difficult to believe, when we consider the barely
concealed industrial installations that supply the drug traffickers,
that there are not also clandestine weapons factories. Furthermore,
there is no such thing as a pistol that cannot be surreptitiously and
retrospectively issued with an official stamp, however invisibly
introduced. When a whole continent such as South America, for
example, estimates that it contains at least 80 million weapons, it
becomes impossible not to believe in the poorly disguised complicity of governments, complicity that must be affording cover to
importers and exporters alike. The blame, at least to some degree,
lies with contraband operations on a grand scale, if you leave aside
the fact that for a thing to be smuggled, the rule *sine qua non* is that
the thing has to exist in the first place. Add to that the fact that
anything can be smuggled.

All my life I have lived in the hope of seeing a strike, every tool
downed in every weapons factory, but I have waited in vain, for
no such prodigious occasion has come to pass, nor ever will. This
was my one pathetic hope, that humanity might yet be capable of
changing its path, its direction, its destiny.

May 27: *Music*

Yesterday weapons, today musical notes. Clearly, we are making progress. The idea, according to what I think I understood, came from the Calouste Gulbenkian Foundation, jointly with the Municipal Chamber of Amadora and the National Conservatory: bring children living in the worst slums together and teach them to read music and play an instrument. The proposal was hardly original; we only need to bear in mind the recent example of the Simón Bolívar Youth Orchestra of Venezuela, known now throughout the world, but it would only have been a mistake to imitate a foreign idea that was in some way harmful or prejudicial. This one would be worth its weight in gold, if an idea—so good, so rich in content—could be weighed. I have just attended the presentation of a video showing a group of children, most of them black, playing instruments that they'd once had no hope of holding in their hands even in their wildest dreams, managing bows and brass stops with a dexterity that astonished me. It was inevitable that I should recall the time, however brief, when I attended the Academy of Music Lovers, where I managed to do no more than stutter out a few vague scales and let my fingers stumble across the piano keys. (My future was clearly not there.) In the same way, not all of those children may have a future in music, yet I am sure they will never forget the hours spent in rehearsal rooms, or the routes they took to get there, carrying their own instrument cases, tiny for the flautists, manageable for the violinists, less comfortable for the cellists. I could see in the seriousness of their expressions, even when their faces broke into a smile, and by the light in their eyes, and the gravity with which they responded to questions, confirmation of an old theory of mine, that happiness is an extremely serious matter. Deeply attentive, utterly immersed, they rehearsed some sections of Beethoven's Ninth. I believe those among them who come to read these pages will find themselves in agreement with me, that music is giving them a good start for the life ahead of them.

May 28: *Clean Hands?*

Baltasar Garzón is one of the most influential people to have
emerged from Spanish society in the second half of the twentieth
century. We owe Judge Garzón some of the most illuminatingly
democratic moments we know: the legal process against General
Pinochet of Chile and the investigation of the war crimes of the
Francoist government. In the second case, Garzón considered
that Franco, together with the forty-four members of his Falange,
committed "crimes against the Highest Organisms of the State"
along with the "illegal detention and the disappearance of individuals, classed in the field of crimes against humanity." It so happened
that the investigation into these crimes exasperated the Francoists,
who still exist in Spain, to the point where they accused Garzón
of prevarication, because he had instigated these legal processes,
they said, knowing that those responsible were already dead. The
protest was signed by a man named Bernard, a former director of
the Fuerza Nueva, an ultra-right-wing group particularly active in
the repression of the anti-Francoists, and the current president of a
trade union that they cynically described as "defending" the right-
wing state and to which they gave the name Clean Hands, after the
forever unforgettable Italian initiative.

What did Baltasar Garzón do? If you set it apart from the judicial associations, with their intrigues and confrontations, and from
the rage (not merely political) that the Francoists unleash against
any initiative that societies may adopt in seeking to rid themselves
of dictatorship, what we see is a process intended to introduce
common sense into our tribunals. Here is one courageous judge
who, instead of covering himself in laws intended to justify silence
and omission, seeks out the necessary resources permitted by law
for the victims of the Civil War and its legacy of Francoism, so
that they can recount their own memorable experiences and have
their rights recognized. Garzón understood that they had a right
to recover the bodies buried in communal graves, to learn where

children violently seized from their families had been taken, and to this end he opened this process, which then led to other ramifications. Yet it is vital that we do not lose sight of the fact that he was the first to begin it. What is terrible, and incomprehensible, is that the heirs to Francoism have met with sympathy in the Supreme Court of Spain, where Garzón will be obliged to declare himself committed to the anti-Franco cause. The Supreme Court determined that "without ascribing value or prejudicing what is to follow, it must be understood that there are no terms under which the admission of this plea can be rejected," and further determined that the hypothesis of prevarication was neither absurd nor irrational. This is what five magistrates have decided, five of them, in the Supreme Court. We now need to wait and see what Spanish society, ever passionate in the defense of just causes, has to say about this. Will it permit, without its voice being heard, that the Fuerza Nueva, with its dirty Clean Hands, should thus use and abuse the law? Will it allow, without protest, concepts such as the rule of law, for which the anti-Francoists fought so hard, to be used against Franco's victims, once again allowing them to fall into oblivion? This is no longer simply about Garzón, to whom I pay a friend's respects, but about these people not entertaining themselves at our expense. To act to widen the terms of the Act is not an act of prevarication. Prevarication would have been a failure to act in this instance. It is a travesty of justice to allow the Francoists to come and lecture us on our democratic scruples.

May 29: *Disenchantment*

Every day species of plants and animals are disappearing, along with languages and professions. The rich always get richer and the poor always get poorer. Each day there is a minority that knows more, and another that knows less. Ignorance is expanding in a truly terrifying manner. Nowadays we have an acute crisis in the distribution of wealth. Mineral exploitation has reached diabolical proportions. Multinationals dominate the world. I don't know whether shadows or images are screening reality from us. Perhaps we could discuss the subject indefinitely; what is already clear is that we have lost our critical capacity to analyze what is happening in the world. We seem to be locked inside Plato's cave. We have jettisoned our responsibility for thought and action. We have turned ourselves into inert beings incapable of the sense of outrage, the refusal to conform, the capacity to protest that were such strong features of our recent past. We are reaching the end of a civilization and I don't welcome its final trumpet. In my opinion, neoliberalism is a new form of totalitarianism disguised as democracy, of which it retains almost nothing but a semblance The shopping mall is the symbol of our times. But there is still another miniature and fast-disappearing world, that of small industries and artisanry. While it is obvious that everything has to die in the end, there are many people who were still hoping to build their own happiness, and these are being squeezed out. They are losing the battle for survival, and they are not capable of surviving under the rules of the new system. They depart like the vanquished but with their dignity intact, merely stating that they are withdrawing because they do not like this world we have made for them

June 2009

June 1: *A Statue in Azinhaga*

There I was, sitting in the middle of the square, book in hand, watching the world go by. They had made me slightly larger than life, I suppose so as to make me stand out all the more visibly. I have no idea how many years I'll be spending there. I have always said that a statue's ultimate fate is to be taken down, even though I'd like to think they'd leave me in peace as someone who had to come to earth twice over, first in person and then in bronze. This was something that sent my mind into the most ludicrous delirium, for I had never previously dared to entertain the prospect that a statue would be erected to me one day, on the very land where I was born. What had I ever done for this to happen? I wrote a few books; transported the name of Azinhaga[1] around the world with me; above all, I made sure that I never overlooked those who bore and raised me: my parents and grandparents. I spoke of them in Stockholm[2] during an illustrated public lecture, and was understood. What we see of a tree is a mere part of the thing: its most important aspect is undoubtedly its roots. My biological roots bear the names Joséfa and Jeronimo, José and Piedade, but I have others, bearing the names of cities and places—Casalinho and Divisoes, Cabo das Casas and

---

1 Saramago's birthplace.
2 Where Saramago was awarded the Nobel Prize for Literature in 1998.

Almonda, Tejo and Rato dos Cagados, and others named for olive
groves, willow trees, poplars, and ash; of hunting parties navigating
the rivers, fig trees laden with fruit, pigs taken to pasture and piglets,
sleeping in the same bed with my grandparents, to stop them freez-
ing to death. I am composed of all these parts, and every part was
included in the composition of the bronze in which they cast me.
Yet you need to be aware that this was not a spontaneous gestation.
Without the determination, the effort and the tenacity of Vítor Guia
and José Miguel Correia Noras, the statue would not be there. Out
of the deepest depths of my gratitude I here bestow on them my
embrace, extended to include all the people of Azinhaga, together
with this other son of theirs, whom I leave in their care and who is
none other than I.

June 2: *Marcos Ana*

There are some people who seem not to belong to either the world
or the period into which they were born. Like so many of his
generation dragged into the prisons of Fascist Spain, Marcos Ana
suffered indescribably in both body and spirit, escaping in extremis
two death sentences and becoming, in every sense of the word,
a survivor. Prison could not defeat him though he spent twenty-
three years of his life there, deprived of his liberty. The book that
he has just launched in Portugal is his account, at once objective
and impassioned, of this dark period. The title of these memoirs,
Tell Me What a Tree Is Like, could hardly be of greater significance. Over time, the harsh reality of his imprisonment ended
by superimposing itself upon external reality, shrouding it in a
vague mist that every passing day he had to make fresh efforts to
dispel in order not to lose faith in his increasingly fragile inner self.
Marcos Ana saved not only himself but many of his imprisoned
comrades, raising their spirits, solving their problems and arguments, acting as a new kind of justice of the peace. Steadfast in
his political convictions, yet without allowing his critical faculties

to be affected, Marcos Ana gave everyone with whom he came into contact an irrepressible sense of hope, as if they all ended by concluding, "If he's like that, then so, too, might I be." On regaining his liberty, he did not simply go home to rest. He returned to the political struggle, risking further imprisonment, and launched an impressive project to help and support those still remaining in jail. In Spain, friends and admirers of this exceptional character (among them, the Nobel Prize–winner Wole Soyinka) have put him forward as a candidate for the Prince of Asturias Concord Prize. Nothing could be more appropriate, and it is all the more necessary to demonstrate to the Spanish people that this historical memory persists, alive and among us.

June 3: *Journeys*

We left Lanzarote last Saturday, flying out to Seville and then continuing by car to Lisbon. On Sunday, as I have explained, we went to Azinhaga on the occasion of the unveiling of a statue. The plane tree standing in front of our house had a splendor all its own, a range of rich greens drawing me into lengthy contemplation and making me think, "Don't ever move, just let yourself stay put as it does." A useless desire, when we observe the heat of summer, the first chills of autumn, the leaves falling and the tree's splendor extinguished, and then its falling asleep until a fresh spring comes to take the place of the one now ending.

These entirely unoriginal thoughts caused me to recall the last brief chapter of *Journey to Portugal*, which, I used to think, had some trace of originality about it. And I deemed it no bad idea to record it here, when we are on the point of another return to the country, this time entering through Coruña. So here we go:

The journey is never over. Only travelers come to an end. But even then they can prolong their voyage in their memories, in recollections, in stories. When the traveler sat in the sand and declared: "There's nothing more to see," he knew it wasn't true. The end of one journey is simply the start of another. You have to see what you missed the first time, see again what you already saw, see in springtime what you saw in summer, in daylight what you saw by night, see the sun shining where you saw the rain falling, see the crops greening, the fruit ripening, the stone moved from one place to another, the shadow that was not there before. You have to retrace your footsteps, either to tread them again, or to plant fresh ones alongside them. You have to start the journey over. Always. The traveler sets out once more.[3]

That's how it is. And so let it be.

June 4: *Secularism*

I'll now approach the question of secularism, in my opinion never very clearly expressed, because the fundamental question that should dominate the debate is usually overlooked: whether or not to believe in the existence of a god who not only created the universe and with it the human species, who will endure until the end of time, but who is also the judge of all our actions upon earth, rewarding those who have performed good ones with admission into a paradise where the elect may gaze upon the face of the Lord for all eternity while, also for all eternity, those guilty of certain other deeds burn forever in the fires of hell. This final judgment will not be easy, either for the god or for those arriving to give an account of themselves, since I don't know of anyone who has performed either exclusively good or exclusively bad deeds in the course of a lifetime. It is our human condition to be uncertain in our purposes and to contradict ourselves from one hour to the next. In the midst of all this, secularism seems to me to be more a defined

---

3 *Journey to Portugal: A Pursuit of Portugal's History and Culture* by José Saramago, translated by Amanda Hopkinson and Nick Caistor (Harvill, 2000), p. 443 (Afterword).

political position based on prudence, than it is the articulation of a profound conviction regarding the nonexistence of god and the impertinence of believing the logic of institutions and their instruments that purport to impose on us ideas contrary to human understanding. We discuss the issue of secularism because we are afraid of discussing atheism. The interesting aspect of the case, however, is that the Catholic Church, conforming to its ancient tradition of doing ill and making moan, continues to bewail its lot as the victim of "aggressive secularism," a new category of the position that allows the Church to attack the whole while pretending to attack only a part. Duplicity was ever a feature inseparable from the diplomatic tactics and doctrinal strategies of the Roman Curia.

It would be a welcome change if the Roman Catholic and Apostolic Church would cease meddling in what doesn't concern it, meaning in people's civic and private lives. We should not, however, be surprised by its behavior. The Catholic Church cares little or nothing for the destiny of souls, and has always had the control of bodies as its primary aim, while secularism has always been the first door through which the body seeks its escape along with the soul, given that one of them cannot set out on a path in any direction without the other. The issue of secularism is no more than a preliminary skirmish. The real confrontation comes when belief and unbelief finally go head to head, when one opponent in the struggle assumes its true name: atheism. All the rest is but a game of words.

June 5: *Carlos Casares*

Carlos Casares, the Galician writer who has brought me to Coruña and will accompany me over the coming days, died in March 2002. A few months after his death, in September of that year, a foundation was established in his name, and in the years that followed that foundation has established an extraordinary program of cultural activities across the region. I have participated in more than one of its Dialogues of Mariñan, and this one, the sixth, was on the theme of the mechanisms of memory and its application to literary creation. My partner in this dialogue was Manuel Rivas, one of the most outstanding heirs to the great tradition of Galician literature, continuing in the steps of Torrente Ballester and Cunqueiro. The auditorium in the Caixa Galicia Foundation, where our session took place, was packed with an audience who displayed the most alert interest throughout, and I consider that Manuel Rivas and I worked well together, not least in offering some straightforward reflections on one another's literary output. The proof is that we do not retreat when confronted with such thorny matters as the unconscious workings of memory . . .

There are around a half dozen foundations in Coruña and they are—as everyone there recognizes—the most active and effective cultural dynamos of the city and the surrounding villages. Every month they organize dozens of cultural activities, as many in the field of literature as in music and the fine arts—not to mention their social dimension, at least as important overall. The population of Coruña *lives* its foundations, which are indispensable to their civil and cultural education. In Portugal, we also have foundations that, happily for them and for the rest of us, enjoy public favor. But there's no shortage, either, of critical outsiders or of the obsessively envious, like a certain opinionated journalist who, when asked what seemed to him the likely reasons for the creation of a José Saramago Foundation (if you'll forgive me for mentioning myself) replied that the sole purpose of any foundation was to launder money and evade taxes. May God forgive him, for we cannot bring ourselves to. . .

June 8: *The Berlusconi-Thing*

This article appeared in yesterday's edition of the Spanish newspaper El País, and was specifically commissioned by them. Given that this blog has already hosted a number of remarks regarding the exploits of the Italian prime minister, it would have been odd not to post this article here. No doubt there will be more in the future, until such time as Berlusconi renounces who he is and what he does. Until that day arrives, neither shall I.

THE BERLUSCONI-THING

I can't see what other name I could give him. A thing perilously close to a human being, a thing that holds parties, organizes orgies, and rules a country called Italy. This thing, this disease, this virus that threatens moral death to the land of Verdi is a deep sickness that needs to be wrested from the Italian consciousness before its venom ends up running through the veins and destroying the heart of one of the richest of European cultures. The fundamental values of communal life are daily trampled into the ground under the sticky feet of the Berlusconi-thing, which, among its numerous other talents, has a theatrical capacity for abusing words, perverting both their sense and intent, as in Partida della Libertà (Freedom Party), the name of the coalition he heads, which has seized power in Italy. I chose to call this thing a criminal, and see no need to repent of the word. For reasons to do with normal or social semantics, which I leave to others who can elucidate them better than I, in Italian, the term for *criminal* has a negative weight far stronger than that in any other language spoken in Europe. It was to translate what I thought of the Berlusconi-thing in a clear and incisive manner that I employed the term, accepting the meaning that the language of Dante had habitually granted it, even though it is now more than dubious that Dante ever employed the term *delinquenza* himself. Criminality, according to my Portuguese mother tongue, signifies—and here I make reference to dictionaries as well as to common parlance—"the act of committing crimes, disobeying laws or moral imperatives." This definition fits the Berlusconi-thing without a solitary wrinkle or a single crease, to the point where it seems more like its skin than the clothes that cover it. For many years now, the Berlusconi-thing has been seen to commit a variety of crimes, always of demonstrable seriousness. That said, it not only disobeys the law but, worse still, manufactures new laws to protect its public and private interests, which are those of a politician, a businessman and an escort of minors; and as for moral standards, there's little point in mentioning those, since there's no one left in Italy or the rest of the world who is unaware that the Berlusconi-thing has long since sunk into the most abject and utter depravity. This is the Italian Prime Minister, this is the thing that the Italian people have now twice elected to serve as their model, this is the road to ruin they have taken, dragging through the dirt the values of liberty and dignity imprinted in the music of Verdi and informing the political actions of Garibaldi and of all those who created the country of Italy in the nineteenth century during the struggle for unification, values that helped make Italy a spiritual guide to Europe and the Europeans. And this is what the Berlusconi-thing wants to cast onto the rubbish-heap of history. Are the Italians really going to permit this to happen?

June 9: *Paradoxical*

At various times I have asked myself where the left was going, and today I have the answer: it is out there somewhere, still counting the miserable and humiliating number of votes cast for its candidates and seeking an explanation as to why that number should be so small. A movement that in the past succeeded in representing one of the greatest hopes for humanity, capable of spurring us to action by the simple resort of an appeal to what is best in human nature, I saw, over the passage of time, undergoing a change in its social composition, displaying a growing tendency to stray and make mistakes, creating its own internal perversions, daily moving further away from its early promises, becoming more and more like its old adversaries and enemies, as if this were the only possible means of achieving acceptance, and so ending up becoming a faint replica of what it once was, employing concepts to justify certain actions, when it formerly used to argue against precisely the same actions. With its increasing slide toward centrism, a shift once proclaimed by its protagonists to be a demonstration of brilliant tactics and peerless modernization, the left does not appear to have noticed that it has become very much like the right. If, at the end of all this, the left is still able to learn a new lesson, that has to be that in creating a pan-European front it has sold out to the right, and once it realizes this, it can ask itself what has created the entrenched distance between it and its natural supporters—the poor, the needy, but also the dreamers—in relation to what still remains of its principles. For it is no longer possible to vote for the left if the left has ceased to exist.

Curiously enough, and this is the real paradox, the politics that the title of this article describes are precisely those that at the moment are determining the destiny of the country that for so very long has been busy devising a form of politics both imperial and conservative in every significant aspect: Barack Obama's. This provides food for thought. A political act that, as I have said, does little beyond attempting to rearrange the furniture in the White House, where a rapacious capitalism on the point of devouring itself resides, now increasingly appears to us almost as the realization of a left-wing dream. All the more so, given that so many people, including progressives, socialists, communists, and the rest, are currently going around asking themselves: "And if Obama were the leader of my party . . . ?" Perhaps it is situations such as these that give rise to discussions of the term *the irony of history*. . . Or perhaps it may also be simply due to his personal charisma.

June 10: *A Good Idea*

Perhaps it was nothing more than a drop of fresh water falling into the bitter ocean of skepticism and indifference, but I think we still need to rejoice over the good idea currently on the march across

Spain. To be precise, the idea, which originated in the province of Granada, is to hold an annual celebration of the lowering of the age of majority—not only officially but also in terms of civic recognition—to the age of eighteen. Each newly enfranchised young person will be handed copies of the Universal Declaration of Human Rights, the Spanish Constitution, and the Statute of Andalusian Autonomy. Obviously, there will be other, perhaps more jocular—or at least somewhat less solemn—celebrations, but since serious matters should only be treated seriously, you could consider that seeing the eleven thousand young people who are expected to attend supplied with such guidance, as one by one they step forward into the future, will teach all of us something about their civic responsibilities. "Equip them," I say, "with these three essential texts, and you won't have failed to provide them with a more solid and substantial education, well fitting them to be citizens of the present and future." The idea is a good one, and let us hope it will spread further. To turn it into a collective and civic holiday will require considerable creativity and effort, but these, we can be sure, will not be in short supply.

The drop of freshwater referred to at the start of this post did not fall into saltwater, but onto my hand. I sipped it like one dying of thirst on one of those days when frustration descends upon us all, as we observe how the forces of the right—including the ultra-right—are rejoicing in their political victories across the length and breadth of Europe. Democracy is as yet not in danger, but it relies on us to prevent it from becoming so. Granada is on the right track.

June 11: *Epitaph for Luis de Camões*

> What do we know about you, if all we have are your verses,
> What memory remains in the world that you knew?
> Between birth and death did you conquer each day,
> Or did you lose your life in the verses you left us?

These questions are taken from my book *Os Poemas Possíveis* [*Possible Poems*], published in 1966. Today, more than forty years later, I am still seeking the answer. Perhaps I will never find it. I write this on June 10, the anniversary of the death of the author of *The Lusiads*, arguably the most fundamental book in Portuguese literature. Although Camões died poor and forgotten, today those writing in Portuguese can still obtain the unique and exclusive honor of receiving the prize that bears his name.

June 12: *The Body of God*

Also known as Corpus Christi, this is a "holy day of obligation" for Roman Catholics, as well as a public holiday. All the faithful are expected to attend Mass in order to bear witness to the real and substantive presence of Christ in the Host. Woe betide you if you have any doubts concerning the Divine Presence within the wheaten wafer, as did a priest called Peter of Prague back in the thirteenth century: the last thing you want is any repetition of the ghastly miracle of actually seeing the host transformed into flesh and blood, not symbolic but real. Nor do you want to have to carry the bloody evidence around in a solemn procession to the Cathedral at Oviedo, as Wikipedia so kindly explained that Peter was obliged to, as I learnt when I had recourse to consult the site on such a complicated topic. The world was an extraordinarily fascinating place in that period. Today the miracle of economic recovery and resurrection of the banks is effected by printing millions of dollars and putting them into circulation at vertiginous speed, thereby filling one vacuum with another, or, to use less risky terminology, substituting for a lack of value a merely assumed value that will last only as long as the consensus obtained on its so-called value in the first place.

Yet it was not this crisis I wanted to write about. In any case, as you will now see, my mention of the Body of God is not a gratuitous or easy pretext to preach heresy, as is my custom when I follow my own canonically expert opinions. A few days ago, on May 28 to be precise, a Bolivian aged thirty-three called Fraans Rilles, an immigrant "without papers" and with no work permit, who nevertheless worked in a bakery in Gandia, Spain, was the victim of a serious accident: a kneading machine severed his left arm. It is true that the bakery owners had the charity to take him to the hospital, but they left him some 200 yards from the door with the injunction, "Should you be asked, don't mention our bakery." Quite properly, the doctors requested the arm so that they could try to reattach it, but were forced to abandon this project because of the arm's poor condition when they found it. It had been thrown onto the rubbish heap.

In conclusion, I realize that I did not really want to write about the Body of God. As is my wont, I have let one thing lead to another, and it was the Body of Man of which I truly wanted to write, this body that since the first dawning of time has been maltreated, tortured, despised, humiliated, and violated in its most basic physical condition; a body from which now an arm has been torn, and the man who lost it ordered to keep silent in order not to damage a business. I only hope that today the faithful who hurry to Mass will read their newspapers and spare a thought for this man's suffering flesh and spilled blood. I am not thinking of what is set out on the altar. I only think that those churchgoers should consider this man and so many others like him. They say that we are all God's children. It's not true, but this falsehood affords consolation to many. God did not help Fraans Rilles, the victim of the kneading machine and of the cruelty of the unscrupulous people who grossly exploited his labor. That is the way of the world; there is no other.

June 15: *Miguéis*

I got to know José Rodrigues Miguéis some time after I began working at Estúdios Cor publishers in 1959. The company was co-owned by Correia and Canhão, and the literary director was Nataniel Costa. A year earlier, Miguéis had published a collection of short stories and novels called *Léah*, which was extremely well received by both the public and the critics of the time. This was the first work of his I read, and I don't need to tell you how much it filled me with enthusiasm. I'm not exactly sure when I first came to know Miguéis in person, for he would have been living in the United States at the time. What I do know is that, from the appearance of the novel *Um homem sorri à morte com meia cara* (*A Man Smiles at Death With Half a Face*), published in 1959, right up to that of the novel *Nikalai! Nikalai!*, which appeared in 1971, and through *A Escola do Paraíso* and *O passageiro do Expresso*, both in 1960, *Gente da terceira classe* in 1962, and *É proibido apontar* in 1964, I was in more or less continual contact with José Rodrigues Miguéis: in daily contact whenever he was in Portugal, and in frequent contact by letter whenever he returned to the United States. This correspondence, judged worthy of selection by José Albino Pereira for his doctoral thesis (and on the same level as I would put my literary exchanges with Jorge de Sena) gives me the right to say that I have not cut a bad figure in this world. My epistolary relationship with Miguéis was only broken when I left the publishing house, toward the end of 1971. Thereafter I saw him only occasionally; there were no more letters that I remember, but he always remained in my memory as an extraordinary person, endowed with exceptional oratorical skills, and with a mind capable of describing the most complex situations in the fewest words. An everyday conversation with him was a real gift, and entering into dialogue with such a brilliant mind made his fellow conversationalist appear all the more intelligent. Speaking personally, and without wishing to boast about it, I made the most I could of those occasions. He died almost thirty years ago, yet I remember it all as if it were yesterday.

June 16: *Netanyahu*

I only spoke because it was impossible to remain silent any longer. Brought to the wall by the president of the United States, the Israeli prime minister agreed (or rather condescended), finally,

to the creation of a Palestinian state. It was no more explicit than
that. Or rather, yes, he additionally demanded that his future state
(should there really be one at some point) should not be permitted
an army, and that its air space should be controlled by Israel—in
other words, that Israel would have the means to oppress and maintain the Palestinians in the state of forced political marginalization.
However, the other essential aspects of Barack Obama's position,
regarding both settlements and settlers, did not merit a single word
from Netanyahu. Everyone knows that on the West Bank the
"national" land theoretically belonging to the Palestinian people is
covered with settlements, some "legal" (meaning sanctioned and
constructed by the government in Jerusalem), others "illegal" (not
sanctioned, but to which the same government turns a blind eye).
Altogether they amount to more than 200 settlements inhabited by
around a half-million settlers, who according to everyone involved
present the most serious obstacle to peace, even greater than obtaining recognition of the Palestinians' right to an independent and
viable state. Bush Senior himself had suggested as much in his time,
when he obliged the Israeli government to realize that to talk of peace
and condone the settlements at one and the same time was an insane
contradiction. Ex–Prime Minister Ehud Olmert also appeared to be
aware of this when, in quotes supplied to the *Haaretz* newspaper in
November 2007, he said that if a two-state solution were not rapidly
reached, "the State of Israel would be finished." Yet he did nothing
at all to resolve the problem while his words stayed hanging in the
air. They help us to understand how the settlers have always served
as a Sword of Damocles suspended over the Israeli government, and
now—with somewhat more pressing reasons—over the head of
Netanyahu. I think that many Jews in Israel are obsessed by a fear of
returning to the Diaspora, that worldwide dispersal that has seemed
to be their destiny. This prospect brings me no pleasure whatsoever,
yet it remains to be seen whether Israel's rulers will prove capable
of forging peace. Ask them as often as you like, the answer remains
negative.

June 17: *The Elephant on His Travels*

My readers will recall that the names of the two villages encountered on the expedition to Figueira de Castelo Rodrigo were never mentioned by the narrator of that story. These villages, as described, were mere inventions necessary to the narrative and did not bear then, any more than now, any relationship to actual reality. It would therefore be an insult to devotees of historical rigor to learn that today Solomon was being prepared for a journey that, although not an actual documented historical fact, could well have happened, even though not a trace of it remains. Life is filled with chance events, and one cannot exclude the possibility that, in this or another instance, the history just happens to tally with the story. It is true that history does not record Solomon trampling over the earth at Castelo Novo, Sortelha or Cidadelhe, but it is equally impossible to swear that it could never have happened. We at the José Saramago Foundation availed ourselves of this obvious truth in order to plan and organize the journey that sets out today from the Hieronymite monastery at Belém and takes us all the way up to the frontier, where the incident of the Austrian cuirassiers who attempted to bring the elephant to the archduke took place. What an arbitrary itinerary, the reader may protest, while we, for our part, will have none of it, preferring to describe it as simply one of innumerable possibilities. Let us go away for a couple of days, and let us weave a story out of our travels. Who is to go? Let the whole Foundation set out, along with a few of Solomon's best friends and some Portuguese and Spanish journalists, good people all. Let us go in peace. Until we return, farewell, farewell.

June 18: *In Castelo Novo*

Over thirty years ago I wrote:

> Castelo Novo is one of the most moving of the traveler's many memories. Perhaps he will go back there one day, perhaps he

won't, or perhaps he'll deliberately avoid it, just because some experiences cannot be repeated. Castelo Novo, like Alpedrinha, is built on a mountainside. If you continued on up, you would soon arrive at the summit of Gardunha. The traveler has no need to reprise his account of the time of day, the light, the damp air. He simply asks that all this be not forgotten while he is busy climbing the steep streets, past the simple houses and the palaces like this one from the seventeenth century, with its portico, its balcony, the deep archway leading to the yard. It would be hard to find a more harmonious construction. So there is the light and the hour, as if held suspended in time and in the sky: the traveler will be able to see Castelo Novo.

I also wrote about specific people thirty years ago:

The traveler asks an old woman who emerges onto her doorstep where the wine trough is. The old woman is deaf, but understands if she is spoken to loudly and she can watch your lips. When she grasps the question, she smiles and the traveler is amazed, for although her teeth are false, the smile is so genuine, and she is obviously so pleased to be smiling that he feels like hugging her and asking her to do it again.

Of José Pereira Duarte, one of the most generous people I have ever met in my life, I wrote that he looked on the traveler as one would on a friend who turns up after many years' absence. His one regret, he said, was that his wife was ill in bed: "Were she not so ill, I would really enjoy entertaining the traveler for a while in my house."

Today we're with José Pereira Duarte's daughter and grandson. The old lady is no longer there, but other friendly faces are to appear in Castelo Novo, and I will depart again in the same high spirits as when I left thirty years earlier. If Solomon the Elephant happens to pass this way, those who make up his retinue will feel the same thing. You cannot invent the warmth of a welcome like this.

June 22: *Return*

The elephant rejoiced in what he saw and let it be known to the assembled company, although there wasn't a single point on our own chosen itinerary that might have coincided with those he guarded so zealously in his elephantine memory. An elephant who, we have been told, traveled north with the soldiers of the cavalry division almost as far as the frontier, at a time when the roads were in a truly dreadful state. Compared to the journey in those days, ours was a walk in the park: good roads, good lodgings, good restaurants. The archduke himself, however well accustomed to all the luxuries of Central Europe, would have been pleasantly surprised. The expedition was a working one, but it was as enjoyable as if it were a holiday. Even the long-suffering porters, obliged to carry over fifteen pounds of equipment on their shoulders, were enchanted. What was interesting was that none of our friends, and none of the accompanying journalists, were already familiar with the places we visited. All the better for them, then, since they could gather so much material to recount and record. We started from Constância, where it is believed that Camões lived and made his home, and where through his windows he must have seen the embrace of the Zêzere and the Tejo over a thousand times, whose gentle backwaters inspired his most sublime verses. From there we went on to Castelo Novo to see the Casa da Câmara,[4] dating from the time of the thirteenth-century King Dinis, and the Joannine fountain that sits tranquilly beside it. We also saw the tub, a kind of open-air vat excavated from the bare rock, where grapes were trodden in times that are now reckoned to be prehistorical. We

---

4 House of Chambers—the town hall, built in Saramago's preferred Romanesque style.

stayed overnight at the Foundation, which is set in an excellent region for cherries, and the next day went on to Belmonte, where Pedro Alvares Cabral was born, and where we went straight to the church of Santiago, to which I am particularly devoted. It contains one of the most moving Romanesque sculptures on the face of the earth, a roughly painted pietà made of granite, with the lifeless Christ spread across the knees of his mother. Set against this, Michelangelo's famous pietà from the Vatican is barely more than a last gasp of Mannerism. It was not easy to drag our fellow travelers from the ecstatic trance into which they had fallen, but we succeeded in enticing them away to view the architectural enigma of Centum Cellas, the building whose unfinished state was and continues to be the subject of the most heated arguments. Could it have been a watchtower? Or a hostelry for passing travelers? Or perhaps a prison, despite the quantity of broken windows that remain, surely unusual for a jail? No one knows. Our hunger for images satisfied for the time being, we proceeded to Sortelha, with its gigantic city walls, where a thunderstorm unlike any other assailed us with striated rays of lightening, thunder to match, rain in buckets, and hail like machine-gunfire. We never managed to get our coffee, as the electricity was cut off. It took an hour before the skies began to clear. It was still pouring when we came out onto the motorway, heading for Cidadelhe, on which I will not now write. I simply refer the interested and well-disposed reader to the four or five pages dedicated to that place in *Journey to Portugal*. Our companions' eyes were dazzled by the 1707 *palio* and afterward, on a tour of the village, by the bas-reliefs over the doorways to the houses and the tombs in the mother church, with its portraits of saints. They returned transfigured by happiness. Now all that yet remained for us to see was Castelo Rodrigo. The president of the council chamber of Figueira de Castelo Rodrigo was waiting for us on the bridge over the River Côa, not far from Cidadelhe. I retained an image of Castelo Rodrigo, from the first time I went there, thirty years ago, of an old town in decline, where the ruins were already ruins of ruins, as if it were all intended as some kind of a multiple disguise. Nowadays Castelo Rodrigo is home to 140 souls, the streets are clean and accessible, the façades and interiors have been restored, and—above all—its sadness has decidedly disappeared, and its new mood is now its best advertisement. One has to return to these historic places, for they can come to life again. That is the lesson of this journey.

June 23: *Sastre*

I met the playwright Alfonso Sastre more than thirty years ago. It was our one and only meeting. I never wrote to him and I never received a letter from him. I was left with the impression of a dour and harsh character, with nothing kindly about it, which did nothing to make our conversation easier, although neither was it exactly difficult. I never heard more of him, other than through occasional and inexpressive press reviews, which always referred to his political militancy in the ranks of the Basque nationalists. In recent weeks the name of Alfonso Sastre reappeared at the head of the list of candidates for the European elections, as part of a recently formed International Initiative. The group failed to obtain representation in the Strasbourg parliament.

A few days ago, the ETA assassinated a policeman by the name of Eduardo Pelles, using that nearly foolproof device, a bomb placed under the chassis of his car. His death was hideous; the fire horribly burnt the body of the unfortunate man, whom no one was able to help. The crime provoked general indignation, right across Spain. Or rather, not so general. Alfonso Sastre has just published a threatening article in the Basque daily *Gara*, where he speaks of "times of great pain rather than peace" while seeking to justify the attacks as integral to the "political conflict," adding that there would be further attacks should political negotiations not be reopened with ETA. I can hardly credit what I am reading. It was not Sastre who attached the bomb to the chassis of Eduardo

Puelles's car. All the same, I never expected to see him justifying murderers like these.

June 24: *Sabato*

Nearly a hundred years, ninety-eight to be precise, are what Ernesto Sabato is celebrating today. I first heard his name in the old Café Chiado in Lisbon, way back in the 1950s. It was uttered by a friend whose literary tastes tended toward the then little-known literatures of South America. The rest of our gathering—we met every day in the late afternoon—favored, almost unanimously, a sweet yet immortal France, except for the occasional eccentric who boasted of knowing by heart what was being written in the United States. To this friend, whom in the end I lost sight of, I owe the initial curious impulse that led me to Julio Cortázar, Borges, Bioy Casares, Miguel Angel Astúrias, Rómulo Gallegos, Carlos Fuentes, and so many others who slip from my memory when I attempt to recall them—Sabato among them. For some strange reason I associated those three rapid syllables with a staccato stab from a dagger. Considering what this familiar Italian word actually means, my association might seem all the more incongruous, but truths are there to be told, and this among them. *El túnel* [*The Tunnel*, also translated as *The Outsider*] had been published in 1948, but I had never read it. At that point in time, as an innocent and youthful twenty-six-year-old, I still had a great many roads to travel before I discovered the sea route that would bring me to Buenos Aires. . . Meanwhile, *El túnel* became my unforgettable companion at many a café table, where I sat musing and perusing, Sabato's novel in hand. Its very first pages showed me exactly how far an audacious association of ideas had come to bring me from surname to dagger. Any subsequent readings of Sabato's works, whether novels or essays, only served to confirm my initial impression of an encounter with a tragic and outstandingly lucid writer who was able to open up a path through the labyrinthine corridors of his readers' souls and would never permit them, even for an instant, to turn their eyes away from the most obscure nook or cranny of their being. Did this make the works difficult to read? Perhaps, but it also made them all the more fascinating. The mixture of surrealism, existentialism and psychoanalysis that provided the theoretical underpinning to the prose composed by the author of *Sobre héroes y tumbas*[5] should not allow us to forget that this self-proclaimed enemy of reason (called Ernesto Sabato) used his own fallible and humble human reason to describe what was right before his eyes during the apocalypse of bloody repression inflicted on the Argentine people.[6] Works of fiction that recall definite historical periods in objectively named places, such as *El túnel*; *Sobre héroes y tumbas*; *Abbadón el exterminador* [*Abbadón the Exterminator*], not only force one to hear the cries of a conscience afflicted by its own impotence and see the prophetic vision of a sibyl terrified by the future foreseen, but also remind us, like Goya (better known as a painter than as a philosopher) in his famous engravings of the *Caprichos* of indelible memory: it is always the sleep of reason that bears, grows and makes prosperous an inhuman race of monsters.

Dear Ernesto, this is the tremor and the terror running through all of our lives, and yours is no exception. Perhaps nowadays we are not confronting a situation as dramatic as those you lived through, and for which, endowed with a sense of humanity as you are, you have refused to absolve your own species. You are someone for whom it has become impossible to forgive even his own human condition. No doubt some will not be pleased by this

---

5 *Of Heroes and Tombs*, now out of print in English, but a classic text of twentieth-century Argentine literature.
6 The three military dictatorships of Generals Videla, Viala, and Galtieri, which took place between 1976 and 1983, and the "dirty war" they waged on the civilian population, resulted in the "disappearance" of 10,000 to 30,000 people. In 1984 Ernesto Sabato published a book of the victims' testimonies, called *Nunca Más* (published in Britain as *Never Again* [Faber & Faber 1986, trans. Nick Caistor]).

violence of feeling, but I beg you not to disarm yourself of that
dagger. Nearly a hundred years old. I am certain that the century
we have left behind will become known as the century of Sabato,
at least as much as that of Kafka or Proust.

June 25: *Formation (1)*

I am not unaware of the fact that the main duty of education in
general, and especially education at the university, is what we call
formation. The university prepares the student for life, transmitting the knowledge necessary for the effective exercise of a chosen
profession within the range of the demands placed on it by a given
society, a profession that might once have been a vocational calling, but which increasingly frequently now is based on scientific
and technological advances, along with pressing business interests.
In either case, the university will always have reason to think it has
fulfilled its obligations by delivering up to society young people
ready to receive and integrate into their body of knowledge the
lessons that yet remain to be learned, meaning those that experience (the mother of all things human) will teach them. Nowadays a
university, as is its duty, forms you, and if this so-called formation
continues to do the rest, the inevitable question arises: "Where is
the problem?" The problem is that I have limited myself to discussing the formation necessary to professional development, leaving
aside that other formation, the formation of the individual, the
person, the citizen—that earthly trinity, all three in a single body.
It is now time to touch on this delicate subject. Any action that
is performed presupposes, obviously, an object and an objective.
The object—or perhaps we should here say subject—is the person
who is the object of that formation, and the objective lies in the
nature and aims of that formation. A literary formation, for example, gives rise to doubts only as to the teaching methods employed
and the greater or lesser receptiveness of the student. The question, however, changes radically when we start discussing the

formation of individuals, always given that we want to inspire that person whom we have designated as our "object," and not restrict ourselves to merely supplying the materials appropriate to this particular discipline or that particular course. This then involves us in including the whole complex of ethical values and theoretical or practical relationships indispensible to any professional activity. However, forming individuals is not, of itself, a soporific. An education that propounded notions of racial or biological superiority would be the perversion of this intrinsic concept of value, replacing the positive with a negative, replacing ideas promoting respect for humanity with intolerance and xenophobia. Both ancient and recent human history is not short on examples of this. Let us continue.

June 26: *Formation (2)*

Where might I be going with this discourse? To the university. And also toward democracy. The university, because it is quintessentially the home of excellence, responsible for dispensing the knowledge necessary to the formation of citizens and the education of individuals in the values of a shared humanity and respect for peace, preparing them for liberty and for the responsible and healthily critical discussion of ideas. You can argue that an important part of this task should devolve upon the family as the basic social nucleus, yet, as we know, the institution of the family is undergoing its own identity crisis, which makes it ineffectual in confronting any of the changes that characterize our times. The family, with rare exceptions, tends to lull our social consciences to sleep, until we reach the university, where, as we meet new people and discover diversity, the necessary conditions for a practical and effective apprenticeship in the fullest democratic values come together, starting with what appears to me to be the most fundamental value of all: the issue of democracy itself. We have to find a way to reinvent this concept, to drag it out from the paralysis into which routine and disbelief have sunk it, both amply assisted by the economic and political powers that find it convenient to maintain the decorative façade of the democratic edifice without allowing the rest of us to check whether there is actually anything still behind it. In my opinion, whatever remains is almost always more heavily employed in bolstering lies than in defending the truth. What we call democracy is beginning, sadly, to resemble the funeral cloth covering the urn in which rest the remains of a putrefying corpse. Let us then resurrect democracy, before it is too late. And may the university assist us in doing so. Will it want to? And will it be able to?

June 29: *Black Spain*

Black Spain [*España negra*] is the title of a book by the artist José Gutierrez Solana (1886–1945). This book is sometimes difficult or discomforting to read, not because of an abstruse style or poor syntactic construction, but because of the brutality of its portrait of Spain, which it traces simply by the translation of his images to the written page, images previously described as gloomy and ugly, reflecting the degraded atmosphere of rural Spain at that time, revealing all in pictures without shirking the most atrocious, obscene or cruel examples of human behavior. Influenced by the darkest Baroque style, most especially that of Valdés Leal, and also informed by Goya's "black pictures," Gutiérrez Solana's Spain is in the highest imaginable degree sordid and grotesque, for no other reason than that this was what he found in his observations of the so-called popular feast days and the costumes and customs of his homeland.

Today Spain is no longer the same; it has become a developed and cultivated country, able to teach the world a few lessons in civil society, as the reader of the above paragraph will protest. I do not deny that this view might hold water in Castelhana, in the halls of the Prado Museum, in the neighborhoods of Salamanca or on the avenues of Barcelona; yet there is no dearth of places where

Gutiérrez Solana, were he still alive, could set up his easel and paint the same pictures in the same shades as before. I mean those towns and cities where, by public subscription or with the financial support of local town halls, bulls and bullrings are provided for the delight and delectation of the local population every time a local feast day comes around. The delight and delectation does not simply consist in killing the bull and distributing its steaks to the most needy. Despite high unemployment levels, the Spanish people enjoy an abundant diet. Delight and delectation also have another name. The bull charges blindly, streaming blood, pierced by lances in both flanks, perhaps scorched by the flaming *banderillas* that were used in eighteenth-century Portugal, and then is chased into the sea, there to drown: the bull has effectively been tortured to death. Small children cling to their mothers' necks and clap their hands, excited husbands grab their excited wives, for it so happens that the people are made happy whenever a bull tries to flee its executioners, trailing rivulets of blood in its wake. It is atrocious, it's cruel, and it's obscene. But surely what really counts is whether Cristiano Ronaldo is going to play for Real Madrid? What does something like this matter when the whole world is crying over the death of Michael Jackson? Or what does it matter that a city subjects a defenseless animal to premeditated torture, on a popular holiday that will be relentlessly repeated the following year? Is this culture? Is this civilization? Or isn't it more like barbarism?

June 30: *Two Years*

Yesterday our Foundation was two years old. As it is customary to say, it really does only seem like yesterday that we got started. If we attempted to draw up a balance sheet of all we did and all we dreamed of doing, we'd have every justification for assuring you that we never had a moment's rest. In the first place, there was the worry over deciding how best to nurture the newborn, in order for its next stages of development to be healthy and full of promise. Then came all the hard work of convincing those of little faith that we were not here to devote ourselves to contemplating the patron's navel, but rather to work for the good of Portuguese culture and society as a whole. We are not so presumptuous as to assume we changed your minds then or are going to change them now, but the task of public clarification affords us the chance to offer our ideas and proposals to people of goodwill, who fortunately are not lacking in this country, however badly it gets spoken of at times. The Foundation is now in a position to present its portfolio of services to be rendered, which looks not only worthy but also promising. The work at the Casa dos Bicos, which we visited three days ago, is making steady progress, and it is highly likely that within six months or not much longer we'll hold the key in our hands and will be able to freely come and go at the house that is already ours but will be all the more our own once its program is fully under way. We hope that the Campo das Cebolas, where it is situated, will become a regular part of people's daily walks, including those for whom culture is more than a superficial spiritual ornament. We recently had occasion to remember the work and life and José Rodrigues Miguéis. Next, perhaps in January 2010, we will celebrate Vitorino Nemésio. And after him, Raul Brandão. Our country's laws, however unjust at times, do provide opportunities and outlets in the literary marketplace, in an age when, all too often, great writers of the recent past are no longer spoken of in the literary world. We shall do all we can to stem, and even reverse, this harmful tendency. We have a great deal of work ahead of us. Two years are nothing, but the infant is in good health, and deserves praise.

July 2009

July 1: *Agustina*

Some forty years ago, over the course of a few months, I worked as literary critic for the *Seara Nova* [*New Cornfield*], a task I was hardly born to do but that two kind and generous friends thought would be within my abilities. They were Augusto Costa Dias, whose idea it was, and Rogério Fernandes, at the time the director of the much-missed review. On the whole I don't think I was responsible for any serious injustices, apart from the lack of care I took when giving my opinion on José Cardoso Pires's *O Delfim* [*The Dauphin*]. Later I would often ask myself what was going on in my head that day. They say that anyone can make a mistake, but that wasn't merely a mistake, it was (if you will excuse the vulgarity of the word) a complete screw-up. Years later, in Rome, when with Jorge Amado's valuable assistance in the battle I fought as hard as I could in the jury's argumentative skirmishes over whether Cardoso Pires should receive the Latin Union Prize, it's perfectly possible that I was being impelled by this painful recollection from my past. And Cardoso Pires's competitor was none other than Marguerite Duras. . .

It is important to note that my list of credits on coming to the *Seara Nova* didn't amount to much: I had published *Terra do Pecado* [*Land of Sin*] in 1947, and *Os Poemas Possíveis* [*The Possible Poems*] in 1966. Nothing else. There wasn't a writer in Portugal who hadn't done much more and much better than José Saramago. I understand that there were those who saw my decision to accept my unwise friends' invitation as an inexcusable impudence for someone so little known. And it was probably this that Agustina Bessa-Luís must have thought when, leafing through the *Seara Nova* (did Agustina Bessa-Luís read the *Seara Nova?*), she found herself looking at a review of her new book, with my byline. I wouldn't blame her if that was what she thought, even though her sense of what was due to her might have been more gratified by the words that immediately followed. I quote them from memory: "If Portugal has one writer who partakes of genius, that writer is Agustina Bessa-Luís." That is what I said, and I repeat it today. It's true, I did subsequently write, "Let us hope she does not fall asleep to the sound of her own music." Might there have been a touch of malice in that comment? Possibly, but that is quite excusable, when we're talking about a rookie critic looking to find himself a niche in the literary marketplace. . .

Did she fall asleep? Did she not? I think not. It would be understandable for some of her readers to have wished that Agustina, with her inexhaustible freedom of spirit (for that she had) had launched herself into other literary adventures and onto new paths, but what Agustina seems to have been most interested in, recording the *comédie humaine* of the Entre Douro e Minho province, she accomplished in an exemplary fashion. To say that there is a sociological reading of Agustina Bessa-Luís's powerful work, among its many other readings, is not to diminish it. Each on their own territory, each in their own time, each according to their own personal and artistic characteristics, Balzac and Bessa-Luís were doing the same thing: observing and recounting. You can understand the French nineteenth century better by reading Balzac. The light that radiates from the work of Agustina helps us to see more clearly the mentality of a particular society in the twentieth century—and the end of the nineteenth, too. Truly, truly, this wasn't the work of someone who had fallen asleep . . .

July 2: *Translating*

To write is always to translate, even when we are using our own language. We convey what we see and feel (assuming that *see* and *feel,* as we usually understand them, are something more than just the words with which it has been relatively possible for us to express the experience of sight and feeling) by means of a conventional code of signs, writing, and we hope that circumstance and the vagaries of communication allow them to reach the reader's intelligence, if not intact, as the entire experience we meant to transmit—inevitably our words convey mere fragments of the reality on which our experience fed—then at least with a shadow of what in the depths of our soul we know to be untranslatable: the pure emotion of an encounter, the wonder of a discovery, that fleeting moment of silence before the word is produced that will remain in the memory like the traces of a dream that time will never completely erase.

The work of someone who translates, therefore, is to render into another language (his own, usually) something that in the work and in the original language was already a translation, that is, a given perception of a social, historical, ideological and cultural reality, a reality that is not that of the translator, and a perception substantiated by a linguistic and semantic context that is also not his. The original text is just one of the possible "translations" of the author's experience of reality, and the translator has to convert this translation text into a text translation; this inevitably creates some ambivalence, since, having begun to grasp the experience of reality that is the object of his attention, the translator then has to undertake the greater task of importing it intact into the linguistic and semantic context of the (other) reality into which he is supposed to translate it, showing due respect simultaneously to both *where it has come from and where it is going*. For the translator, the moment of silence that precedes the word is therefore like the threshold of an alchemical transmutation in which "the thing that it is" must be transformed into something else in order for it to *remain* "the thing that it was." The dialogue between author and translator, in the relationship between the text *that is* and the text *to be*, is not only between two individual personalities who have to complement one another, it is above all a meeting of two collective cultures that must acknowledge one another.

July 6: *Review*

In his review of *O Caderno* [*The Notebook*], published in the latest issue of *Expresso*, José Mário Silva says that I am not a real blogger. He says this and demonstrates it: I don't include links, I don't have a direct dialogue with my readers, I don't interact with the rest of the blogosphere. This is something I knew already, but from now on whenever people ask me I will use José Mário Silva's reasons as my own and sort the subject out once and for all. In any case, I'm not complaining about this review, which is polite, appropriate, and revealing. There are, however, two points that have brought me out of my bunker, against my original decision—which hitherto I have fulfilled to the letter—never to respond to, or even comment on, any criticism of my work. The first point relates to the apparently simplistic nature of my analysis of problems. I could answer that space doesn't allow for more, but it is really because I don't allow myself to do more, as I lack the essential competencies required of a profound analyst, like those profound economists from the Chicago School, who, although very gifted, failed utterly, the notion never going through their privileged brains of a catastrophic crisis that any simplistic analyst would have been well able to predict. The other point is more serious, and this point alone I think justifies my somewhat unexpected intervention. I refer to my alleged excesses of indignation. I would expect anything but this from an intelligent man like José Mário Silva. So my question is just as simple as my analyses: Does indignation have limits? And further, how can one talk of excesses of indignation in a country where it is specifically lacking, with consequences for all to see? My dear José Mário, think about this and enlighten me with your opinion. Please.

July 7: *The Subject, on Himself*

I don't think I have ever divided my identity as a writer from my conscience as a citizen. I believe that where one goes, the other should go, too. I don't recall ever having written a single word that contradicted the political convictions I uphold, but that does not mean that I have ever placed literature at the service of my ideology. What it does mean, however, is that in every word I write I seek to express the totality of the man I am.

Let me repeat—I do not separate my role as a writer from my role as a citizen, but neither do I confuse the role of the writer with that of the political militant. It is true that I am better known as a writer, but there are also some people who, independently of any significance they may or may not find in my work as a writer, believe that what I say as a common citizen is of interest to them and matters to them. Even if it is the writer and no one else who bears on his shoulders the responsibility for expressing that voice.

If he is a person of his time, if he is not chained to the past, a writer must know the problems of the age in which he happens to live. And what are these problems today? That we do not live in an acceptable world; on the contrary, we live in a world that is going from bad to worse and that does not function humanely. But please note—do not confuse my complaints with any kind of moralizing; I am not saying that the purpose of literature is to tell people how they ought to behave. I am talking about something else, about the need for ethical content without the least trace of demagoguery. And—this is fundamental—a literature that never holds itself aloof when a critical point of view is needed.

July 8: *Castril*

The river that flows through Lisbon is not called the Lisbon, but
the Tejo; the river that flows through Rome is not called the Rome
but the Tiber; the one that flows through Seville is not the Seville
but the Guadalquivir. . . but the river that flows through Castril
in Spain, yes, this one is called the Castril. Any inhabited place
quickly acquires the name by which it comes to be known, but not
so rivers. For thousands and thousands of years all the rivers of
the world had to wait for someone to turn up and baptize them, so
that they might then appear on maps as more than just an anonymous sinuous line. For centuries and centuries all the waters of
an unnamed river passed stormily through the place where one
day the village of Castril would appear, and as they passed, they
glanced up at the mountains and said to one another, "This is not
yet it." And they continued on their way down to the sea, thinking, just as patiently, that age follows age and that new waters
would appear one day to find women beating their clothes against
the rocks, children learning how to swim, men fishing for trout
and whatever else came to their hooks. At that moment the waters
would know that they had been given a name, that from that day
forth they would be not the river in Castril but the *Castril River*, so
strong would be the lifelong pact that would unite them to those
people putting up their first simple homes on the terraced slope,
and who would then put up second and third groups of homes,
some next to the others, some on the ruins of others, generations
following generations, right up to this day. Now tamed, held back
by a huge wall that has made them into a lake, the waters of the
Castril no longer hurl themselves furiously against the rocks, they
no longer roar as they once did between the tall, narrow rock walls
with which for millennia the mountain had tried uselessly to choke
them. Instead, the development that will make Castril grow and
prosper has tamed that current. The people best able to calculate
what has been gained and lost are the Castrilenses, whose roots are

there, while I am merely that quiet and discreet Portuguese man who appeared one day, led by the hand of the person I most love in the world, and who since then has been honored with the title of adoptive son of the land and has gone up and down, from village to river and river to village, walking along the banks and the ancient footpaths that still retain the memory of the bare feet that walked them, as though he, too, also barefoot, were again walking the path of his own childhood in a different land, not of mountains and a river capable of jumping over crags, but of plains and winding watercourses, the Tejo, the Almonda, sheets of water momentarily reflecting the clouds that passed across the sky and hurried on, making way for the clouds behind them. In spite of all the time— so, so much time gone by—the old man I am today looks with the same innocent eyes at the mountains and the Castril River, the village's narrow sloping streets, the low houses, the olive trees that remind him of other olive trees in whose shade he has sheltered and whose fruit he has gathered, the paths between herbs and flowers, a startled animal running to hide, leaving behind it the quick shiver of a plant it has brushed past. Some people spend their lives looking for the childhood they have lost. I think I am one of them.

July 9: *A Parting in the Hair*

José Manuel Mendes and I were lamenting the incurable weaknesses of our country, in that way we have of being a sort of Wailing Wall for one another, not in Jerusalem but in the Arco do Cego neighborhood, and when we had gone over all the ghosts and ghouls of national politics and rounded off, each in his own style, with appropriate comments about the horns[1] of Manuel Pinho (godspeed), a heavy silence settled between us. I even thought of bringing up the fact that Michelangelo's Zeus, which

---

1   On July 4, 2009, Minister of the Economy Manuel Pinho made the rude gesture of that name at a Communist opponent in front of the parliament and was forced to resign.

is in Rome, also has homes, but thought it would be mixing apples and oranges, so I kept my mouth shut. I imagine it was just out of desperation, just to break the uncomfortable silence that seemed to be trying to crush us, that José Manuel Mendes made an observation, casual rather than truly interested, on the common use of the terms center-right and center-left and the difficulty of finding real differences between the parties, groups, and people who use these terms to define and classify themselves. That was when I came up with the joke of the day, a day that was already beginning to draw to a close. I said: "My dear Zé Manel, politics is like the parting in a person's hair, sometimes in the middle and sometimes off to one side. Even those partings slightly off-center are an indication of the shortsightedness of the person who has made them. The political life of our dear country is all about that: partings and myopias, myopias and partings. The only thing that doesn't change is the haircut." We both laughed and changed the subject. It was a good gossiping afternoon.

July 10: *Summer Reading*

It is as sure as destiny that when the first summer heat begins there will be newspapers and magazines, as well as the occasional television program with eccentric tastes, coming to ask the writer of these lines which books he would recommend for reading over the summer. I have always dodged a reply, since to me reading is an important enough activity to occupy us all year round, this year and every year to come. But on one occasion, at the importuning of a persistent journalist who wouldn't let go of my front door, I decided to get past the question once and for all, and defined for him what I then called my spiritual family, in which, it goes without saying, I would be the littlest cousin. It wasn't just a list of names, for each one was annotated, so that my choice of relatives might be better understood. In the *Lanzarote Notebooks* I included the final version of the "family tree" I had daringly presumed to sketch out, and I reproduce it here for anyone who is curious. In first place came Camões, because, as I wrote in *The Year of the Death of Ricardo Reis*, all Portuguese roads lead to him. He was followed by Father António Vieira, because the Portuguese language was never more beautiful than when this Jesuit was writing it; Cervantes, because without the author of *Quixote* the Iberian peninsula would be a house without a roof; Montaigne, because he didn't need Freud to know who he was; Voltaire, because he lost all his illusions about humanity and managed to survive his disgust; Raul Brandão, because you don't have to be a great genius to write a great book, like his *Húmus* [*Humus*]; Fernando Pessoa, because the door you take to find him is also the door you take to find Portugal (we already had Camões, but we still needed a Pessoa); Kafka, because he demonstrated that man is a beetle; Eça de Queiroz, because he taught the Portuguese irony; Jorge Luis Borges, because he invented virtual literature; and finally Gogol, because he contemplated humanity and found it to be sad.

How's that? Allow me to make a suggestion to my readers. Make up your own list, define the literary "spiritual family" you feel closest to. It will be a good way to pass the time, one afternoon on the beach or in the country. Or at home, if the money won't stretch to a holiday this year.

July 13: *Academician*

Please forgive my vanity in making an announcement: I am an associate member of the Brazilian Academy of Letters, given the place vacated by the death of the French writer Maurice Druon, whom I remember reading countless years ago, in a Portuguese Arcádia edition, if memory serves, of his novel *Les grandes familles*, written in the best tradition of nineteenth-century fiction. I learned the pleasing news from Alberto da Costa e Silva, a fine poet who is also an ambassador, posted in various countries including Portugal, and an able historian of African subjects—whoever doesn't know him should, for example, read the excellent work *A enxada e a lança: a África antes dos portugueses* [*The Hoe and the Spear: Africa before the Portuguese*]. So here I am, member of the Academy in the country I love most after my own, Brazil. It is like being at home, with the not at all insignificant difference of feeling surrounded by affection, something that our own country sometimes forgets to express, as though having managed to be born in Lisbon or Azinhaga were honor enough. I will be going there in October to present a new book, and to sit in the shadow of the statue of Machado de Assis. And people say there are no good things in life. . .

July 14: *Aquilino*

The Romanesque work of Aquilino Ribeiro was the first, and perhaps the only, work to look without any illusions at the Beira region of Portugal's rural world. Without illusions, but with passion, if by passion we understand—as in the case of Aquilino—not the immodest display of tenderness, nor the gentle tear so easily wiped away, nor even the simple pleasures of feeling, but a certain rough emotion that prefers to hide itself behind a brusqueness of voice and gesture. Aquilino had no successors, though there was no lack of people who declared themselves or suggested themselves as his disciples. I do not think this claim of discipleship was anything worse than a mistake made in good faith. Aquilino is a huge boulder, solitary and vast, who burst from the ground in the middle of the main garden path that ran through our flourishing and often fluid literature of the first half of the century. He was not the only spoilsport, but speaking artistically, and also in terms of his own virtues and defects, he was surely the most coherent and persistent. On the whole the neorealists didn't know how to understand him, stunned by the master's somehow archaic verbal exuberance, disoriented by the "instinctive" behavior of many of his characters, as accomplished in good as they were in evil, and

234 The Notebook

even more accomplished when the time came to swap around the meanings of evil and good in a kind of startling, jolly game, but a game that was above all cheekily human. Perhaps Aquilino's work was an extreme point in the history of Portuguese literature, an apex, perhaps suspended, perhaps interrupted in its deepest impulse, but awaiting new readings to get it moving again. And have these new readings taken place? Or to be more precise, have new readers appeared to carry them out? Aquilino will survive, and we will survive, those of us who write today about the loss of memory, not only the collective but the individual memory of the Portuguese people, of each Portuguese person now indulging in this insidious and fundamentally imbecilic binge of modernity that confounds the circulation of our ideas and addles the minds of the Portuguese world with its lies. Time, which knows everything, will tell. We cannot understand that if we neglect our own memory, and out of resignation or mental laziness forget what we used to be, the vacuum that this will create will be (and is already) occupied by memories that are not ours but that we will begin to consider our own; they will start to become the only memories, and we the accomplices and the victims of a historical and cultural colonization that cannot be reversed. You might say that Aquilino's real and fictional worlds died. Perhaps so, but those worlds *were ours,* and that should be the best reason for their continuing to be so. When we are reading, at least.

July 15: *Siza Vieira*

All architecture presupposes a certain relationship between the natural opacity of most commonly used building materials and external light. In thick Romanesque walls it was difficult to create openings that would let in enough daylight to cast the shadows that would have made sense of spaces that seemed to reject them. It is shadows that make it possible to read light. Gothic walls were split vertically by stained-glass windows that let in light and in the selfsame moment altered its color to re-create the mysterious effects of shadow. Even in modern times, when walls are largely replaced by openings that almost negate them, that make them disappear in ludicrous glass cladding that dilutes their volume through a process of kaleidoscopic reflections and projections, the human eye, seeking the support it cannot do without, looks anxiously for a solid point where it can rest and which it can contemplate.

I don't know of any expression of modern architecture in which the primordial wall is so important as in the work of Siza Vieira. At first glance those long, closed walls rise up like implacable enemies of light, and when they do finally let light through they do so as though grudgingly obeying a pressing demand that the building be functional. However, the truth as I understand it is different. A wall in Siza Vieira's work is not an obstacle to light, but rather a space for contemplation, where the light from outside does not stop at the surface. We have the illusion that materials become porous to light, that our gaze can pass through the solid wall and join together what is outside and what is inside in a single aesthetic and emotional awareness. Here opacity is turned into transparency. It takes a genius to be able to merge these two irreconcilable opposites so harmoniously. Siza Vieira is that conjuror.

July 16: *The Colors of the Earth*

When hands work in the earth they get mixed up with it. There are painters who approach the easel with their hands stained with earth. There are painters who cannot forget the colors of the earth, nor would they ever want to, when they set out to paint a face, an undressed body, the shine of a piece of glass, or nothing more than two white roses in a pot. Light exists for these painters too, but they apprehend it as though it had come up to them from inside the dark earth. When they arrange it on the canvas, or on the paper, or on a wall, what they conjure up are the hot muted tones of clay, the darkness of humus, the brown of the roots, the blood of red

ochre. They paint humanity and what belongs to it with the colors
of the earth because it is these colors and no others that are fundamental. You would never say that a picture painted in the colors of
the earth (like those painted by Cézanne) was a likeness: it is not
like but identical, identical to the original, identical in its essence;
the greater or lesser likeness it might offer us should be what
matters least. Figures painted in the colors of earth will always
have something of the rough wholeness of flint in their faces, their
hair swirls like cornfields tossed and moved by the wind, and their
hands seem to have just pulled up the deepest fruits of the earth.
Colors, all colors, of both earth and air, always seek out the shapes
they need in order for us to see more in them than mere color.
Colors have always both challenged and embodied the contradictory impulses implicitly found in shapes, in which an eternal battle
is waged between chaotic rebelliousness and passive submission
to custom. Without doubt, all this is less noticeable in paintings
that offer themselves as mimetic transpositions of apparent reality;
such pictures aspire above all to be recognized, identified, classified, but sooner or later end up being prisoners of the decaying
effect of a vision that, bit by bit, reduces them to insignificance.
In contrast, by protecting itself against forms that are easily identifiable with common representations of the surrounding reality,
abstract art—either directly or at least with a tendency that way—
"protects" and generally "liberates" the relative independence of
color; it does not "strangle" it in a squeezing constraint of compositions that are more or less predictable or of what are generally
agreed to be correct social models.

It was no accident that I used the word *tendency* when referring
to a certain kind of pictorial practice that, though it is unmistakably
established in the category of what we tend to describe too generally as abstract art, refuses to demolish completely the bridges to
the world of signs and symbols, whether archetypical or modern.
All this sprang up spontaneously in my spirit while with eyes of
wonder, feeling an emotion I had rarely experienced before, I

contemplated the murals with which Jesús Mateo had covered
the cold walls of the church of San Juan Bautista de Alarcón. Was
Jesús Mateo an abstract painter with a "tendency" toward realism?
Or, on the contrary, a realist painter with a "tendency" toward the
abstract? And are those bridges I referred to above only practicable
for connecting "abstract" art with the signs and symbols created
through the various inquiries to which reality has been subjected,
or might they exist also to connect "realist" art with a continually
expanding universe of abstractions? It occurred to me then that
Jesús Mateo, at the same time he freed himself from the constrain-
ing bonds of a strict realism in order to give himself up to an essay
on forms that themselves had a tendency toward freedom, and in
spite of my way of understanding, adhered to a consistent chro-
matic logic, also managed, thanks to his intelligently and carefully
measured introduction of easily identifiable signs and symbols, to
create a unique, one could almost say unified expression, a chorus
of many simultaneous voices, like a polyptych whose perspectives
meet at a single vanishing point, the enormous walls rising up from
the ground drawing all the muted colors of the earth upward to
meet the luminous colors of the air. Faced with such an immense
and amazing work, concepts such as abstractionism and realism
lose some of their current independent significance, and become
a left and a right hand harmoniously modeling the same piece of
clay. I don't know whether the church of San Juan Bautista de
Alarcón will come to be seen as the Sistine Chapel of our day, but
I do know that Jesús Mateo was born of the family tree whose best
fruits were Hieronymus Bosch and Breughel the Elder. Like them,
Jesús Mateo has explained man. Through what is visible, and what
is invisible.

July 17: *Stories of Migration*

Let him who has not a single speck of migration to blot his family
escutcheon cast the first stone. . . To paraphrase the big bad wolf

in the fable who accuses the innocent little lamb of muddying the water of the stream where they are both drinking: if you didn't migrate then your father did, and if your father didn't need to move from place to place, then it was only because your grandfather before him had no choice but to go, put his old life behind him in search of the bread that his own land denied him. Many Portuguese people drowned in the Bidassoa River one dark night while trying to swim over to the far bank, where it was said the paradise of France began. In the so-called cultured, civilized Europe beyond the Pyrenees, hundreds of thousands of Portuguese people had to submit to disgraceful working conditions and insulting wages. Those survivors able to withstand the same old violence and new forms of deprivation, living disoriented in the midst of societies that despised and humiliated them, lost in languages they could not understand, started, bit by bit, with almost heroic self-denial, to sacrifice coin after coin, cent after cent, to build their descendents' future. Some of these men and women have neither lost nor want to lose their memories of the times when they had to suffer all the humiliations of badly paid work and all the bitterness of social isolation. They should be thanked for managing to maintain the respect they owe to their past. Many others, the majority, have burned the bridges that linked them to those dark hours; they are ashamed of having been ignorant, poor, sometimes wretched; in short, they behave as though a decent life only really began for them on that blissful day when they were able to buy their first car. These are the people who are always ready to treat with cruelty and scorn the immigrants who are crossing this other, broader and deeper Bidassoa, the Mediterranean, where plenty drown and will become food for the fish if the tide and the wind do not wash them up onto the beach and the police come along to take the bodies away. The survivors of these new shipwrecks, those who reach land and are not expelled from it, can look forward to the eternal Calvary of exploitation, intolerance, racism, hatred of their skin, suspicion, and moral degradation. He who was once exploited and

has lost his memory of being exploited will become an exploiter.
He who was scorned and pretends to have forgotten will refine his
own scorn. He who was insulted yesterday will today insult others
more bitterly. And there they all are, all together, throwing stones
at the people who reach the near bank of the Bidassoa, as though
they had never been immigrants themselves, nor their parents, nor
their grandparents—as though they had never suffered hunger
and despair, anguish and fear. And in all honesty, in all honesty
I tell you, there are certain ways of being happy that are simply
loathsome.

July 20: *Jardinisms*

Since the announcement of the constitutional reform law proposed
by the unspeakable Alberto João, as he is affectionately called by
his friends and followers, it has been clear that there is something
concealed inside it, something there is no point in trying to hide.
We compliment him on his frankness. Jardim does want to be
president of the region, keeping the right of veto for any excuse
however trivial, and it would be reasonable to believe that he was
already nurturing the idea in his head some time back when he
signaled—albeit cautiously, with some degree of verbal vagueness—his decision to leave politics, giving us a pleasure that,
like Malherbe's roses, would be bound not to last very long.
Jardim's intelligence is nothing spectacular, but in compensation,
his cunning is apparently limitless. Limitless, just like our own
naïveté. Imagining this Madeiran Berlusconi anywhere but in the
halls and offices of power would be like trying to imagine what
one might call absolute nonbeing, a contradiction in terms. Jardim
was born to command, and he will command until his last breath.
Hating Portugal as he does, he will never agree to be president of
the republic; it will be enough for him to be president of Madeira,
Porto Santo, and the Savage Islands. Deep down, what the
proposed law seeks to do is establish a constitution in Portugal that

is shaped in his own image—that is to say, short, round, pointless.

One of the inconvenient protuberances that Madeira's dear leader would like to chop off the current body politic is the despised Communist Party. I fear he may crack his teeth in the attempt. The Communists have a long, hard experience of living in secret; making them illegal would effectively mean having to lift up every one of the rocks scattered across all of Portugal to see whether there might be one hiding underneath. What will be most interesting in the coming hours will be the festival of fake patriotism that will explode across the Regional Assembly, with public speakers embracing local emblems and possibly trampling and burning the flag displaying the Portuguese arms because the red two-thirds of that have inflamed Jardim's rubicund cheeks even more. It will also be interesting to watch how Manuela Ferreira Leite,[2] that lynx of continental politics, will manage to wriggle out of this one. I would suggest to the four people who are reading this that they keep an eye on events. You will have something to tell your grandchildren.

July 21: *Moon*

Forty years ago I didn't yet have a television set at home. I only bought one, a tiny little one, five years later, in 1974, to follow the news about that other kind of moon landing that the experience of the April revolution was for us. So for the original touch-down I had recourse to some friends who were closer to the cutting edge of technology, and in that way, maybe drinking a beer and chewing on dried fruits, I watched the moon landing and the disembarkation. Around that time I was writing columns in the recently revived evening paper *A Capital* [*The Capital*], which some time later were collected in a book under the title *Deste mundo e do outro* [*Of This*

---

2 Portuguese politician and economist, leader of the country's Social Democratic Party.

World and the Other]. I devoted two of the pieces to commenting
on the North Americans' achievement in a tone that was neither
dithyrambic nor skeptical—as would quickly become the fashion.
Reading them again now, I have come to the sad conclusion that
no great step for humanity was taken after all, and that our future is
not in the stars, but always just here on the earth where we place our
feet—as I said in the first of these columns, "Let us not lose the earth,
for this is the only way for us not to lose the moon." In the second
column, which I called "A Leap in Time," imagining the earth float-
ing as the moon is now, I started by writing that "It all seemed to
me like merely an episode in a technically elementary science fiction
film. Even the movements of the astronauts clearly resembled the
movements of marionettes, as though their arms and legs were being
pulled by invisible threads, extremely long threads attached to the
fingers of the technicians in Houston, with which, across space, they
made the necessary movements up there. Everything was planned
to the last second, and even the danger was included in the plan. In
the greatest adventure in history there was no room for adventure."

And that was where my imagination took over completely, and
informed me that the journey to the moon had not been a leap in
space but a leap in time. It claimed that the astronauts, launched on
their flight, had traveled across a timeline and come to land back
on earth, not this earth we know—white, green, tan and blue—but
the future earth, an earth that still occupies the same orbit, rotating
around an extinguished sun, also dead, bereft of men, birds, flowers, without laughter, without a word of love. A useless planet, like
an ancient story with no one to tell it. The earth will die, it will be
what the moon is today—that was how I ended it. At least the long
saga of misery, war, hunger, and torture it has been to this day will
not last forever. Lest we start trying to say from today onward that
man did not deserve his fate after all.

The reader will agree that, for good or ill, it would seem that my
ideas have not changed much in forty years. I honestly don't know
whether I should congratulate myself or tell myself off.

July 21: *Montaña Blanca*

Now that my legs have started gradually recovering their strength and their ability to walk normally, thanks to the combined efforts of their owner and of Juan, my devoted physiotherapist, I am glad to recall that May afternoon when, without having thought of it earlier, I set off to climb Montaña Blanca, though at first without any confidence at all that I would make it to the top. This was sixteen years ago, in 1993, and at the time I was exactly seventy years old. Montaña Blanca, which rises a couple of kilometers away from my house, is the tallest mountain on Lanzarote, which isn't saying much, seeing that the island, although extremely bumpy, with its hundreds of extinct volcanoes, does not rejoice in anything that could be set alongside Teide in Tenerife. Its height, in relation to sea level, is a little over 600 meters, and it is shaped like an almost perfect cone. If I was able to climb it, anyone could climb it—you do not need to be a consummate mountaineer. However, it would be right to put on suitable boots, the kind with metal spikes on their soles, as the slopes are very slippery. Every three steps, you lose one. Though I say so myself, I whose own shoes have had their soles polished by domestic rugs. . . Reaching the foot of the mountain, I asked myself, "And what if I were to climb this?" In my head, climbing it meant going up twenty or thirty meters, just to be able to tell the family that I had been on Montaña Blanca. But by the time those first twenty meters had been conquered, I already knew that I would have to get to the top, whatever it cost. And that was how it was. It took me more than an hour to ascend to the rocky outcrops that crown the peak of the mountain and that must be the remains of the ancient volcanic crater. "Was it worth it?" people ask. If I had the legs today that I had then, I would abandon this piece of writing right now to go up again and contemplate the island, all of it, from the Coroa volcano in the north to the plains of the Rubicón in the south, the La Geria valley, Timanfaya, the rolling of the countless hills that the fire has left bare. I had the wind in my face, drying the sweat from my body, making me feel happy. It was 1993 and I was seventy years old.

July 23: *Five Films*

I was asked to talk about five films I really remembered. I was not to worry about whether or not they were the best, the most famous, the most often referred to. It would be enough that the films had particularly struck me, as one might be struck by a gaze, a gesture, a tone of voice. Choosing them was not difficult; on the contrary, they presented themselves to me quite naturally, as though I would never have thought of any others. Here they are, then, but in an order that is not any indication of merit, nor should it be taken as such. In first place (I had to start the list somewhere), Herbert Biberman's *Salt of the Earth*, which I saw in Paris in the late seventies and which moved me to tears; this story of the strike by the Chicano miners and their brave wives struck me to the depths of my spirit. Next I nominate Ridley Scott's *Blade Runner*, which I also saw in Paris, in a little cinema in the Latin Quarter, not long after its world premiere, and which at the time did not seem to have much of a future. No one can have any doubts about Fellini's *Amarcord*, an absolute masterpiece, possibly the Italian master's finest film, in my opinion. Then comes Jean Renoir's *La Règle du jeu*, which dazzled me with its impeccable editing, the direction of its actors, its rhythm, its finesse, its "timing"—well, anyway. And to conclude, a film that appears in my memory as if it were coming from the fireside stories told on the first night of history: a silent comedy about two millers, played by Pat and Patachon, those sublime (no exaggeration) Danish actors who when I was six or seven made me laugh more than anyone else. More than Chaplin, Buster Keaton, Harold Lloyd, or Laurel and Hardy. If you haven't seen Pat and Patachon you don't know what you're missing . . .

July 24: *Chapter for the "Gospel"*

It has been said of me that after Jesus' death I repented of what were called my heinous sins of prostitution and became a penitent for the rest of my life, and this is not true. I have been placed upon the altars clothed only in the hair that goes right down to my knees, my breasts shriveled and my mouth toothless, and if it's true that the years did end up drying up the smooth tautness of my skin this is only because in this world nothing can prevail against time, not because I had disdained and offended that same body that Jesus had desired and possessed. Whoever tells those untruths about me knows nothing of love. I stopped being a prostitute on the day Jesus came into my house with his injured foot, asking me to heal it, but as for those human acts that they call sins of lechery, I have no reason to repent, since it was as a prostitute that my beloved met me, and having tasted of my body and knowing how I lived he did not turn his back on me. When Jesus kissed me once, many times, in front of all the apostles, they asked him why he loved me more than them, and Jesus replied: "Why is it that I do not love you as much as I love her?" They did not know what to say, because they would never have been able to love Jesus with the same absolute love that I felt for him. After the death of Lazarus, Jesus' distress and sadness were so great that one night, under the sheet that covered our nakedness, I said to him, "I can't reach you where you are, because you have closed yourself off behind a door that was not made for the strength of a human being," and he said, with the lamenting and groaning of an animal who has hidden himself away to suffer, "Though you cannot enter, do not leave me, keep your hand always stretched out toward me even when you cannot see me, for if you do not I shall forget about life, or life will forget about me." And a few days later, when Jesus went to meet the apostles, I said, walking beside him, "I will look at your shadow, if you do not want me to look at you," and he replied, "I want to be where my shadow is, if your eyes are there." We loved one another and we spoke words like these, not only because they were beautiful and true, if it is possible to be both one and the other at the same time, but because we sensed that the time of shadows was arriving and while we were still together we had to begin to get used to the darkness of permanent absence. I saw Jesus brought back to life, and for that first moment I thought that the man I saw was the person who took care of the garden where the tomb was, but now I know that I will never see him from the altars where they have placed me, however high they may be, however close they may reach the sky, however adorned with flowers and scented with perfumes. It was not death that separated us; what separated us forever was eternity. Then, embracing one another, united in spirit and in the flesh of our mouths, Jesus was not what he was proclaimed to be, nor was I what I was spurned for being. To me Jesus was not the son of God, and I, to him, was not Mary of Magdala, we were just that man and this woman, both trembling with love, with the world circling us like a vulture dribbling blood. Some said that Jesus had expelled seven demons from my entrails, but that, too, is untrue. What Jesus did do was awake the seven angels that slept in my soul waiting for him to come to ask me for assistance: "Help me." It was the angels who healed his foot, it was they who guided my trembling hands and wiped the pus from the wound, they who put on my lips the question without which Jesus could not help me: "You know who I am, what I do, how I live," and he replied, "I do." "You did not need to look, and you knew," I said, and he replied, "I know nothing," and I insisted, "I am a prostitute." "I know that." "I lie with men for money." "Yes." "Then you know everything about me," I said, and he, his voice calm, like the smooth surface of a murmuring lake, said, "This is all I know." I still did not know then that he was the son of God, nor did I even imagine that God wanted a son, but at that moment, with the dazzling light of understanding in my soul, I understood that only a Son of Man could have spoken those five simple words, "This is all I know." We looked at one another, not even having noticed that the angels had already gone, and from that moment on, through words and silences, through night and day, through sun and moon, through presence and through absence, I began to tell Jesus who I was, and I was still far from reaching the depths of myself when they killed him. I am Mary of Magdala and I loved. There is nothing more to say.

July 27: *A Male Problem*

I see from the surveys that violence against women is number fourteen on the list of Spanish people's concerns, in spite of the fact that you will run out of fingers if you try to count on them the number of women murdered every month by those who believe themselves to be their owners. I see too that society, via state advertising and various civic activities, is coming to assume— albeit only gradually—that this violence is men's problem, and it's men who have to solve it. A while ago we received news from Seville and Spanish Extremadura of a good example: men demonstrating against violence. Until then it had been only women who came out into the public squares to protest against the ill-treatment they were suffering at the hands of their husbands and partners (*partners*, that's a sad irony), and although in so many cases they suffered cold-blooded, deliberate torture, they didn't flinch at the possibility of incurring worse: of being strangled, beaten to death, burned by acid or fire, or having their throats slit. The violence that has always been exerted against women has turned the place of cohabitation (let us not call it a home) into a prison, an ideal space for daily humiliation, for regular beatings, for psychological cruelty as a tool of domination. It's women's problem, they say, but that is not true. The problem is men's: men's egotism, men's unhealthy feelings of possessiveness, men's poltroonery, that wretched cowardice that allows them to use force against someone who is physically weaker than they are and whose capacity for psychological resistance has been systematically weakened. Just a

few days ago in Huelva a group of adolescents, aged thirteen and
fourteen, fulfilling the roles usually taken by their elders, raped a
girl of the same age who was mentally disturbed, perhaps believing that they were entitled to the crime and to the violence, that
they were right to use what they believed to be theirs. This fresh
act of gender-based violence, along with those that took place this
weekend—a girl murdered in Madrid, a thirty-three-year-old
woman killed in front of her six-year-old daughter in Toledo—
should have made the men take to the streets. Maybe a hundred
thousand men, only men, no one but men, should demonstrate
in the streets, while the women stand on the pavement throwing
flowers at them—that might be the signal society needs to begin to
fight this unbearable disgrace, from the inside, and without delay.
And to make gender-based violence, whether fatal or not, one of
our citizens' principal sorrows and concerns. It's a dream, a duty.
It could be more than just utopian.

July 28: *The Right to Sin*

On the list of human creations (there are others that have nothing
to do with humanity, such as the food-attracting design of a spider's
web, or the submerged air pocket that serves as a fish's nest), on
this list, I would argue, there is one thing I haven't seen included,
a thing that used to be the most effective way of controlling our
bodies and souls. I am referring to the judicial system that resulted
from the invention of sin, its division into venial and mortal sins,
and the consequent invention of a roster of punishments, prohibi-
tions, and penances. Though discredited today, fallen into disuse
like those ancient monuments that have been ruined by time but
that retain the memory and impression of their former power down
to the very last stone, the judicial system based on sin continues to
overgrow our consciences, penetrating them with its deep roots.

I understood this better when I saw the controversies raised by
the publication of the book that I titled *The Gospel According to Jesus*

Christ, controversies that were almost always aggravated by the insults and other slanderous ravings aimed at the reckless author. Since the *Gospel* is merely a novel that limits itself to "restaging," albeit obliquely, the character and life of Jesus, it is surprising that many of those who rose up against it actually saw it as a threat to the stability and strength of the foundations of Christianity itself, to the Catholic version of Christianity in particular. It would make sense for us, then, to question the real strength of that other monument inherited from antiquity, were it not obvious that such reactions are essentially the manifestation of a kind of tropism, a reflex of the sin-based judicial system that one way or another we carry within us. The principle reaction, but one of the most peaceable, consisted of protesting that the author of the *Gospel*, being an unbeliever, had no right to write about Jesus. Now, quite apart from the basic right that any writer has to write about any subject, I would add in this case the fact that the author of *The Gospel According to Jesus Christ* restricted himself—if you consider the matter properly—to writing about something that does interest and affect him directly, since as a consequence and a product of Judeo-Christian civilization and cultures, he is, in all ways and every way, as far as his mentality is concerned, a "Christian," even if he defines himself philosophically and behaves in day-to-day life as what he also is— an atheist. It would thus be fair to say that I had just as much right as the most devout, observant, and militant Catholic to write about Jesus, incredulous as I am. I can see only one difference between us, but to this difference—and it's an important one, that of writing things down—I have added, of my own accord and at my own risk, another that is forbidden to Catholics: the right to sin. Or in other words, the most human right to heresy.

Some would say that this is all water under the bridge. However, since in relation to this matter my next novel (I won't call it a story this time) will not be less controversial; quite the contrary, I thought it might be worth taking some preemptive measures. Not to protect myself (something that has never concerned me) but because, as we say around these parts, he who forewarns is no traitor.

July 29: *"E pur si muove"*

With the results of the survey still warm, the newspaper El País *was already asking me for my comment on the eventual union of the people who make up the Iberian peninsula. What follows is what I sent to Madrid on this tricky subject. This tricky, delicate, controversial, and provocative subject on which it has been possible to agree at least enough for us to discuss it seriously.*

"And yet it does move." These are the words that Galileo Galilei said in a barely audible whisper at the end of his reading of the abjuration he had been forced to make by the Inquisitors-General of the Catholic Church on June 22, 1633. As you will know, this was an attempt to make him deny, condemn, and repudiate publicly what had been and continued to be his deeply held conviction, that is, the scientific truth of the Copernican system, which affirms that it is the earth that rotates around the sun and not the sun around the earth. The text of Galileo's abjuration should be studied with all due attention in every educational establishment on the planet, whatever the prevailing religion, not so much in order to confirm what is now evident to everybody, that the sun is immobile and the earth moves around it, but as a way of preempting the development of new superstitions, brainwashing, *idées fixes* and other assaults on intelligence and common sense.

The main subject of this piece is not, however, Galileo, but something closer to us in time and space. I am referring to the "Hispano-Luso Barometer" survey from the Center for Social Analysis at the University of Salamanca, published today, which examines the possibility of ultimately creating a union between the two countries of Iberia with a view to forming a Hispano-Portuguese Federation. Regular readers of these and other comments of mine will be reminded of the controversy, decorated with a number of choice insults and a number of accusations of treason to my country, that my prediction of such a union evoked some time ago. But no, according to the University of Salamanca's survey, 39.9 percent of Portuguese and 30.3 percent of Spaniards would support this union. The percentages show an appreciable advance—in both countries—in terms of the most recent calculations. Those who reject the idea make up a little more than 30 percent of those who were asked, that is, 260 of the 876 citizens interviewed for this purpose in the months of April and May of this year.

In spite of what people usually say, the future is already written; it is just that we do not yet have the necessary science to read it. Today's protests might turn into tomorrow's accord, or the opposite might happen, but there is one thing that is certain, and Galileo's phrase fits it perfectly. Yes: Iberia. *E pur si muove.*

July 30: *The Abjuration*

For anyone who might be interested:

I, Galileo Galilei, son of the late Vincenzo Galilei, of Florence, seventy years of age, having been brought personally to judgment and kneeling before you, most eminent and reverend Cardinals Inquisitors-General of the entire Christian community against heretical depravity, having before my eyes the Holy Gospels, which I touch with my own hands, I swear that I have always believed, and with God's help will in future believe, in each of the articles that the Holy Catholic Church of Rome supports, teaches and preaches. But because this Holy Office has ordered me completely to abandon false opinion, which maintains that the sun is the center of the world and immobile, and prohibits the holding, defending or teaching in any way of the said false doctrine [. . .] I wish to remove from Your Eminences' minds and the minds of all Catholic Christians that correctly held suspicion against me; so out of sincerity of heart and true faith I abjure, curse and detest the said mistakes and heresies, and in general all other mistakes and sects which are contrary to the Holy Church, and I swear that never again in the future will I say or claim anything, verbally or in writing, that might raise similar suspicions against me, but if I learn of any heretic or anyone suspected of heresy I will denounce him to this Holy Office or to the Inquisitor and Ordinary of whatever place I am in. Besides this I swear and promise to fulfill and observe all the penances that have been or will be imposed by this Holy Office. But if by chance I were to violate any of my aforesaid promises, judgments or protestations (may God forfend), I shall subject myself to all the pains and punishments that have been decreed and promulgated by the holy canons and other general and particular decrees against such offenders. Therefore, with the help of God and His Holy Gospels, which I touch with my hands, I, the undersigned, Galileo Galilei, have abjured, sworn, promised and morally committed myself to what is written above, and in pledge of which with my own hand I have signed this document of my abjuration which I have recited word for word.

July 31: *Álvaro Cunhal*[3]

He wasn't the saint that some people worshipped, nor the devil that others abhorred; he was—though not simply—a man. His name was Álvaro Cunhal, and for many years his name was synonymous with a kind of hope to many Portuguese. He embodied convictions toward which he maintained an unshakable fidelity; he was a witness to and an agent of the times when they prospered; he was present when ideas decayed, judgments withered, and practices were distorted. The personal memoirs that he refused to write down might perhaps have helped us to better understand

---

3 Portuguese politician (1913–2005), for three decades secretary-general of the Portuguese Communist Party.

the basic truths about the puny tree in whose shadow today we
find the Portuguese sheltering while ingesting the wordy prov-
ender that they believe is feeding their souls. We shall not read
Álvaro Cunhal's memoirs, and that loss is something we have to
get used to. Nor shall we read what would probably—looking at
the past from where we are now—have been the most instructive
of all documents that might have been born from his intelligence
and his fine artist's hands: a reflection on the grandeur and deca-
dence of empires, including those we construct within ourselves,
those frameworks of ideas that keep us upright and call us daily to
account, even when we refuse to heed them. Instead, as though one
door had closed and another had opened, the ideologue became a
writer of novels, the retired political leader fell silent on the question of the possible and probable destiny of the party for which
he had been for many years a constant and almost sole reference.
Whether on a national or an international level, I have no doubt
of the bitterness of the hours and days that Álvaro Cunhal lived
through. He was not the only one, and he knew it. Sometimes the
militant that I am disagreed with the secretary-general that he was,
and I told him so. At this distance, however, everything seems to
fade, even the reasons we were using (with no noticeable result)
to try to convince one another. The world continued on its way
and left us behind. To grow old is to be imprecise. We still needed
Cunhal when he retired. Now it is too late. We cannot get away
from this feeling of being orphaned that overtakes us whenever
we think of him. Whenever I think of him. And I understand, I
assure you that I do understand, what Graham Greene once said to
Eduardo Lourenço: "As to Portugal, my dream would be meeting
Álvaro Cunhal." The great British writer gave voice to what so
many were feeling. You must understand how much we miss him.

August 2009

August 3: *Gabo*

Writers can be divided (assuming they could ever agree to be divided. . .) into two groups: the smaller group includes those capable of forging new paths in literature, and the larger one consists of those who make their own way following in the first group's footsteps. It was ever thus since the world began, and the (legitimate?) vanity of authors is powerless in the face of such clear evidence. Gabriel García Márquez used his talent to open and establish the route of what was later (and wrongly) named magic realism, and along that path have advanced by turns multitudes of followers and, as always happens, detractors. The first of his books to fall into my hands was *One Hundred Years of Solitude*, and the shock it gave me was such that I had to stop reading after the first fifty pages. I needed to get my thoughts into some order, discipline my pounding heart, and, above all, learn to control the compass with which I hoped to be able to navigate my way along the paths of the new world that had just appeared before my eyes. In my life as a reader there have been remarkably few occasions on which an experience as intense as this has arisen. If the word *traumatized* could have a positive significance, I would apply it willingly in this instance. But now this word has been written, I will leave it as is. I trust it will be understood.

August 4: *Patio do Padeiro (Baker's Patio)*

I think I must have lived in Lisbon's Penha da França neighborhood for about twelve years, first in the Rua do Padre Sena Freitas,
then in the Rua Carlos Ribeiro. For many years thereafter, until
the death of my mother, to me the neighborhood was a continual
extension of all the other places I would come to live in. I have
memories of it that are still vivid today. Then, even the Vale Escuro
[Dark Valley] lived up to its name, for it was a place of adventure
and discovery for young people, a natural enclave just starting to
be threatened by the first new buildings being constructed, but it
was still possible to savor the acidic taste of the sweetened tubers of
the roots of a plant that grew there whose name I never managed
to learn. And it was also a battlefield where Homeric wars could be
staged . . . There was the Patio do Padeiro (which did not belong
to Penha de França, but to Alto de São João. . .), where "normal"
people did not dare to enter, and where, or so I was told, even the
police stayed away, turning a blind eye to the supposed or genuine illicit behavior of the inhabitants. What was certain was that
this degree of fear and mistrust was caused by the closed-in nature
of that little world, segregated from the rest of the neighborhood,
whose words, gestures and attitudes clashed with the quiet, self-
effacing comportment of the fearful souls walking in its squares.
One day, between dawn and dusk, the Patio do Padeiro disappeared, possibly razed by a municipal wrecking-ball, but more
likely by the earth diggers of the building constructors, and in its
place unimaginative buildings were raised, each one a replica of
the next, that would already look old within a few years. At least
the Patio do Padeiro had an originality and a physiognomy all its
own, however dirty and malodorous. If I could have shared, had
I but had the courage to share, the lives of those people and learn
about them, I would like to reconstruct the life of the Patio do
Padeiro. But it would be a labor lost. The people who used to live
there have become dispersed, and their descendants either remade

their lives for the better, or else perhaps forgot or no longer wished to remember the tough lives of those who used to live there. The memory of Penha de França (or of the Alto de San João) no longer retains a space for Patio do Padeiro. Some people are born and live their lives without luck. Not one of them left any trace behind them. They died and passed on.

August 5: *Almodóvar*

I came to *la movida*[1] late, when she had already left behind her urban-Harlequin catsuits, her fake tears rimmed with black mascara, her false eyelashes, her wigs, her laughter, and her sorrows. I don't mean that *las movidas* by definition have to be sad, or to say that great efforts are needed to stop the definitive question, "What am I doing here?" from slipping through their lips in the midst of a fiesta or an orgy. Please take note, I am telling you a story that is not my own. I was never a man for *las movidas*, and if I ever let myself be seduced, I am as certain as can be I would cut no better a figure than Don Quixote in the duke's palace. Ridiculousness is a matter of fact, not merely a point of view. Given that this is the case, I do not think I am greatly mistaken when I imagine Pedro Almodóvar, the reference point par excellence of *la movida* in Madrid, asking his little soul (all souls are little, almost to the point of invisibility), "What am I doing here?" He has given us the answer in his films, which make us laugh at the same time as they produce a lump in our throats, and which insinuate that behind the images lie things that invite us to speak their names. When I saw *Volver* I sent Pedro a message in which I told him, "You touched perfect beauty." Perhaps (or no doubt) out of modesty, he did not reply to me.

I need to draw this to a close. In an unexpected manner, for whoever is wasting their time reading these lines, I will summarize

---

1 "La movida" is a Spanish cultural movement that arose with the new democracy following Franco's death and was epitomised, in cinema, by Almodóvar s racy, eclectic, and outrageous films.

them as follows: one expects Pedro Almodóvar to provide us with the great film about death so lacking in Spanish cinema to date. There are a thousand reasons for this, but most of all because it would be a way of rescuing the ultimate meaning of *la movida* from the shadows.

August 6: In the Shadow of the Father (1)

In his *Theory and Aesthetics of the Novel*, Mikhail Bakhtin wrote: "The principal subject of the genre of the novel, that which epitomizes it, that which creates its originality, is the man who speaks and the words he uses." I believe there has rarely been an assertion of this general theory as precise as that of the literary and human example of Franz Kafka. I wish to leave aside those theorists who, while not devoid of reason, have revolted against the "romantic" tendency to search for a writer in the autobiographical code he left in his work, and in turn search for the meaning of the work in the details of the life. Kafka does not conceal a single example (more, he seems to go so far as to raise noteworthy questions about every example) in his depiction of the factors determining the course of his dramatic life and, consequently, of his work as an author: the conflict with his father, his misunderstandings with the Jewish community, the impossibility of abandoning the celibate life for marriage, and his illness. I consider that the first of these factors, meaning the antagonism that sets son against father and father against son, something he never overcame, is what constitutes the keystone of the whole Kafka oeuvre, and that from it derives—just as the branches of a tree derive from the main trunk—the profound and intimate unease that led him in a metaphysical direction, the vision of a world agonized by absurdity, and the mystification of consciousness.

The first reference to *The Trial* can be traced to his *Diaries* and was written on July 29, 1914 (the First World War had been unleashed the day before), and opens with the following words:

"One night Josef K., son of a rich trader, following a lengthy argument with his father. . ." So he announced, as he had in those three rapid lines of *Metamorphosis*, written nearly two years earlier, what would become the central theme of *The Trial*. When Gregor Samsa, transformed overnight, without explanation, into a loathsome insect—somewhere between a beetle and cockroach— complains of the underserved sufferings that befall the commercial traveler in general, and himself in particular, he expresses it in a manner that leaves no room for doubt: "frequently he is the victim of mere rumor, chance mention, or of a gratuitous complaint, and it is totally impossible for him to defend himself, since he no longer has the least inkling of what he is being accused." The whole of *The Trial* is encapsulated in these words. It is true that the father, the "rich businessman," disappears from the story, and the mother is only mentioned in two sketchy chapters—fleetingly and without filial affection—but it does not seem to me to be overly audacious (unless I am totally wrong regarding the intentions of Kafka as an author) to imagine that the omnipotent and threatening paternal authority could have been, via the stratagems of fiction writing, converted into the overweening might of an Ultimate Law that without precisely specifying what crime has been committed against its codes is implacable in imposing its punishment. The simultaneously anguished and grotesque episode of extreme aggression when Gregor Samsa's father expels his son from the family's living room, pelting him with apples until one gets stuck in his carapace, describes a nameless agony that is the death of all hope of communication.

August 7: *In the Shadow of the Father (2)*

A few pages earlier, the scarab Gregor Samsa had painfully uttered the last words his insect mouth was capable of pronouncing: "Mother, mother." Then, as if dying a first death, he entered into the muteness of a voluntary silence, an essential sign of his irremediable animal nature, a part of which was his definitive relinquishing of any possession of a father, mother, or sister in his insect world. When at the end the servant sweeps the dried-up shell that is all that remains of Gregor Samsa into the rubbish, his absence from that day forward only serves to confirm the oblivion to which his family had already relegated him. In a letter dated the August 28, 1913, Kafka would write: "I live in the midst of my family, among the best and most loving people one could imagine, but as someone more strange than a stranger. In recent years I have not spoken more than an average of twenty words a day to my mother, and never exchanged more than a passing greeting with my father." One would have to be a completely disengaged reader not to notice the pained and bitter irony contained in the words ". . . among the best and most loving people one could imagine," which seem to be there only to be contradicted. One would need to be similarly inattentive, it seems to me, not to attribute a particular significance to the fact that Kafka had proposed to his editor, on April 4, 1913, that *The Stoker* (the first chapter in his novel *America*), *Metamorphosis* and *The Verdict* should be published in a single volume under the single title *The Sons* (something that, as a matter of fact, was only done much later, in 1989). In *The Stoker*, "the son" is expelled by the parents for having offended against the family's honor by making a servant pregnant; in *The Verdict*, "the son" is condemned to death by drowning by the father; and in *Metamorphosis*, "the son" simply surrenders his existence, allowing his place to be taken by an insect. . . More than the *Letter to a Father*, which was written in November 1919 but which never reached its addressee, it is these stories, as I understand it—most particularly *The Verdict* and *Metamorphosis*—that, precisely by dint of being literary transpositions, where the trick of showing and concealing functions as a mirror of ambiguities and reversals, offer us the most accurate description of the extent of the incurable wound that the conflict with his father had opened up in the spirit of Franz Kafka. *The Letter* assumes, in a manner of speaking, the form and tone of a libelous accusation, set out like a final reckoning of accounts, a balancing act between the owing and owning of two confrontational existences, two mutual oppositions, making it impossible to reject the hypothesis that they are based on exaggerations and distortions of actual facts, particularly when Kafka, at the end of the book, suddenly switches to using the father's voice as narrator, in order to accuse himself. . . In *The Trial* Kafka can rid himself of the paternal figure, objectively described, but not of his patriarchal law. And, just as in *The Verdict* the son commits suicide in accordance with the prescription of a patriarchal law, so in *The Trial* it is the accused himself, Josef K., who ends up leading his executioners to the place where he will be executed and where, in his last moments when death is already approaching, he will still admit the thought, like a final regret, that he never learned how to fulfill his role until the end, and that he never succeeded in sparing the authorities any trouble. . . That is to say, succeeded in sparing the Father.

August 10: *Yemen*

Laura Restrepo, the Colombian author and our friend with whom we share our hearts and ideas, asked Médecins sans Frontières [Doctors without Borders] if she could accompany them to Yemen, in order to provide an account of what she saw, heard, and felt there. This account has now been published in *El País Weekly*, in an impressive report that opens, like many others previously made on the subject of Africa, with a narrative that Laura—rejecting, as befits her nature as a writer, the emotive affectations of the writer who deliberately appeals to the reader's sensibilities—expresses in a way that insists on an obstinate search for truths beyond the reach of most observers. Her descriptions of the boats arriving from Somalia, overladen with fugitives who hoped they could find in the Yemen a solution to the problems that had impelled them toward the sea, have a rare and informative impact. In them you can still see the men, accompanied by women and children as always, but Laura Restrepo does not hesitate to demonstrate how common it is to speak of these men without making mention of the women and children too, and how once you mention the children, it is impossible to avoid also speaking of the mothers who bore them, and who carry more still in their bellies. The situations in which these women find themselves when they disembark in the Yemen demonstrate the whole catalogue of moral and physical humiliations to which they are subjected simply because they were born as women. Behind each word Laura writes of them are tears, groans and cries that would keep us all awake at night if our highly flexible consciences had not grown accustomed to the idea that the world is going where those who control it want it to go, and it is enough for us to cultivate our own patches the best we know how, without troubling ourselves about what may be occurring on the other side of our living room wall. This, after all, is the oldest story in the world.

August 11: *Africa*

Someone said that in Africa the dead are black and the weapons are white. It would be hard to construct a better epigraph for that succession of disasters that is, and has been for centuries, what is meant by existence on the African continent. The part of the world believed to be the birthplace of humanity was certainly not a terrestrial paradise when the first European "discoverers" disembarked there (contrary to what the Bible myth tells us, Adam was not expelled from Eden; he simply never entered it), but for the blacks the arrival of those white men opened up the gates of hell one after another. These gates remain implacably open, and generation after generation of Africans have been thrown through them into the flames, thanks to the barely concealed indifference or else the careless complicity of world public opinion. A million blacks dead as a result of war, hunger, and curable diseases will always weigh little in the balance with any neocolonialist country, and take up less space in its newspapers than the fifteen victims of a serial killer. We know that horror, in every one of its manifestations—however cruel, atrocious or shameful—shadows and darkens each day like a curse on our unfortunate planet, but Africa appears to have returned to its accustomed place as the laboratory for our experiments, a place where horror is most often experienced as the committing of crimes we would for the most part deem inconceivable elsewhere, as if the African populations had been marked out at birth to be guinea pigs, so that by definition every violence against them is allowed, every torture justified, every crime absolved. Many of us persist in our naïve belief that neither God nor history will come to judge these atrocities committed by men against men. The future, forever willing to decree the type of general amnesty afforded by oblivion disguised as a pardon, is also adept at giving official recognition, tacitly or explicitly, whenever it suits the new economic, military, or political order, to the life-long impunity of the direct or indirect authors of the most monstrous actions against flesh and the spirit. Therefore it is an error to consign to the future the duty of bringing to judgment those responsible for the suffering of the victims of today, for this future will also not fail to produce victims of its own, and will equally not resist the temptation to postpone until yet another future that still more distant or wondrous moment of universal justice, when many of us will attempt to justify ourselves in the most facile and hypocritical manner, disclaiming responsibilities which were ours alone, and are ours this present day. Does anyone really understand a man who excuses himself by saying: "I didn't know"? How even more unacceptable, therefore, would it be for us to say: "I would prefer not to know"? The way in which our world operates is now no longer the complete mystery it once was; the machinations of evil have been exposed for all to see; the hands doing the operating do not have gloves big enough to conceal the bloodstains. It should therefore be easy for someone to distinguish between truth and lies, between respect and disdain for another fellow human, between those who are for life and those who are against it. Unhappily, events hardly ever unfold that straightforwardly. Personal egotism, indolence, lack of generosity, the petty daily instances of cowardice, all of these contribute to this pernicious form of mental blindness that consists in being of the world and not perceiving the world, or in only seeing what, at any given moment, is capable of serving our own private interests. In such cases, we can hardly wish for some sign that our conscience will awake and shake us urgently by the arm, asking the point-blank question: "Where are you going? What are you doing? What do you think is going on?" What we need is an insurrection of liberated consciences. But is such a thing still possible?

August 12: *The Man Who Would Be King* . . .

The man who would be king is Dom Duarte de Bragança, someone moderately well instructed, thanks to the tutors in charge of him since birth, but who nonetheless loathes literature in general and what I write in particular, firstly because he considers that my novel *Baltazar & Blimunda* insulted his family, and secondly because the said work is, according to the refined jargon of a pretender to the throne, a "big heap of shit." He has not read the book, but it's obvious he sniffed it out. Please therefore understand that for all these years I have not thought to include Dom Duarte de Bragança, let it be noted, on my select list of political friends. It does not bother me to be the object of a battering now and then, but the Christian virtue of turning the other cheek to the aggressor is one I am not in the habit of cultivating. In fact I have my revenge in my appreciation of his quality as an involuntary humorist, which this nephew of King João V demonstrates every time he opens his mouth. I owe him some of the most cherished belly laughs of my long life. This then ended, the monarchy was restored, and one has need to be extremely cautious that these words do not turn up elsewhere, resuscitated perhaps by Superintendant Pina Manique or Inspector Rosa Casaco. What does this mean, the restoration of the monarchy? my stupefied readers will ask. Yes sir, the restoration, as he who has the best possible reason for saying so will affirm (meaning the pretender in question). Not that he need henceforth to be described as such, for the monarchy has been restored to us with the unfolding of its blue-and-white flag right there on the balcony of the Lisbon Council Chamber. The lads of Armada 31 (as those who scaled the Council Chamber walls describe themselves) have now assured their place in the History of Portugal, alongside the lady baker of Aljubarrota,[2] who—or at least it is currently in dispute—never killed a single Castilian. This is not the current situation. The flag remained there for several hours (had some monarchist infiltrated the Chamber in order to prevent its immediate removal?) while attempts were supposedly made to establish the identity of the authors of the exploit—all of this ending up, as ever, in comedy, in farce, in buffoonery. Dom Duarte does not have the charisma to make rousing addresses to the masses in the city square, ready and prepared to present him with his crown, scepter, and throne.

What a shame that such a glorious deed is going to end like this. But since I am, at heart, a sensible individual, I too will end with a suggestion for Dom Duarte de Bragança. He has already assembled a football team, entirely composed of monarchist players, a monarchist trainer, and a monarchist masseur, every last man a monarchist and, wherever possible, of blue blood. I can guarantee

---

2 According to one version of this story, Brites de Almeida was a valiant woman baker who had been a soldier of fortune before she turned to a quiet life making bread. When Spain invaded Portugal in 1385 she took part in the crucial battle of Aljubarrota, where she lived. On returning from the battle, which Portugal won, she found her oven door shut suspiciously tight and ordered the seven Spanish soldiers hidden in it to come out, and as they did so she whacked each one with her baker's shovel. She also led troops of other women around the region routing out stray Spanish soldiers and rebels. Then she went back to being a peaceable *padeira*.

264

that if they win the league, the country—this land we all know so well—will kneel at his feet.

August 13: *Guatemala*

Each day it becomes even more obvious to the world that the problem with justice is not justice itself, but judges. Justice resides in laws, in the civil code, so applying it ought to be straightforward enough. All it requires is literacy, a comprehension of what is written, and the ability to listen impartially to the statements from the accused and the accuser—in addition to any witness testimonies there may be—and to judge according to the light of one's conscience. Corruption has a thousand faces, and in the case of justice the worst corrupter is in some sense the nature of the relationship between the judge and the judged. A typical instance of judicial perversion occurred very recently in Guatemala, where an editor named Raúl Figueroa Sarti, of the F&G Editores publishing house, was sentenced to a year in prison, commuted to a fine of 25 quetzals a day and the payment of a lump sum of 50,000 quetzals plus the cost of all of the legal proceedings. What was the nature of the crime committed by Raúl Figueroa? He had published a photograph, at the request and in the full knowledge of his author, Mardo Arturo Escobar, in a book that had just been issued by F&G. The accused was presented with copies of the work under discussion. The judges were not in the least bothered that the said Mardo Escobar had acknowledged giving the photograph to Raúl Figueroa, to whom he had also given verbal authority to use it in the book. What did matter to the judges was that the accuser was their colleague: Mardo Arturo Escobar works in the Court of Penal Verdicts, which means he is the colleague of these judges, officials and magistrates. . .

Yet this is not a simple case of base corruption. For two years, the publishing house of F&G Editores had been the target of harassment, a harassment that has to be viewed within the framework of the repressive situation which prevails in Guatemala, where official power is routinely used to silence discordant voices, that is, those voices that regularly and vociferously continue to denounce the human rights violations in that country. It would appear that the old pun on *Guatemala* forever becoming *Guatepior*[3] has some validity. Guatemalan citizens must be hoping that this innocuous pun does not turn into a somber reality.

August 14: *Jean Giono*

I imagine that Jean Giono planted more than a few trees in his lifetime. Only a man who had dug the earth to free up a root in the hopes of nourishing a tree could have written such a unique narrative as *The Man Who Planted Trees*, an indisputable masterpiece of the art of storytelling. Naturally, for such a thing to take place it was essential for Jean Giono to have existed, but that fundamental premise, happily for us all, is already an established and confirmed fact: this author did exist, and it only remained for him to have written the work. For that, it was necessary for time to go by, for old age to arrive, and for him to appear and say, "Here I am." Only then, presumably, at the very advanced age that Giono had by then attained, was it possible to create, as he did, in the colors of a lived reality, a history conceived as the most secretive of fictitious elaborations. Elzéard Bouffier, the tree-planter who never existed, is no more than a character drawn using the two magical ingredients of literary creation—the ink and paper with which he wrote. Thanks to these, we learn to recognize this character from the first reference onward as a man we have been awaiting for a very long time. The fictitious Elzéard plants thousands of trees in the French Alps, and to these thousands, through the action of nature properly assisted, you can add the millions of birds that will

---

3 The Spanish suffix -mala means "bad," and -pior means "worse." In other words, the country thus goes from bad to worse.

return to them, and the numbers of animals that return as well, and the water flowing in a place that once suffered from drought. The truth is that we are all waiting for the appearance of any number of real Elzéard Bouffiers. Before it is too late, for us and the world.

PS: Dom Duarte de Bragança is correct: it was my book *The Gospel According to Jesus Christ*, not *Baltazar and Blimunda*, that he decried, but he's not so correct when he says that in it I attributed the paternity of Jesus to a Roman soldier. Not one of the millions of readers who have read the book up to today would confirm his assertion. I knew of that theory, but thought, due to the exigencies of good taste, I would not make use of it in writing my novel. By way of compensation, I dedicated a number of pages to Jesus' conception by Joseph and Mary, his parents. Allow me to suggest to Dom Duarte de Bragança that he should read my *Gospel*. Go on, don't be shy, dare to give it a try. I promise that it improves with reading.

August 17: *Acteal*

Almost twelve years have already elapsed since the massacre at Acteal, in the southeastern part of the Mexican state of Chiapas. On December 22, 1997, when members of the Tzotzil community of Las Abejas [The Bees] gathered together for prayers in their humble chapel, a rural building of poorly assembled unpainted wooden boards, ninety paramilitaries of the Máscara Roja [Red Mask], deliberately brought there and supplied with firearms and machetes, launched an attack that lasted seven hours. By the time they left the terrain, forty-five of the indigenous men, women and children were dead and many others were wounded. The crime of these victims was to have lent their support to the Zapatista Army for National Liberation. Only 200 meters away there was a police station, from which came not the least movement in the direction of the massacre, not even to see what was happening. They already knew too much about it. Pilar and I were in Acteal only shortly afterward, and we spoke and wept with some of the survivors who had managed to escape. We saw the traces left by the bullets on the chapel walls and the place where the graves were excavated, and we climbed to a cave entrance in a hillside where a number of women had attempted to hide with their children and where they were murdered, some by machetes and some by machine-guns fired at point-blank range. We returned to Acteal a few months later, and you could still smell the terror in the air, but justice was going to be done.

Only in the end it wasn't. Alleging procedural errors, the Mexican Supreme Court ended up freeing nearly twenty members of the Máscara Roja who had done time for (just imagine) the illegal bearing of arms, deliberately ignoring the fact that these arms had been fired and used to kill. In my opinion, those who are still in prison won't be spending much more time there before being released, either. But there is no way to release—or resuscitate—the forty-five dead Tzotzils, murdered with the most extreme cruelty. I wrote only a few days ago that the problem with justice is not justice itself, but judges. Acteal is one more proof of this.

August 18: *Carlos Paredes*

I hadn't thought of it before, when I listened to Carlos Paredes playing his guitar, but remembering his music today, I realize that it was composed of days dawning, the dawn chorus of sparrows heralding the sun. Although we had to wait another decade before another dawning, that of liberty, the unforgettable tune of "Verdes Años" that song of ecstatic joy with its intermingled arpeggios of a muted but irrepressible melancholy, became for us a kind of secular prayer, a call to unite our hopes and desires. That in itself would be something, but it isn't everything. The other thing that we still need to know is the man with fingers of genius, the man who taught us that it was possible to be beautiful and strong to the sound of a guitar and who, besides being an exceptional musician and performer, was an extraordinary example of a character of great simplicity and grandeur. It was never necessary to ask Carlos Paredes to open the gates to his heart. They were already and forever open.

August 19: *Blood in Chiapas*

All blood has its history. It runs tirelessly through the labyrinthine interior of a body, without losing either sense or direction, suddenly reddening or increasing the pallor of a face when it flees; it roughly breaks out in a scratch to the skin's surface, before turning into the protective coating over a wound; it floods battlefields and torture chambers, and transforms the asphalt road into a river. Blood is our guide, it swells in us; we fall asleep to the rhythm of our blood and rise to it next morning; we can be either lost or saved through blood; our blood is our life, and it can be our death. It turns into milk to feed infants at their mother's breast; it turns into the tears shed over the murdered; it turns to rebellion, and is raised in a clenched fist holding a weapon. Blood helps our eyes to see, understand, and judge; helps our hands to work and caress; helps our two feet to go wherever duty calls or directs them. Blood belongs to both man and woman, whether they are dressed for mourning or for feasting, with flowers in their belts, and when it assumes names that do not belong to it, it is because these names belong to all those who share the same blood. Blood knows a great deal; blood knows the blood it bears. There are times when blood mounts a horse and smokes a pipe; times when it looks out from eyes that are dry because pain has withered the power to weep. Sometimes it smiles with a wide grin or closed lips; and there are other times when it conceals a face but allows a soul to be bared; a time when it beseeches mercy from a dumb, blind wall; a time when it is a bleeding child being carried in a pair of arms; times when it outlines vigilant figures on house walls; times when it occupies the fixed stares of these figures; times when it binds, and times when it unleashes; times when it becomes gigantic in order to climb walls; times when it boils, times when it calms; times when it's a furnace burning all around it; times when it is an almost gentle light, like a sigh, a dream, a head resting in the shadow of blood just there beside it. There is blood that burns until it freezes. This kind of blood is as eternal as hope itself.

August 20: *Sadness*

An irresistible and already automatic association of ideas always causes me to recall Dürer's *Melancolia* whenever I think of the work of Eduardo Lourenço. If *Só* [*Only*] by Antonio Nore is the saddest book ever written in Portugal, we had yet to reflect and meditate on the sadness it contains. Then along came Eduardo Lourenço, who explained to us who we are and why we are this way. He opened our eyes, but the light was too strong for us. That was why we decided to shut them again.

August 21: *A Third God*

I consider that Huntingdon's thesis on the "clash of civilizations," attacked by some and lauded by others ever since it first appeared, now deserves a more meticulous and less impassioned study. We have become accustomed to the idea that culture is some kind of universal panacea, and that cultural exchanges are the best route to conflict resolution. I am a little less optimistic. I believe that only a manifest and active desire for peace can open the door to this multidirectional cultural flow, without the will to dominate emerging from any one of its parts. The desire for peace may well exist out there, but there are no means to forge it. Christianity and Islam continue to behave like irreconcilably estranged brothers incapable of reaching the long-hoped-for nonaggression pact that could somehow bring a degree of peace to the world. Ever since we invented God and Allah, with all the disastrous consequences we know of, perhaps the solution lay in creating a third god with sufficient powers to oblige the importunately wayward to set down their arms and leave humanity in peace. And then this third god could do us the favor of withdrawing from the scene, where the old tragedy continually unfolds: an inventor, man, is enslaved by his own creation, god. It is most likely, however, that there is no remedy for any of the above and that civilizations will continue to collide, one against another.

August 25: *Playing Dirty*

Young and innocent as I was all those many, many years ago, someone persuaded me to take out a life insurance policy, no doubt of the most rudimentary kind then on the market—twenty reis that would be returned to me twenty years later if I hadn't died, and naturally without the company being obliged to provide me with any account of the eventual profit from the interest accrued by my miniscule investments, still less to permit me to share in the proceeds. Alas for me, however, if I failed to pay my premiums. At that time, those twenty *reis* represented a considerable sum to me; I needed to work hard for almost a year to earn that much, so I was looking forward to seeing a fair return on those earnings, although I never quite managed to avoid the disagreeable feeling of distrust that told me, insistently, that I had been swindled, even though I did not know exactly how. In those days, it was not only the proverbial small print that deceived us, even the large print amounted to little more than a fistful of dust thrown in our eyes. Those were other times, when ordinary people—among whom I include myself—knew little of life, and even this little was of little use. Who would dare to argue not only with the actuary but also with the investment company broker or claims adjuster, who always had the gift of the gab?

Nowadays things are very different. We have lost our innocence and would not dream of avoiding a dispute, flaunting the strongest convictions, including on subjects of which we may only have the remotest idea. Let them not come to us afterward with their stories, for we have learned to know you well, O Mask. The bad thing is that masks change and change hugely, but what lies beneath them never alters. Nor can it even be taken as certain that we have lost our innocence. When Barack Obama, in the heat of his presidential campaign, announced a health reform that would afford protection to the 46 million people in the United States excluded from the system that currently provides coverage to the rest (meaning those who, directly or indirectly, pay their various insurance policies), we hoped a wave of enthusiasm would sweep across the United States. This did not occur, and now we all know why. The processes that were to lead (or would lead?) to the establishment of this reform had barely begun when the sleeping dragon awoke. As Augusto Monterroso wrote, "the dinosaur was still there."[4] It was not merely a matter of the fifty North American insurance companies that control the current system gunning against the project; it was the whole gang of Republican senators and representatives, along with an appreciable number of Democratic senators and congressmen and women. The real underlying philosophy of the United States establishment has never been more exposed than by this: if you are not rich, it has to be your own fault. Forty-six million North Americans do not have the money to pay for health insurance, 46 million poor people who, it would seem, don't even have a place to fall down dead. How many more Barack Obamas will we need to bring the present scandal to a close?

August 26: *Two Writers*

Their names are Ramón Lobo and Enric González. Their profession is journalism, and they exercise it at the highest level of any

---

4 This is the final part of what is known as (because it isn't obviously, of course) the shortest story ever written: "On waking the dinosaur was still there," by the Guatemalan author Tito Monterroso (after Ernest Hemingway).

journalism you can find in the pages of any newspaper. However, I prefer to view them as writers, not because I want to separate and grade the two professions hierarchically, but because what they write expresses emotions and defines sentiments that, at least in principle, are naturally found in literary works of high quality. I have been reading Ramón Lobo for many years, but Enric González is a recent discovery. As a war correspondent, Ramón possesses the exceptional ability to place every word according to its precise terms of reference—eschewing rhetoric and sensationalist oratory—in the service of what he sees, hears, and feels. It seems so obvious, but it's not as easy as it sounds to achieve, and only an exceptionally sure command of the language he deploys allows him to succeed. Enric González was not someone I had read before. I saw his column in *El País*, but my curiosity was not strong enough to lead me to include his entire body of work in my daily reading. At least, not until the day when I found myself with his book *Stories of New York* in my hands. The word "dazzling" would not be an exaggeration. Books about cities are almost as common as stars in the sky, but as far as I know, there's not another like this one. I thought I knew Manhattan and its surroundings reasonably well, but the extent of my error became clear from the very first pages of his book. Few literary experiences have given me as much pleasure in recent years. Take this brief text as a homage and a demonstration of gratitude to two exceptional journalists who are, at the same time, two noteworthy writers.

August 27: *Republic*

It was nearly a hundred years ago, on October 5, 1910, when a revolution broke out in Portugal that overthrew the old and collapsing monarchy and proclaimed a republic that, between decisions and errors, between promises and failures, and by way of nearly fifty years of a fascist dictatorship and with all the sufferings and humiliations that imposed, has survived until today. In the course of the confrontations involved, seventy-six people—soldiers and civilians—were killed, and 364 were wounded. One incident in this revolution in a small country on the extreme western tip of Europe, on which the dust of a century has now accumulated, happened to lodge in my memory—something I read long ago and cannot resist recalling to mind. Fatally wounded, a civilian revolutionary was in his final agony on a street right beside a building on the Rossio, the main square in Lisbon. He was alone, and knew he had no hope of rescue, since no ambulance would dare come and pick him up, for crossfire prevented the safe arrival of any emergency services. So this humble man, whose name, as far as I know, history has not recorded, traced with trembling fingers—almost fainting and falling as he did so—on a wall in his own blood, using the blood streaming from his wounds: *Long live the Republic!* He wrote the word *Republic* and died, and this one word said, as much as if he had written them too: *hope, future, peace.* He left no other will or testament, he left no riches to the world, just one word that to him, at that moment in time, perhaps signified *dignity*, a thing one can neither sell nor permit others to buy, and which is the greatest thing a human being can possess.

August 28: *The Carburetor*

It is now over sixty years since I should have learned to drive a car. I knew well, in those remote times, about how those generous work and leisure machines functioned. I would dismantle and reassemble their engines; clean their carburetors; tune their valves; investigate differentials and change gearboxes; replace the brake shoes and renew tire inner tubes—in short, beneath the precarious protection of my blue overalls, which afforded me the best protection they could from oil splashes, I managed to perform with reasonable success nearly any operation a car or a truck might be obliged to undergo from the moment they entered the garage for a checkup, mechanical or electrical or any other kind. All I needed to do was sit down one day behind the steering wheel and receive the practical lessons of a driving instructor, which were supposed to culminate in an exam and the long-awaited approval that would permit me to enter into the daily growing social order of licensed motorists. However, this remarkable day was never to arrive. That was not merely a question of the legacy left by the infant traumas that condition and influence adult identity, for those suffered during adolescence can also have disastrous consequences, and, as happened in the present case, radically and negatively determine the future relationship of the trauma victim with something as everyday and banal as a motor vehicle. I have solid grounds for believing that I am the deplorable outcome of just such a trauma. Furthermore I wish to add that, however paradoxical such a thing might appear to those for whom the connection between cause and effect seems like a wholly elementary concept, had I not spent the green years of my youth working as a blacksmith and mechanic in a garage, I would today probably know how to drive a car, and I would be a proud driver rather than one of the humble driven.

Over and above the operations I mentioned to start with, and as a compulsory component of some of them, I would also change the carburetor, meaning those fine plates lined with copper leaf, without which it would be impossible to prevent leaks of a gaseous mixture of air and combustion between the engine head and the cylinder block. (If the language I am employing seems ridiculously archaic to those who understand only modern cars, more controlled by computers than by the brains of their drivers, it is not my fault: I speak of what I know, not what I don't know, and you'll be in luck indeed if I don't set about describing the construction of wooden wagon wheels and the best ways of harnessing draught animals to the yoke. The subject in which I had a degree of competence is equally archaic.) One day, having completed my work and put the engine back in place, and having deployed the full force of my nineteen years to unscrewing the nuts that joined the engine head to the block, I set about accomplishing the last phase of the operation, meaning that of filling the radiator with water. I struggled to remove the plug and began pouring water into the radiator opening from an old watering can I had filled in the garage for just this or a similar purpose. A radiator is a container; it has a limited capacity and cannot hold even a millimeter beyond the precise quantity of water it is designed for. Any more water you continue pouring into it will spill over the edges. But something strange was happening with this radiator: the water went in and in, and the more water I poured into it, the less seemed to bubble up at the lip of the opening, the one sign that the filling process was nearly completed. The water I had already tipped into the insatiable throat beneath should have been sufficient to satisfy two or three big-truck radiators, yet it had vanished without a trace. Sometimes I think that today, sixty or more years later, I would still be attempting to fill that tunnel of the Danaides if at some point I had not finally registered the sound of cascading water, rather as if a small waterfall had just appeared inside the garage. I went to take a look. From the car's exhaust pipe there emerged a large jet of water that beneath my astonished eyes gradually diminished in volume to a few final and melancholy drops. What was going on? I had badly joined up the carburetor, jamming the engine head and the block that should have been left open, and, much more seriously even than all this, opening up passageways where there shouldn't have been any. I never found out what moves I had managed to make to get the poor water to find an escape route through the exhaust pipe. Nor do I wish to be told now. The shame is grave enough as it is. Perhaps that was the day when I first considered becoming a writer. It is a career in which we are at the same time engine, water, steering wheel, speedometer and exhaust pipe. Perhaps, in the end, the trauma was worth it after all.

August 31: *Farewell*

The motto says that all things, good and bad, must pass, and that fits like a glove the work that is ending here and the person who

did it. You may find something good in these posts, and on that
I congratulate myself, without vanity; and others may encounter
something bad, and for this I apologize—but only for not having
written of certain subjects better, not for having failed to write of
different subjects, since, if you will excuse my saying so, that was
never an option. Farewells are always best when briefly bidden.
This is no opera aria into which can now be inserted an intermina-
ble *addio, addio*. Farewell, however. Until another day? I sincerely
think not. I have begun another book and wish to dedicate all my
time to it. You will see why, if it all goes well. Meanwhile, you will
have my *Caim* [*Cain*].

PS: On second thought, there is no need to be so drastic. If one day
or another I feel the need to comment or opine upon something or
other, I may come and beat a path to the *Notebook*, that place where
I can most express myself according to my desires.